D0467178

PRAISE FOR *THE RED WIDOW*

"*The Red Widow* is much more than a page-turning true crime narrative. It is a deeply researched social history that brings to rich and complex life the much mythicized world of Belle Epoque Paris. Most of all, it is an unforgettable portrait of a woman who became one of the most notorious figures of her day and whose scandalous story sheds fascinating light not only on her own tumultuous time but ours as well."

Harold Schechter, author of *Hell's Princess: The Mystery of Belle Gunness, Butcher of Men*

"In this tawdry little tale, Horowitz recounts the fascinating life of Marguerite 'Meg' Steinhell. Sex, lies, murder—Meg was willing to use everything at her disposal to amass fame and fortune. Reveling in every lurid detail, Horowitz takes readers on a rollicking ride through the depraved world of the Parisian elite. Wonderfully researched and exquisitely written, Horowitz's book is a reminder that truth really is stranger than fiction."

Nimisha Barton, award-winning author of *Reproductive Citizens: Gender, Immigration, and the State in Modern France, 1880–1945*

"Historian Sarah Horowitz has taken what could be easily dismissed as an unsympathetic and salacious subject and reveals a potent and poignant story about womanhood and self-fashioning in late nineteenth-century France. Deeply researched and beautifully written, we hear and see Meg in all her maddening glory: sometimes vain and defiant, sometimes perplexing and ridiculous, but always profoundly human. In our persistent obsession with true crime narratives, we often forget the very real people behind our moralistic outrage. Settle in, because once you pick up Horowitz's book, you won't be able to put it down. She has written one hell of a book, and *The Red Widow* is one hell of a ride!"

Robin Mitchell, author of *Vénus Noire: Black Women and Colonial Fantasies in Nineteenth-Century France*

THE

RED

WIDOW

THE SCANDAL THAT SHOOK PARIS AND THE WOMAN BEHIND IT ALL

SARAH HOROWITZ

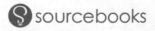

For Lucie, toujours

Copyright © 2022 by Sarah Horowitz
Cover and internal design © 2022 by Sourcebooks
Cover design by *the*BookDesigners
Cover images © PVDE / Bridgeman Images, René Dazy / Bridgeman Images
Internal design by Holli Roach/Sourcebooks

This publication is designed to provide accurate and authoritative information in regard to the subject matter covered. It is sold with the understanding that the publisher is not engaged in rendering legal, accounting, or other professional service. If legal advice or other expert assistance is required, the services of a competent professional person should be sought. —*From a Declaration of Principles Jointly Adopted by a Committee of the American Bar Association and a Committee of Publishers and Associations*

Published by Sourcebooks, an imprint of Sourcebooks
P.O. Box 4410, Naperville, Illinois 60567-4410
(630) 961-3900
sourcebooks.com

Library of Congress Cataloging-in-Publication Data

Names: Horowitz, Sarah, author.
Title: The red widow : the scandal that shook Paris and the woman behind it all / Sarah Horowitz.
Description: Naperville, Illinois : Sourcebooks, [2022] | Includes bibliographical references and index.
Identifiers: LCCN 2021055947 (print) | LCCN 2021055948 (ebook) | (hardcover) | (epub)
Subjects: LCSH: Steinheil, Marguerite, 1869-1954. | Mistresses--France--Biography | Faure, Félix, 1841-1899--Death and burial. | Sex scandals--France--History--19th century. | Widows--France--Biography | Female offenders--France--Biography. | Murders--France--Paris--History--20th century.
Classification: LCC DC342.8.S82 H67 2022 (print) | LCC DC342.8.S82 (ebook) | DDC 944.081092 [B]--dc23/eng/20211123
LC record available at https://lccn.loc.gov/2021055947
LC ebook record available at https://lccn.loc.gov/2021055948

Printed and bound in the United States of America.
WOZ 10 9 8 7 6 5 4 3 2 1

CAST OF CHARACTERS

BEAUCOURT

Marguerite "Meg" Steinheil, born Marguerite-Jeanne Japy

Édouard Japy, her father

Émilie Japy, née Rau, her mother

Juliette Herr, Meg's older sister

Julien Japy, Meg's older brother

Émilie "Mimi" Seyrig, Meg's younger sister

Lieutenant Gustave-Édouard Sheffer, Meg's first love

MEG'S HOUSEHOLD IN PARIS

Adolphe Steinheil, a painter

Marthe Steinheil, Meg and Adolphe's daughter

Mariette Wolff, the cook

Rémy Couillard, the valet

LOVERS AND FRIENDS

Camille-Joseph Bouchez, Adolphe's best friend and Meg's first lover, a
    former magistrate

Berthe Lefèvre, a relative of Bouchez, a friend of Meg, and possibly her lover

Paul Bertulus, a judge and Meg's lover

Joseph Lemercier, a judge and Meg's lover

Léon Bonnat, a painter and friend of the Steinheils

Antony Aubin, a lawyer and occasionally a guest at Meg's salon

André Paisant, another lawyer and friend of Meg and Adolphe

Louis Lépine, the head of the Parisian police and a guest at Meg's salon

Félix Faure, president of the Republic from 1895–1899 and Meg's lover from
    1897 until his death

Berthe Faure, his wife

Émile Chouanard, an industrialist and Meg's long-term lover in the 1900s

Monsieur and Madame Buisson, family friends

Pierre Buisson, their son and Marthe's fiancé

Dominique-Marie-Joseph de Balincourt, a grifter

Maurice Borderel, a wealthy landowner

Roger de Chateleux, a journalist and the ghostwriter of Meg's memoirs

Monsieur and Madame Chabrier, cousins who moved into the Impasse
    Ronsin after the murders

Madame Thors, the wife of a banker and maybe one of Meg's lovers

Robert Scarlett, Lord Abinger, Meg's second husband

THE INVESTIGATION

Alphonse Bertillon, the crime scene photographer

Octave Hamard, Paris's top detective

Joseph Leydet, the examining magistrate for the double murder

Pouce, a detective

Burlingham, an American journalist

Davidson, an American artist

Noretti, a singer and Burlingham's mistress

Marcel Hutin, a journalist for *L'Écho de Paris*

Georges de Labruyère, a journalist for *Le Matin*

Henri Barby, another journalist for *Le Matin*

Souloy, Meg's jeweler

Alexandre Wolff, Mariette's son and a horse trader

Jean-Louis André, the second examining magistrate for the double murder

SAINT-LAZARE

Sister Léonide, a nun

Firmin, Meg's cellmate

THE TRIAL

Bernard-Théodore-Médéric de Valles, the presiding judge at Meg's trial

Paul-Adolphe Trouard-Riolle, the prosecutor

PREFACE

AS THE MORNING LIGHT shone through the large windows of her drawing room on Impasse Ronsin in Paris, Marguerite Steinheil, more commonly known as Meg, was surrounded by men. She was used to male attention and had received presidents, royalty, and many of France's most powerful men in this room. Usually, the men around her were paying her court, begging for the attention of this beautiful, charming woman. Usually, they were wealthy, urbane, and in search of a night or more of pleasure. Not this time, though. On the morning of May 31, 1908, the men around her were dressed for a day of police work as opposed to a society event. They weren't engaging in witty, flirtatious banter but besieging her with questions.

What had she seen? What had she heard? What had she done?

Meanwhile, she could hear the footsteps of other detectives searching for clues upstairs. One floor above, the corpse of her husband, Adolphe, lay on the threshold between his bedroom and the bathroom. He was on his back, his knees bent underneath him, with a rope around his neck. In another room, Meg's mother's body was sprawled on her bed with her legs dangling off it, her mouth stuffed with cotton wadding. A cord was also tied around her neck and her eyes were still open, staring blankly at the detective taking photographs of the crime scene.

Meg was the only survivor of the attack—and the only witness. The police wouldn't let her see the dead bodies, partly out of a sense of delicacy. Society women like her needed to be shielded from the harsher realities of life. Later that day, the two corpses were whisked away to the morgue for autopsies. She wouldn't get the chance to say a last goodbye.

That morning, she was racked with fear and anxiety. How could she explain what had happened? She also remembered how she had been tied to a bed for much of the night. Her urine stains were still on the mattress, serving as a humiliating reminder of her powerlessness as she lay bound and had no choice but to relieve herself on the white sheets.

A few years back, Meg had been one of the most powerful women in France. Money and jewelry flowed into her hands. That life seemed far away at the moment. Instead, an uncertain future awaited her: rumor, suspicion, imprisonment, perhaps even a death sentence and the guillotine.

Right now, though, she had to deal with the detective's questions: What did she know about how her husband and mother had been murdered? Was it a burglary gone wrong? A family feud? A jealous lover?[1]

Everything depended on how she explained what she had seen. Although the story she told that day strained belief, it was not as wild as the story of her life up to that point—and certainly nothing compared to what would happen to her in the coming months.

PART 1

BETWEEN SCANDAL AND RESPECTABILITY

"Mme Steinheil, who is very pretty, fascinating, and wanton"[1]

CHAPTER I

DECADES BEFORE THAT TERRIBLE morning in Paris, long before her life as a wife, high-society hostess, political fixer, and mistress to prominent men, she was quite simply Marguerite-Jeanne Japy, always Meg to her family and friends. Born in April 1869 to Édouard Japy and his wife, née Émilie Rau, she was the third of four children and grew up in Beaucourt, a small town in eastern France with around four thousand residents.[1]

Beaucourt had its pleasures—forests with majestic trees, a chilly winter perfect for snowball fights and sleigh rides, and a smattering of graceful mansions. It was, however, primarily an industrial town, one dominated by the Japy family, whose firm manufactured wrought-iron goods such as clocks and locks and whose coal-fired factories sent pollution billowing into the air.

Édouard's great-grandfather Frédéric Japy began the family business in the late eighteenth century. At the time of Meg's birth, Japy Brothers, as the firm was known, employed a sprawling network of

Frédéric's descendants as well as over five thousand factory workers, making them one of the largest industrial firms in France.[2]

To be a Japy meant something. They were Protestant and proud of their commitment to hard work, thrift, and sobriety. Japy Brothers was known for its paternalism, and it built houses and schools for workers and provided them with medical care and day care.[3] It was an approach that mixed altruism with a good deal of self-interest. The Japys hoped that their workers would be less likely to strike or descend into alcoholism, sin, and laziness—all of which were seen as constant temptations for members of the working class.

Édouard was a Japy twice over: his father, Julien, and mother, Émilie, were both grandchildren of Frédéric. Marriage between cousins was not uncommon for Japys and other industrial dynasties, for it served to knit the kin tighter and keep capital within the family.[4] Like many of his male relatives, Édouard worked as a manager for the family firm.

But every family, especially one that holds itself up as a moral exemplar, has its black sheep. For the Japys, that was Édouard. He showed no propensity for morality, temperance, or sobriety, displays of which were fundamental to the values of his family and the French bourgeoisie more generally.[5]

In the euphemistic language of his day, he had "a slightly turbulent youth"—too much carousing, too much alcohol, too many women, too many fights.[6] A certain level of skirt chasing was acceptable, and bachelors were allowed to live lives that were "wild" and "devoted to pleasure," as one conduct manual put it.[7] Édouard went much, much too far, though, and his behavior embarrassed the family. How would they claim that they owed their wealth to their adherence to a strict moral code when one of them was flouting all the rules? It was made even worse by the fact that Beaucourt was a small town where workers and managers lived in close proximity.

In 1860, Édouard committed the worst crime against his family they could have imagined: he married the wrong sort of woman. Two years earlier, when he was twenty-six and staying at an inn in Montbéliard, a city not far from Beaucourt, the fourteen-year-old daughter of the inn-keeper caught his eye.[8] Even he knew that she was much too young, and Édouard packed her off to boarding school for two years. He must have convinced her father that this was in her best interest, that he would take care of her, that the Raus would now be connected to one of the most powerful families in the area. And Édouard made good on his promise: when Émilie turned sixteen, he married her.[9]

To us, the age difference between a twenty-eight-year-old man and a sixteen-year-old girl is what is most shocking. Indeed, Émilie was young by the standards of the day. Although a marriage at sixteen wasn't unheard of, she was just one year older than the legal minimum age of marriage.[10]

Édouard's family, though, focused more on the class difference. Japy marriages were carefully scripted arrangements meant to promote the family's interests. Had his parents gotten their way, he would have likely married a young woman from one of the other Protestant indus-trial dynasties of eastern France.[11] As a daughter of the people, Émilie brought neither money nor connections into the match.

There was also the foolish business of marrying for love. According to the logic of the time, passion was an unstable foundation for a mar-riage and would be too fleeting to sustain a household.[12]

The Japys initially kept Émilie at arm's length and always enjoyed gossiping about the errant Édouard.[13] Nor were the young couple particularly close to Émilie's relatives, though this was a choice that Émilie and Édouard made. Émilie's brother lived nearby, but he reported that he had little contact with his nephew and nieces and that Meg treated him as beneath her, since he was from the poor side of the family.[14]

Still, they had each other. They were a handsome couple, Édouard with his slicked back hair, wild beard, and sharp features, Émilie with dark hair that went down to her feet and a softness to her face and demeanor. And as Meg wrote, "Édouard adored Émilie, Émilie adored Édouard, and all was for the best in the best of all possible worlds."[15]

Édouard and Émilie Japy

Their personalities were a study in contrasts. He was domineering, charming, generous to a fault, the life of every party.[16] According to Meg, Émilie was passive, "of a quiet and sunny nature, kind, serene, and smiling. She ignored evil, was exquisitely artless, and never understood a great deal of the realities of life, because she did not see them. She… went through life a simple and happy being, knowing neither great exultation nor deep depression, incapable of sustained effort or serious worry."[17] Meg blamed her mother for being docile. But from another perspective, Édouard never gave Émilie the chance to mature, be anything but passive, or confront some of the more distressing realities of her married life.

Meg was utterly and completely her father's daughter. He was her sun and her moon; she was the apple of his eye. She inherited his charm, his zest for life, his abundant energy that tipped into restlessness, his inability to follow the rules, and his desire to live life exactly as he liked.

Mother and daughter were not as close, however. For all that Édouard appears as a vibrant, larger-than-life character in Meg's memoirs, her mother seems almost absent from her passages on her childhood. Later, she found that Émilie's passivity was a burden. Meg loved her mother but was often disappointed with her and seemed to define herself in opposition to a woman who accepted what fate had given her.

———

Édouard, Émilie, and their four children—Juliette (b. 1862), Julien (b. 1863), Meg, and Émilie (b. 1873, known as Mimi)—lived in one of the large mansions in Beaucourt, one that still bears the name Château Édouard. Three stories high with a roof of blue-gray slate and a limestone exterior that gleams in the sunlight, it rises up from the closely trimmed grass and white gravel that surround it, as if to announce the solidity of the family's fortunes.[18]

Which were, in truth, not as solid as they seemed to be. Because of his marriage to Émilie as well as his temper and his erratic behavior, Édouard was excluded from working for the family firm. He lived as a gentleman farmer, and at the time of his death, he owned about fifty acres. Many of his relatives were wealthier, and Édouard's real talent was for spending money, not making it.[19]

Eventually, Meg would experience the consequences of her family's strained fortunes, but as a child, she enjoyed the fact that her father had more leisure time than he would have had if he had been a hardworking manager of Japy Brothers. She could be his chief preoccupation, and although Juliette and Julien were sent away to boarding schools, Meg and her younger sister were educated at home after a stint at the local primary school.[20]

Meg wrote in great detail about the education her father gave her in her memoirs. Although they are unreliable and often present the rosiest possible picture of her life, it's hard to miss Meg's pride at being the center of Édouard's world. Her sister Mimi, for instance, never appears in the passage where she discusses her schooling. It's always only Meg. In her telling, her father gave over a large, light-filled room of Château Édouard to his favorite daughter's education and filled it with books, blackboards, and a globe. He hired the best tutors he could find but put little faith in them. Instead, he listened at the door and burst in often with suggestions about how they should be teaching Meg: "What, you are drawing in this room, in this weather! Run down into the garden: that's the ideal place where to draw." Her tutors might be annoyed, but Meg was convinced that in all cases, "my father was absolutely right."[21]

Meg had lessons in history, geography, literature, drawing, music, and aesthetics. She cared the most about the last two, and it's no coincidence that these were the subjects closest to her father's heart. She learned how to play the violin, the piano, and the organ. Édouard also insisted that she be able arrange flowers and "recognize and appreciate things beautiful, ancient or rare—old furniture, old tapestries, old china, old pewter. He showed me the hall-marks on silver, he made me caress cameos and enamel-work and touch embroideries and old lace reverently."[22]

These were all important subjects for a proper young lady. As was typical for the period, her education was designed primarily to help her be a good wife, mother, and society hostess, as opposed to open up professional opportunities.[23]

Édouard also focused a great deal on her comportment. He made her "go up and down a staircase ten, twenty times in succession" and told her how to walk upstairs as gracefully and coquettishly as possible, how to look back at her admirers at just the right moment. As he told her, "You see, darling, any one can go down steps without being ridiculous, but to go up a staircase, that's another matter. Now then, come down—that's it—raise your head—go slowly—like a queen in books of long ago. Look as though you came down from Heaven and had wings, and didn't press upon the carpet!"[24] He also had strong opinions on how she should style her hair and what jewelry she should wear.[25]

This level of paternal attention was highly unusual for the time. Mothers typically directed their daughter's education, whereas fathers tended to be distant figures who were absorbed in their work obligations. Few cared so much about clothing and hairstyles.[26] Édouard's laser-like focus on Meg might have had to do with his estimation of Émilie's limits. Her time at a boarding school and her years as mistress of Château Édouard had not entirely obliterated the traces of her origins growing up in the rough-and-tumble world of her family's inn, and she was in no position to train Meg how to be a proper lady.[27] It also speaks to Édouard's overinvestment in Meg, suggesting that he wanted her to make up for all the faults that he saw in Émilie.

After the lessons, father and daughter made music together and wandered far and wide in the countryside around Beaucourt. If she was stuck at home with tutors or doing chores and he set off before her, she would run out to find him as soon as she could. "Instinct led me in the right direction" and once finding him, she could throw herself into his arms.[28] "We had endless surprises, and we laughed at everything, often for no reason at all. A word, a common thought, the shape of a leaf or of a cloud, sent us into fits of ecstasy or laughter."[29] He told her "I love you every day more than yesterday and less than to-morrow" and called her "puppele" (little doll or poppet).[30] He implored her, "Try to love me as long as you possibly can. A father like the one you own is worth all the husbands in the world."[31]

Meg remembered her childhood as bliss. She was the beloved daughter of two parents who adored each other. Yet as is so often the case with her, her account of her life often reflected her fantasy of what she wished was true, not the more complicated reality.

For one, all members of her household, save perhaps Meg's mother, Émilie, struggled with severe mental illness. Édouard had extreme swings between depressive states and manic ones; today we might diagnose him as bipolar.[32] Her older brother, Julien, also had manic episodes, including ones in which he ate hundred-franc notes.[33] Mimi was diagnosed with neurasthenia, a catch-all syndrome that was tied to exhaustion, and spent time in a mental institution, and one observer noted that Juliette had "a tormented mind" and was "excessively irritable."[34] Family members recounted that Meg began to have psychological difficulties when she was an adolescent.[35] Although diagnoses of mental illness were routinely slapped on women who were regarded as difficult or unable to conform to the strict standards for womanly behavior, Meg did seem to have real troubles.[36] As an adult, she suffered from repeated mental breakdowns that confined her to her bed for months at a time.[37]

The atmosphere of Château Édouard was also fraught with violence, family discord, and illicit sexuality. According to residents of Beaucourt, Édouard was "rude, brutal, a partier and an alcoholic." His mistresses were legion and included household servants and women in the town. He had at least one child out of wedlock. Édouard also had unfounded suspicions that Émilie was having affairs right and left and was furious at the prospect of her infidelity.[38]

Plenty of men of his station maintained this same double standard. Bourgeois husbands were certainly not expected to remain faithful to their wives. Men were seen as having physical needs that would be dangerous not to satisfy, and their extramarital pursuits were taken as proof of their masculine power.[39] In contrast, bourgeois women were often regarded as essentially asexual and were supposed to be the guardians of their family's morality.[40]

Yet Édouard's philandering went past the tolerated limits. He also physically abused his wife during his fits of jealousy, and townspeople noted that she "often bore the marks of his brutality."[41]

Moreover, observers noted that he "had improper conversations in front of his children" and spoke to them about sexual matters.[42] It was one thing to have affairs outside marriage but quite another to be so open about them and about sex more generally. It showed that you weren't ashamed of your actions. After all, if you were going to break the rules, the least you could do was keep your transgressions hidden.[43] It was especially bad to talk about sex in front of girls and young women, who needed to be shielded from all sexual knowledge lest any awareness of sex corrupt them.[44]

Of Édouard and Émilie's children, it was Julien who both was the most like his father and had the worst relationship with him. Both were violent alcoholics who chased women. Neither had any aptitude for work. Meg described her brother as "bright, witty, a little irresponsible, and very much of a *mauvais sujet* ['bad seed']"—a description that could just as easily have been applied to Édouard.[45] Julien had joined the army, where he was heartily disliked by his superiors. But one of the Japy cousins was a general and made sure that Julien never really suffered from the consequences of his actions, which included frequent brawls and a penchant for breaking windows and glasses.[46]

When Julien was home, father and son exploded into conflict. In one instance, Julien was having a liaison with Édouard's illegitimate daughter. (That is to say, Julien was sleeping with his half sister.) When Édouard scolded his son, Julien "answered ironically by saying that there was no harm in seeing his sister."[47] Julien was throwing Édouard's impropriety back in his face: how could his father possibly rebuke him for his liaisons when Édouard's own behavior was so egregious?

For all Meg's fond memories of her childhood, the truth was that she grew up in a family where sex was a weapon and where she and her siblings had to contend with their father's domineering personality, violence, and flagrant impropriety.

In this light, the idyllic portrait of the father/daughter bond that she paints in her memoirs takes on a more sinister cast. There were the lessons about walking up the staircase as alluringly as possible, the insistence that she love him more than any future husband, and even the unusual attention to her dress and comportment. Was Édouard grooming his daughter in the way that he had groomed her mother, so many years his junior?

Indeed, rumors circulated among the Japy cousinage that Édouard routinely sexually assaulted Meg, beginning when she was fourteen. This might just be malicious gossip: at the time, sexual abuse of children was taken as a sign of the child's immorality as well as the adult's.[48]

Yet Meg's own memoirs provide considerable evidence of a sexual charge to her relationship with her father. She describes the visits from Édouard's friend M. Doriand and how her father flew into a jealous rage when he thought Doriand was paying too much attention to Meg.[49] At her first dance when she was seventeen, she showed up in a plain blue dress with flowers in her hair. Her father told her, "I distrust all these young men. Your entrance has caused a sensation, and all the officers of the garrison are staring at you. I hate it, but, on the other hand, I would have been furious if my daughter had passed unnoticed."[50] She was only permitted to dance with her brother. She told her father he was being a hypocrite, since he loved music, dancing, and partying. His response: "When one loves, one is illogical, and you don't know, my 'Puppele,' how I love you."[51]

In both cases—Meg's relationship with Doriand and her first ball—there was the same dynamic. Édouard was jealous when other men paid attention to her, and Meg saw his rage as a sign of love. She even sought to cultivate it at times. Doing so may have allowed her to feel that it was appropriate and that she had some measure of control over their relationship.

Meg's comportment more generally was highly sexualized, which can be a sign of childhood sexual abuse. Tongues wagged in Beaucourt about her habit of brazenly flirting with factory employees and her father's agricultural workers.[52] Such behavior was strictly forbidden for girls of Meg's station, who were supposed to demonstrate their purity through displays of restraint and by walking demurely with their eyes lowered, refusing to respond to male attention.[53] They definitely were not supposed to bat their eyes at working-class men who might then think that bourgeois girls and women weren't quite as morally pure as they claimed to be. Meg hadn't learned these lessons. Instead, her childhood had taught her that sexual attention was love and a form of power.

When she was fifteen, the flirting extended to a secret romance with the son of a grocer in Beaucourt. They went on long walks in the woods and exchanged letters through her family's cook, a woman who had plenty of secrets of her own, as she was one of Édouard's many mistresses.[54] When her parents found out about Meg's relationship, they were none too happy. After all, it could only have sparked Édouard's jealousy.

Yet for all Édouard's overbearing ways and overinvestment in Meg, he was quite lax in certain respects. Bourgeois girls were typically closely supervised, never left alone with a member of the opposite sex or allowed outside the house unaccompanied. Otherwise, they might fall into temptation and sin.[55] While Meg was disinclined to follow the rules, her parents were just as disinclined to enforce them. Neither Édouard nor Émilie cracked down on Meg's behavior or tightened restrictions on her after they discovered her first romance.[56] Perhaps they were too absorbed in their own troubles, or perhaps Meg was able to convince them not to do so.

This flirtation was a foretaste of what was to come. Only the next time, the consequences would be severe and would shape the rest of her life.

CHAPTER 2

TROUBLE CAME IN THE form of an army lieutenant named Gustave-Édouard Sheffer, who was one of Julien's friends and classmates. Unlike Julien, he was hardworking and liked by his superiors. Beginning in 1885, when he was twenty-one and Meg sixteen, he started coming to Beaucourt with Julien, enjoying the boundless hospitality on offer at Château Édouard. In exchange, Édouard and Émilie hoped that the winning ways of Lieutenant Sheffer would rub off on Julien, their problem child.[1]

They didn't, but the young officer's visits became even more frequent over the next couple of years. How could they not? Meg had inherited her father's charisma and expansive nature as well as her mother's features. She had large, light blue-green eyes and masses of long hair that was dark brown or auburn, depending on how the light hit it.[2] She was charming, spirited, and, in the words of observers, "already very captivating."[3]

In a photograph taken when she was seventeen—the moment

when Lieutenant Sheffer's courtship of her began—she seems delicate, almost fragile. Her fine features and pose show off her tiny waist and slender hands and feet. The lacy white dress with frills and bows and the precarious pose, where she seems to be sliding off a rock, heighten the sense that she could at any moment fall from grace. She seems awkward, not quite at ease with herself, a reminder that her boldness masked her innocence and vulnerability.

Meg at seventeen

Meg was enthralled with her new beau. She found him "charming and clever," as did everyone else who met him. His fellow army officers considered him "very intelligent, educated, a good dancer...and bold with women"—more or less the male version of Meg.[4]

Meg related that over the course of Sheffer's visits to Beaucourt, "there grew between us a kind of poetical intimacy." During the day, they read to each other in the gardens of Château Édouard and took long walks around her family's property. At night, they sang together.[5] He wrote poetry for her and sent her love letters when he returned to the army barracks in the nearby town of Belfort.[6]

Of course, Meg's parents knew why the young army officer's visits were so frequent. They, too, were very fond of him. But Édouard could neither entertain the prospect that Meg was serious about this—or any other—suitor nor say no to her. Instead, he only "uttered vague words" when she spoke about her hopes for a future with the army officer.[7]

The two love birds, though, ignored Édouard's equivocation and rushed into their romance with their whole hearts. His widowed mother came to Beaucourt from Geneva to meet Meg and her family, as sure a sign as any that the couple were thinking of marrying. Mme Sheffer was "modest and gifted" and had "silvery hair" and a "smooth pure brow." It's not hard to imagine that Meg saw her as an ideal mother-in-law, some-one who was as loving as her own mother but had a practical sense and worldliness that Émilie lacked.[8]

Meg and her beau hid their intentions, however. He sent letters to her via *poste restante*, or general delivery, which were picked up by the family cook to avoid prying parental eyes. They also got engaged in secret.[9] Meg hoped that with time, her father would come around and bless their union. It's true that Sheffer had little money and that the life of a wife of an army officer wasn't a particularly easy one, but he was from a respectable family.[10] With the ardor of youth and with Meg's impetuousness, none of that mattered, anyway—their love would over-come any hardships they encountered, although if Édouard agreed to a generous dowry, that would help. After all, she regarded her parents' marriage as a great love affair. Her mother and father had conquered the odds and built a family and a life for themselves despite their age and class differences. Meg and Lieutenant Sheffer had even fewer barriers to surmount. Meg must have thought that her father, so loving and indulgent, would never deny her the chance to marry the man of her dreams.

Meg and the young officer were so in love that they threw caution to the wind. One day, her art teacher, Mlle Ringel, inadvertently walked in on the two. She opened the door to one of the grand rooms on the first floor of Château Édouard and "found Marguerite nonchalantly lying on a couch" with Sheffer. He jumped up and quickly "grabbed a book in order to give me the impression that he was reading," but Mlle Ringel knew from their flustered faces and hurried excuses that they were not.[11]

Mlle Ringel couldn't keep the information about what she had seen to herself. For one, she was "known in the area for having a mean tongue and for having broken plenty of hearts, since she is jealous of everyone," in Meg's estimation.[12] Furthermore, to have not told Meg's parents about their daughter's session on the couch with her lieutenant would have been to condone Meg's behavior.

And that behavior was very, very bad. Young women of Meg's station had to remain virgins before marriage. Indeed, many of Meg's peers got married with no understanding of what sex was or what they would be expected to do on their wedding night.[13] To have sex before marriage was a sign that a young woman was immoral and not a proper member of the bourgeoisie. This was the type of trouble that working-class women—always presumed to be less virtuous than their wealthy counterparts—supposedly got into.[14] Meg's parents' lenient oversight of their daughter was also regarded as a sign of their moral laxity and a dereliction of their duty to maintain her purity.[15]

Then there were the marital plans. Engagements weren't promises whispered in secret between two young people but involved extensive negotiations between the two families.[16] At the very least, Meg's beau needed to have secured Édouard's permission to ask for her hand.

Most parents would have been upset with Meg. Her father was furious. In the words of one of the family's servants, "For two nights, no one in the house was able to sleep."[17] What Meg had read as love was revealed as an obsession with control. Édouard was incensed that she had tried to escape his domination by entering a secret romantic relationship with a man of her choice.[18]

The consequences were quick and severe. Quite obviously, the engagement was off. Édouard and Juliette's husband also requested that Sheffer give them Meg's letters.[19] The return of letters was a standard end to many a romantic relationship, and it prevented any compromising letters from falling into the wrong hands. It was also one way that Meg's father asserted that he was in control of her.

Another was to send her away. She was put on a train to Bayonne, where Juliette lived with her husband and children. This was a city in the southwestern corner of France, about as far from Beaucourt and Sheffer as Meg could get in metropolitan France. Her father hoped that distance would keep the lovers apart. It was also a form of punishment and a way to remove her from his sight so he could recover from his favorite child's monstrous betrayal.[20]

The young couple was devastated, all their hopes and dreams of a life together dashed. To see her one last time, Lieutenant Sheffer went to the train station as she was leaving for Bayonne. He was wearing a marguerite daisy on his lapel, a sign that the relationship was over but his love for her was not. When he arrived, she was no longer on the platform but was already seated, as if in a metal cage. They said a tearful goodbye as she was whisked away to her life in exile.[21] He would see her one more time, decades later, under the most adverse circumstances.

Years after, Meg stated that "it was in this moment, in this moment of dreadful sadness…that I can say that my life was broken."[22] She would not marry the man she loved, would not move easily from her father's home to the one she made with a dashing, kind army officer who met her energy and passion with his own.

The fallout of her broken engagement didn't stop there. With Meg in Bayonne for an indefinite amount of time, Mlle Ringel couldn't resist explaining her former pupil's absence by claiming that Meg had run away with Sheffer, gotten pregnant, and given birth to an illegitimate son.[23] It was just another rumor about the most wayward daughter of the Japy family's black sheep.

To cap it all off, in November 1888, two months after he sent her to Bayonne, Édouard Japy died suddenly. He was drinking a glass of water and collapsed.[24] His anger about Meg's behavior, the sadness at her exile, and his distress over the rumors of her nonexistent pregnancy all compounded to kill him. Meg said, "My father died because of his grief… He died of a stroke caused by his suffering."[25]

———

Meg flew back to Beaucourt as fast as she could, out of her mind with anguish. She later wrote of her father's death that she "couldn't believe this atrocious reality, since he was everything to us."[26]

After the funeral, Meg wanted to run away from "the sight of all that my father had touched or loved."[27] Her mother begged her not to, tears streaming down her face; she needed her daughter far too much.

Meg would spend much of that winter taking care of Émilie and Mimi. At age nineteen and deep in mourning, it was up to her to be the adult in the family.[28]

Édouard's sudden death also came with a host of difficulties. Some were financial. Édouard was a terrible manager of money, and the family's finances were increasingly strained. Having Émilie in charge made things even worse. A widow at forty-four, she managed her grief—or made use of her newfound sense of independence—by setting off on elaborate building projects on the property. First to go up were a series of "large, sumptuous and extremely expensive greenhouses." Meg and her siblings "begged her in vain to have the work stopped". Her mother displayed her usual sense of passivity, but this time toward her own behavior, telling her children, "I love bricks, cement, sand, stone. To build has become my passion and at my age, you don't get cured of your passions."[29] Not long after, Émilie would set her heart on "a luxurious piggery, large enough for hundreds of pigs" modeled after what she had seen on a German prince's farm.[30]

There was also the problem of what to do with Meg. At age twenty, it was high time the family find her a husband; if she didn't get married in the coming years, she might become a spinster, a fate that many saw as a kind of social death. Finding a match for a young woman was no small task: typically, bourgeois households mobilized "their entire social and familial network in order to find the right person and be aware of every last detail."[31]

Meg never described how she felt about her family's concern that she be married off promptly. She may have resented the fact that they had first broken off her engagement to the man she loved and were now so preoccupied with finding her a suitable husband. Or she may have accepted that this was how the world worked, that marriage and family were a woman's fate.

In any case, the problem was that Émilie had no kin who could help her out. Given that Meg characterized her mother as "incapable of sustained effort or serious worry," she may not have had the mental resources to undertake this project.

What Émilie could not do for Meg, her sister Juliette would have to do instead. So Meg returned to Bayonne to meet the man that Juliette had in mind for her.

CHAPTER 3

HIS NAME WAS ADOLPHE Steinheil. He was a distant relative of Juliette's husband and was in Bayonne to restore the stained-glass windows of the cathedral.

Adolphe had learned how to do this work from his late father, Auguste. In his day, Auguste had achieved a fair amount of prominence. He had helped restore Notre-Dame Cathedral and Sainte-Chapelle and played an important role in the revival of interest in the medieval era in nineteenth-century France.[1] Auguste's sister was also married to Ernest Meissonier, one of the most commercially successful artists of the time. By the 1880s, the Parisian artistic establishment saw Meissonier as vulgar and out-of-date, but Meg and her family members were unlikely to have made any such judgments.[2]

Adolphe, born in 1850, followed in the footsteps of both his father and his uncle. He had a talent for stained-glass restoration and, like Meissonier, he produced paintings that were scenes of everyday life set in previous centuries. In 1870, he debuted at the age of twenty at the state-run salon, no small feat. He showed regularly at salons for the next twenty years, and in 1882, the government awarded him a medal for painting.[3] Some critics regarded him as an up-and-coming artist who had the potential to go far.[4]

He didn't. By the time Meg met him in 1889, Adolphe's old-fashioned, academic style was increasingly out of step with the latest artistic currents. In any case, he was not a great artist, and in the condescending words of Le Figaro, "he gives proof of his skill: his drawing is precise, correct, always without daring, and his color, although bright, lacks the verve that draws you in."[5]

As was true for the art, so was true for the man. He was passive, easily discouraged, and somewhat disconnected from the world. In this, he failed to live up to the masculine ideal that he be active, energetic, competitive, and always searching to impose his stamp on the world.[6] Even his closest friends had to admit that, well, there was something not quite right with Adolphe. One called Adolphe "a big child, like artists often are, that is to say that he was unaware of the first necessities of life" and so preoccupied with his art that he was frequently "disheartened" and "melancholic."[7]

From the beginning, Meg saw many of his flaws. When her sister showed her a photograph of Adolphe, she exclaimed, "No thank you! I'd never dream of marrying a man like that." She deemed him too old and not particularly handsome: short, "with small eyes, a dark moustache, and a pointed beard."[8] His tired eyes also made him look considerably older than thirty-nine.

Juliette convinced Meg that at the very least she should meet Adolphe. On their first encounter, he greeted her "with a number of quick, jerky little bows" and displayed no social graces. Meg said, simply, "He didn't please me at all."[9]

Still, Juliette would not relent. She was always more serious and sober than the impulsive Meg and continued to arrange occasions for the two to meet. Meg didn't push back too hard and she found she enjoyed talking to Adolphe.[10]

The turning point came when she went to see him work at the Cathedral of Bayonne—as good a place for a conversion as any, with its improbably high arches and narrow windows that let in enough light to make the wooden pews glow. There she found "a tiny man lost in a white smock, like a house-painter." It wasn't an attractive sight. Under his smock, he was wearing "a thick knitted brown sweater" that "reached down to his knees and gave him a most comical appearance." As he gave her a tour of the cathedral and showed her the restoration work that his late father had started and he was now continuing, something changed in her. "He spoke about his father with such feeling that, remembering my own father, I became quite serious, and thenceforth listened with keen attention to all that M. Steinheil said."[11] Suddenly, she saw Adolphe not as a figure of mockery but a man she could sympathize with and one who understood her pain.

After that, she started taking him more seriously as a person, if not yet as a suitor. He called on her and Juliette regularly and tutored her in painting. The lessons continued even after he returned to Paris and she to Beaucourt. There, she received word that he was desperately in love with her, to the point that he "had no longer any desire to live" and was unable to work.[12] He was too afraid to ask her to marry him, knowing that she would turn him down. So one of Adolphe's friends asked in his stead, while one of Meg's aunts went to Paris to investigate what his house was like, how he was regarded in Parisian society, and how he felt about her.[13]

Finally, Meg agreed to consider Adolphe's suit. Her mother and her aunt extolled the benefits of marrying a man almost twenty years older than she. After all, there had been a considerable age gap between her father and her mother, and hadn't they been so very happy? Or as Meg herself stated, "When I married a husband who was older than me, I thought that I would find a source of support and protection in him."[14] Indeed, many in Meg's day believed that a husband had to be older than his wife so that he could better establish his authority over her.[15] She wanted that badly, hoping that he could replace Édouard. Adolphe was an only son who had helped raise his four sisters after his father's death, and Meg thought he must be plenty used to playing a paternal role for the women in his life.[16]

Another appeal: Adolphe's intense love for her. When he came to visit her in Beaucourt, "he was most attentive to me, spoke so convincingly, though without any passion—of the happiness that would be ours, and seemed so desperately anxious to hear me say 'yes' after he had proposed, that I had not the heart to say 'no.'"[17] Disappointing him seemed like too great a burden. What's more, Meg was always mindful of the effects she had on the men around her and relished the power it gave her.

Meg also considered what her father would have thought about the match. Adolphe "seemed grave and kind, two qualities which my father thought essential, and he was a talented artist, to which my father would certainly not have objected."[18]

Paris, of course, offered its own appeal. When asked decades later about why she said yes to Adolphe, she responded, "Parisian life attracted me… I thought that life in the capital would be easy and picturesque."[19] There she could escape the enclosed, gossipy world of Japy relatives. Few would know about her romance with the young army lieutenant or her father's wild ways.

Last but not least, there was the family pressure. This was what her mother and Juliette wanted.[20] They must have known that Meg had very limited options. She was beautiful and charming but without extraordinary wealth. Typically, a suitor and his family would have made extensive inquiries into her background and family life. Had Adolphe or his kin done so, they would have found a field of red flags, including Meg's own scandalous behavior in Beaucourt, her father's alcoholism, which was regarded as hereditary and a stain on one's character, and the family's history of mental illness.[21] In truth, Adolphe was probably the best she could do.

Finally, she said yes.

At least she had a beautiful wedding. It took place in the Protestant church in Beaucourt in July 1890. The young people of the town presented her with roses as she entered the building, while they gave Adolphe a glass to break, a tradition "which is supposed to show that he renounces the joys of bachelordom." As she entered the church, there were even more roses—"a present from the poor of the neighbourhood" in recognition of her and her father's generosity. She could not help but "burst into sobs," cognizant of all that she had lost and all that she hoped for in her marriage to Adolphe.[22]

Meg had no doubt constructed a fantasy life of wedded bliss for her and Adolphe. Although sometimes she managed to impose her desires on reality and make her wishes come true, that would not be the case this time. Instead, her hopes faded quickly. Ten days into her honeymoon in Italy, she decided she had had enough of marriage to Adolphe and fled to her mother in Beaucourt and "begged her to let me stay with her—for ever."[23]

Meg never said why she decided that Adolphe was not for her less than two weeks into her marriage, just that she was "home-sick and depressed."[24] Indeed, this was likely her first time away from her family. What's more, most young bourgeois women had relatively limited contact with their fiancés before marriage. Meg and Adolphe's honeymoon was their first real opportunity to get to know each other, and she may have realized that her first impression—that he didn't please her—still held.

Yet Adolphe pleaded with her to come back, and Émilie, like so many other bourgeois individuals at the time, thought that marriage was supposed to last until death. [25] Finally, Meg resolved that she would give him another try and went with him to his house at 6 *bis* impasse Ronsin in Paris.*

There, she would face the realities of her new life as a twenty-one-year-old bride.

———

We often think of Paris in the 1890s and 1900s—the two decades Meg lived there—as the most exciting and glamorous era in the city's history. The Eiffel Tower had just gone up, the capital was a center of artistic ferment and creativity, and many of the city's residents devoted themselves to pleasure, festivity, and gaiety.[26] These were the years in which Oscar Wilde declared, "When good Americans die, they go to Paris." (The bad ones stayed in America.)[27]

Yet this era was also marked by political strife that sometimes turned violent, as well as anxieties about national decline. This period acquired the name of the Belle Époque decades later: it would be seen

---

* "*Bis*" here meant that the original parcel of land had been split and that there was a building numbered 6 impasse Ronsin as well as a different one that was 6 *bis*.

as a constant party only in light of the horrors of the twentieth century.[28] Paris around 1900 was also marked by intense inequalities. The rich lived in splendor on the western side of the city, but the vast majority of the population, some 80 percent, was poor. Many of them lived in crowded quarters on the eastern side of the city, where disease and hunger were endemic.[29]

Meg's new home in the fifteenth arrondissement was removed from some of these struggles as well as many of the city's pleasures. This area had a reputation for being dull and was light-years away from the glamorous Paris she had dreamed of.[30]

Impasse Ronsin was in a neighborhood of tatty lace curtains and plain, sometimes dirty façades.[31] It had a print shop that ran day and night, which meant the street was always noisy, busy, and filled with workers. The street's inhabitants were largely workers and artists, one of whom was Adolphe's brother-in-law Albert Bonnot. Parallel to Impasse Ronsin was Impasse de l'Enfant Jésus, which was regarded as dodgy and a place for lowlifes.[32] Meg was a tremendous snob, with all the prejudices of a member of the bourgeoisie toward workers and the poor: that they were dirty, lazy, and inclined toward bad behavior. Living so near to them would have held little appeal.

Then there was 6 *bis* impasse Ronsin itself. Adolphe's home was a freestanding villa covered in ivy and had a garden and a conservatory. The entire property, including the garden, was between seven and eight thousand square feet.[33] By Parisian standards, the house was spacious, but it was hardly a distinguished building from the outside, and one newspaper stated that the exterior was "banal" and looked like "the annex of a train station."[34]

When Meg arrived at her new home after her honeymoon, she

realized that her biggest problem was within the house. Adolphe's unmarried sister, also named Marguerite, lived with him. She was at Mass and had taken the keys with her when Meg and Adolphe landed in Paris on a rainy Sunday morning. Marguerite seemed to have forgotten about the new couple—and even Meg's very existence. Meg had no choice but to wait in the rain, "distressed by the smell of fried onions which came from the kitchen." When her sister-in-law finally returned to the Impasse Ronsin, she was wearing "a morning dress which I would not have allowed my maid to wear." Inside, she found that "the hall was very dusty; there was no carpet, and nothing was ready for the arrival of a young wife." As soon as she was in alone with Adolphe in their bedroom, she "burst into tears."[35] The house itself was telling her how very unwelcome she was and how drab her new life would be.

Meg soon realized that her sister-in-law, not Adolphe, ruled the roost.[36] When Meg tried to enliven the drawing room, which she found "cold, dreary, and as unattractive as could be," with flowers and furniture from her home in Beaucourt, Marguerite wouldn't have it. She told Meg, "Never, you understand me, never has the furniture in this room been touched since the death of our venerated father."[37] The house had space for Adolphe, Marguerite, and the memory of their late father, but none, apparently, for Meg.

Fortunately, Marguerite would soon marry and leave Meg the undisputed mistress of the house.[38] But the disappointment didn't stop there.

———————

In coming years, Meg and Adolphe's marriage would produce one great success and many failures. Less than a year after they were wed, their daughter, Marthe, was born. By all accounts, she was an ideal daughter, and a family friend described her as "a kind and loving child."[39]

The problems in the Steinheil marriage were psychological, economic, social, and sexual. Meg was energetic, Adolphe resigned. She had no capacity for self-reflection or self-criticism; he was almost too inclined to be in his thoughts. She had a tendency to lash out at others, he to blame himself. It was a toxic combination, all made worse by the fact that he never stopped loving her while, at best, she could take or leave him.

The household was also under constant financial stress. For the first fifteen or so years of their marriage, Adolphe brought in around twelve thousand francs a year, while Meg's dowry netted them another three thousand.[40] This was five times what it took for the Steinheils to claim a status on the lowest rung of the Parisian bourgeoisie but placed them far from the top. If Meg and Adolphe's total income was considered enough for them to live "honorably," it did not put them in the category of being "rich," according to the terms of the day.[41] To conserve their resources, Meg did domestic labor that servants would have undertaken in wealthier houses. She sewed clothes for herself and Adolphe and did much of the cooking, ironing, and laundry.[42]

Growing up in Beaucourt, she had done plenty of chores with her mother and her sisters; the finances of Château Édouard were so strained that they had fewer servants than other Japy households. That had been her father's doing, though, and she could never be the least bit critical of him.[43] But the drudgery of Meg's life in Paris was something that she deeply resented and blamed on her mother and her husband. In her telling, Émilie had skimped on her dowry, while Adolphe didn't push the issue by asking for more.[44] It was her mother's blissful ignorance of the ways of the world and immoderate spending, as well as her husband's passivity, that were confining Meg to a life of chores.

Then there was the boredom. Many of Adolphe's friends were painters and sculptors who lived nearby.[45] These were not the eccentric, rule-breaking artists who sought to shock the bourgeoisie with their behavior and their art but ones who followed artistic conventions and sought state patronage. All Adolphe's sisters were in the Paris area; one was right next door and another was in the neighborhood.[46] They were between six and twenty-two years older than Meg and, like Marguerite, were all old-fashioned. Meg's sexualized comportment and speech took them aback. One of the brothers-in-law said that she had "a certain freedom to her appearance and language that made her sisters-in-law say: 'Adolphe would not have tolerated a twentieth of what he is allowing her from us.'"[47] Even in Paris, Meg couldn't escape judgmental relatives. It's not hard to imagine that she found this world dull and claustrophobic and dreamed of the broader social horizons that more money and prestige would bring.[48]

Adolphe, though, was perfectly content with this life, with making art that neither sold particularly well nor garnered much attention. He had no hustle and couldn't promote his paintings to save his life.[49] It fell to Meg to make up for the ambition that Adolphe lacked, to be the one to promote and sell his art. In her telling, "I reorganised our home, tried to breathe ambition into my husband, cheered him when he was depressed, surrounded him with comfort and assisted him in his work, made the historical costumes which he needed for his models and sat for him myself. But I failed to rouse him from his apathy or to give him the love of effort."[50] And if he wasn't willing to pay visits to the right people and stroke the right egos, that was something that Meg would eventually come to do as well.

Much to Meg's dismay, she found that she needed to act as the adult in the relationship in so many ways. As she said, "I thought that I had found a protector, but I was obliged to protect him."[51] It was a bitter blow. She had married Adolphe in the hopes that he could serve as some sort of replacement for Édouard. Instead, he was more like Émilie—resigned and out of touch with reality. What's more, Adolphe was in total violation of the principles of the bourgeois family and the French legal code, both of which were based around the husband's role as protector of and provider for his wife and children.[52] In later decades, Meg would grow cruel to Adolphe. But it's hard not to sympathize with her at this point, when she was a twenty-one-year-old woman thrust into parenting a man twice her age.

Last but certainly not least in the litany of their incompatibilities was Adolphe's sexuality. Although he loved her deeply, he wasn't faithful to her. Instead, he pursued sexual relationships with both men and women. He often prowled the streets of Paris, asking individuals if they wanted to pose for him in exchange for a few francs, and recruited his lovers from those who said yes. This was such a low sum that anyone who agreed would likely have been truly down and out.[53] Some of Adolphe's behavior was par for the course. Bourgeois men often turned to Paris's boulevards in search of extramarital sex, and Parisians often regarded their city as throbbing with erotic possibility.[54]

But many would have seen Adolphe's behavior as appalling. In particular, homosexuality was seen as unnatural, a sign of mental illness, and dangerous to the nation. (Bisexuality was regarded as an impossibility.)[55] Meg imbibed these prejudices. In a letter to him, she wrote,

"I have had enough of life with a man who has your morals… You disgust me."[56] She was also repelled by his relationships with women. She told the family doctor that Adolphe "doesn't behave in the way that he should" and that he and his mistress would "masturbate together at her place and he leaves in such a state of overexcitement that he has to drink tea with opium in it in order to sleep."[57] Masturbation was seen as unmanly, a drain on men's vital energy, and a perilous path to other, more degenerate acts.[58] Undoubtedly, too, the fact that many of Adolphe's partners were from the poorest of the poor must have horrified Meg, especially as she was subjected to a constant stream of lowlifes parading through her house on their way to Adolphe's studio.

Then there was the humiliation of it all. Meg sometimes saw graffiti scrawled on the walls near their house that referred to Adolphe's liaisons with men, and the couple received hostile anonymous notes about his affairs in the mail.[59]

What was Meg to do?

The obvious solution was a divorce. This was an option that Meg considered quite seriously when she discovered Adolphe's sexual liaisons with men, soon after Marthe was born in 1891.[60] She even had the evidence of his adultery in the form of letters he had written attesting to his affairs with men.[61]

Meg fled to Beaucourt to make her decision. Her mother begged her to stay married to Adolphe, as did his best friend, a lawyer named Camille-Joseph Bouchez, who Meg had turned to for advice about her legal options. For his part, Adolphe seems to have asked Bouchez to plead his case to Meg. While in Beaucourt, she got letter after letter from the lawyer, telling her to "come back to Paris and to him… Don't divorce, for your child's sake."[62] He could tell Meg that she would probably get custody of Marthe.[63] Did she want to wrench the poor child away from her loving father? And unless Meg wanted to live even more modestly, she would have had to find a new husband relatively quickly. A divorce would leave her essentially right back where she started, except a few years older and with a small child in tow.

Émilie also "had a holy terror of divorce."[64] She had endured so much during her marriage to Édouard. Meg maintained that her mother was utterly devoted to her father, but Émilie may have seen it differently. She may have felt that she sacrificed herself to provide for her children and that her daughter should now do the same. Moreover, Émilie wasn't the only one who thought it was best to avoid divorce at all costs. It was regarded as scandalous, since it required airing the household's dirty laundry in the courtroom.[65] Had Meg taken this option, she would have compromised Marthe's reputation and made her less attractive on the marriage market when she came of age.

After months of deliberation, Meg concluded that she and Adolphe would remain legally married. They would live together, raise Marthe together, but "would henceforth be 'friends,' each living in his or her own way."[66] In other words, she was free to have her own affairs and Adolphe would have no say in the matter.

This arrangement made Adolphe plenty miserable.[67] He, like other bourgeois men of the era, might have seen his own extramarital liaisons as permissible but his wife's as beyond the pale. Yet in many instances, he reacted to Meg's affairs with sadness, not jealousy or rage. He may have wanted a marriage that was more loving and companionate and less about maintaining appearances. If this was not the kind of marriage he wanted, Meg let him know that he was not the kind of husband that she wanted.

With one decision made, there were others to contemplate. Did Meg really want to spend the rest of her life taking care of Marthe and Adolphe and staying within the confines of their preexisting circle of friends and relatives? This was the path of least resistance and probably what most women in her situation would have done. Meg's personality made it utterly unthinkable. She said of this period in her life, "I was quite incapable of dumb resignation. With me, to strive and accomplish has always been a necessity."[68]

Twenty-first-century readers would no doubt counsel Meg that if she wouldn't divorce her husband, a professional career was the easiest route to fulfillment and an income to shore up the household's finances. While women needed their husbands' permission to work and did not have financial control over their earnings, there were a handful of women in Meg's day who were doctors, lawyers, journalists, or other professionals.[69] Yet Meg lacked the formal schooling that might have prepared her for a career in law or medicine. Pursuing any one of these options would have put her in the emerging category of the "New Woman"—someone who had turned her back on tradition, femininity, and domesticity, all of which Meg strongly believed in.[70] There was also the question of class: many women of the bourgeoisie defined themselves by the fact that they did not work for money and regarded work as degrading.[71]

At heart, there is something very conventional about Meg that would have made any attempt at an independent life—divorce, a career—unappealing to her. Her survival strategy was one of dependence and attaching herself to rich and powerful men. Likewise, maintaining some semblance of bourgeois propriety was of paramount importance to her.

It may have been the result of her father's upbringing or the fact that she lived in a milieu that valued outward conformity to social norms above all. It may also have been a realistic calculation about where money and influence lay in a deeply inegalitarian, highly patriarchal society.

Whatever the reason, she set on her own path to achieve her ambitions and escape the tedium of her marriage.

Adolphe Steinheil

CHAPTER 4

BY THE TIME MEG decided to remain married to Adolphe, she was twenty-four.[1] She was just one of many provincials who had come to the capital with dreams of making it, of achieving worldly success and renown, and of penetrating the tightly knit world of Parisian high society. Many, probably most, failed.

Meg was completely undaunted. Not for the last time would she bend fate to her will.

As she set out to scale the heights of the Parisian elite, Meg had a few vital resources at her disposal. Although she had luminous, pale skin, clear and captivating eyes with long eyelashes, she was not a great beauty by the standards of the day. Instead, her assets were more intangible, something no photograph or painting could ever capture. One was her voice, which listeners described as "delicious, caressing, pure," and "musical."[2] She could play it perfectly, adjusting it as circumstances warranted—to reassure, to mock, to impress, and most often to captivate.

Her voice was a perfect match for her personality. Every friend, every society acquaintance, everyone who ever gave an interview to the press about her described her as overwhelmingly charming and seductive. One close friend stated that "Mme Steinheil charmed anyone who was around her. There was something soft, tender, affectionate, even, about her charm."[3] More critically, the diplomat Maurice Paléologue described her as "very pretty, fascinating and wanton."[4] It was a legacy of Édouard: he had taught her how to enthrall others, intuit what they wanted from her, and give that to them.

Adolphe, Meg, and Marthe

To gain access to high society, she would need more than her own personal assets. The man who opened the doors to the drawing rooms of the Parisian elite for her, figuratively if not literally, was none other than Adolphe's best friend, Bouchez.

The two men had met in the mid-1880s when Adolphe painted Bouchez's portrait.[5] At the time, the sitter was the attorney general of Paris, making him one of the most important magistrates in France. He resigned (or was fired, depending on who you asked) in 1889 for failing to prosecute Georges-Ernest Boulanger, a prominent politician and general who had threatened to overthrow the government.[6] He then went into private practice, though he still retained plenty of connections within France's prestigious civil service.[7]

After Bouchez had successfully used all his lawyerly skills to dissuade Meg from getting a divorce, he continued to seek her out. "He called almost every day, read to me, filled my mind with new ideas, introduced all kinds of interesting people to me." She and Adolphe went to receptions at his home "where scores of magistrates and famous barristers gathered" and "very soon I knew what is usually called le Tout-Paris [high society]." Bouchez showed her a world of "statesmen and diplomatists, famous authors and famous composers, generals and admirals, scientists and officials, business magnates and great financiers, State-councillors, explorers, men with historic names, men who were making names for themselves, and judges, a whole body of judges."[8]

This seemed to be part of the bargain he had made with Meg: if she remained married to Adolphe, he'd work to open new social vistas for her. As she wrote in her memoirs, when Bouchez pleaded with her to stay married to Adolphe, he told her that if she did, "We will all do our best to make your life a happy one."[9] The "we" speaks volumes: he would give Meg the life she wanted if Adolphe could not. But of course, he may have had his own reasons for becoming closer to a charming young woman who was seeking an escape from the tedium of her marriage.

In her memoirs, Meg presented her rise in high society as abrupt, writing that one moment she was miserable and bored and the next she was standing at the summit of *Tout-Paris*. It can't have been like that: undoubtedly she spent years hustling, learning the particular codes of high society, figuring out who mattered, who could help her, and how to get an invitation to the next big ball or to take tea with the women who controlled access to elite circles.

Adolphe wasn't much help to Meg. After all, he was timid, preferred a modest life, and wasn't many people's idea of a good time. But some of his friends were society artists who could help her, who knew the right people. And she could tell her husband that if he also knew the right people, then he, too, could earn a steady stream of commissions.

There must have been times when she felt like she was on the brink of failure, that one false step would mean she'd be banished forever from the life she so desperately wanted and sent back to the monotony of her life on Impasse Ronsin. But ultimately, her charm, her connections, and her sheer force of will allowed her to embed herself firmly in *Tout-Paris*.

Meg loved her new life unabashedly and unreservedly. Gone were the days of feeling like she was stuck in some provincial version of Paris, spending her afternoons visiting Adolphe's sisters in their drab houses. Now she was going from one event to another in lavishly appointed spaces where light bounced from the chandeliers to the gilding on the walls to the gleaming parquet floor.

It was a world of glamour but also of enormous wealth and power. France claimed to be democratic and meritocratic, but in fact it was deeply oligarchic, and many vestiges of the old aristocratic order remained intact. For one, there was the sheer scale of economic inequality. In Meg's day, the top one percent of French society raked in twenty times the average income of the rest of the population.[10] Politicians tended to come from wealth, as did the men who occupied the upper reaches of France's powerful civil service, and ties of family, friendship, and education knit them to prominent industrialists. All the receptions and balls to which Meg went bound this world closer together. They were spaces of courtship, of politicking, of currying favor, of trading information, and of affirming who belonged and who did not.[11]

Meg's days in *Tout-Paris* were spent taking tea with other women of high society. At night, she went to balls where men in impeccably tailored white tie and tails whisked women in frothy, pastel gowns from one end of a vast room to another. Or to the opera, where she sat in a friend's loge, a good place to view the performance—and an even better one to see who else was there.

It would have been exhausting for anyone, and the Steinheils' strained resources made it all the more so. When other women entertained, they relied on a small army of servants. Meg had some help but had to do much of the preparations herself. She cooked, she cleaned, she moved furniture, she arranged flowers, she lit candles. This left her with all of five minutes to get dressed before her guests arrived. They'd expect to see her elegantly and calmly welcome them.[12] Seeming harried or distracted by domestic concerns would be a faux pas, though, and raise eyebrows about whether she really belonged in high society.

Meg wouldn't let anything so trivial as time stop her. She was the first to rise in her household and the last to go to bed.[13] Her mother warned her that she was stretching herself too thin, but anything was better than rotting away with Adolphe.[14] In her words, "The Parisian life, brilliant and exhausting, strenuous and artificial, was above all intoxicating, and I needed such intoxication."[15]

She loved the glitz and glamour of it all, of course. She adored feeling like she was in the know, hearing "dreadful secrets from excited ladies." There was also the pleasure of being considered a society broker, arranging advantageous marriages between two illustrious families or helping friends get into the most exclusive men's clubs in Paris.[16] She made sure that her own family benefited from her access to the halls of power. After her brother, Julien, abruptly left the army to run away with a singer, Meg found him a position in the Ministry of Finances.[17] As she moved into the densely connected milieu of Parisian elites, Meg had the impression that she knew everyone who mattered and understood how power operated. It was an unfair system built on insider access, but for her, there was only pleasure in knowing how decisions were made and in being in the room when they did.

All this was made even sweeter by her sense of having triumphed over everyone who had ever disapproved of her. In the words of a journalist, she had grown up "part of a prominent bourgeois family, but from a minor branch, scorned, kept apart" by her "haughty cousins."[18] After she left Beaucourt, she faced Adolphe's disapproving sisters and brothers-in-law. Turns out her loose behavior and talk weren't holding her back from being fêted by the cream of Parisian society.

This world loved her in return. There were any number of rich and powerful men who were delighted with the young, vivacious beauty who had shown up in their midst and who flirted right back at them. Meg now got a sort of male attention that she craved. In her words, "I admit that I very much enjoyed being flattered and adored. I realized that I held a real fascination for men and that made me very happy."[19]

One of these men was, of course, her husband's friend, Bouchez.

As he entreated her to remain married to Adolphe, he had probably offered her a bargain: don't get a divorce, have an affair with him instead.

There was a lot to recommend him as a lover. Twenty-nine years older than Meg, he had enjoyed a meteoric rise to the top of the French judiciary. There, his superiors had remarked on his intelligence, his eloquence, and his "sound and astute judgement."[20] He was tall, with muttonchop sideburns and a craggy face. Meg found him handsome, with a "small, shrewd, and sensuous eye." With his "exquisite courtesy, his self-control, and his capable and masterly way of dealing with affairs," he reminded her of her father's friend M. Doriand. He had a "natural and romantic charm" and "was a witty *causeur* [conversationalist], on whose words every one hung fascinated. People were anxious to be admitted to his salon, and he was a great favourite, especially with women."[21] And he had picked her.

This is all to say that Bouchez was everything that Adolphe was not: successful, admired, urbane, and rich. It's hard to imagine that these men—so different in temperament and circumstances—were best friends. In particular, it's hard to imagine what Bouchez saw in Adolphe—at least until he saw that the painter had a desirable, lonely wife. And ultimately, with his charisma, appeal to the opposite sex, and sexualized manner, he was a great match for Meg.

Bouchez also offered Meg the forms of support that she had so desperately wanted Adolphe to provide. He was her confidante and she was able to tell him "all my anxieties, all my worries about the fact that my marriage was not what I had dreamed of, that is to say that in Adolphe I didn't find what every woman hopes for, a source of support, moral support, a support in all ways, a protector."[22] He also had a worldliness and practicality that Meg and Adolphe completely lacked. Between the two of them, they couldn't make a sound financial decision to save their lives, and they came to rely on Bouchez's good sense.[23] Meg's statement that she wanted "support in all ways" was also a polite way of saying that Bouchez gave her money.

One problem: how was she going to explain where she was on her afternoons at Bouchez's and why she was coming back with so much cash and jewelry in her hands? On his advice, she claimed that she had been visiting an "Aunt Lily." This was one of her newfound society acquaintances for whom she and Bouchez constructed an elaborate backstory. In their telling, Aunt Lily was the wealthy illegitimate half sister of one of Bouchez's relatives, a woman named Berthe Lefèvre (Berthe actually existed, Lily did not). If no one had ever met Aunt Lily, that was because no one could. A respectable woman could never receive someone born out of wedlock, even if they were close relatives. Meg had healed a breach between Berthe and Lily, who then showed her gratitude through generosity.[24]

The story made about as much sense in Meg's day as it does now, which is to say, not much. Adolphe wasn't fooled for long, and he quickly figured out who was giving Meg money.[25] It must have hurt him to know that his best friend, the man he trusted with his most sensitive dealings, was the one sleeping with his wife. Yet he couldn't do a thing. And Adolphe's misery might have been part of the appeal for Meg. It was a slap in the face of a husband who had so disappointed her.

As they settled into their relationship, Meg and Bouchez became more open about it. Adolphe knew, and so did many others. Indeed, she came to have an almost official status as his "lady of the house," entertaining friends, family members, and visitors on his behalf, giving orders to the servants, and embedding herself in his circle.[26] (Bouchez was married, but it's not known where his wife was in all this.)[27]

Within the confines of *Tout-Paris*, Meg's behavior didn't really matter. Married women's infidelities were increasingly acceptable in the

Belle Époque, especially within elite Parisian circles. Men, of course, had long enjoyed such freedoms. Women, though, needed to maintain appearances and a modicum of discretion about their affairs.[28] Some went to elaborate lengths to do so. One chronicler of elite life recounted that to avoid the servants spreading gossip, women had their coachmen take them to a department store. They entered the store and then promptly left from another set of doors and took a cab to their assignation. When they returned a few hours later, they'd tell their coachman that shopping had taken an eternity.[29] Meg's fiction of Aunt Lily was sloppier than this kind of subterfuge, but what was important was that she offered the fiction, not that anyone believed it.

———————

Many women would have stopped there and been content with a generous and kind lover. Meg was not. Instead, she was determined to use the connections that Bouchez offered to earn more money and continue her rise in high society.

What Meg wanted was to be the wife of a prominent society artist. Maybe Adolphe could become like his friend Léon Bonnat, an esteemed painter who had a lucrative business as the portraitist for the French elite. Accordingly, Meg shamelessly solicited every new acquaintance to buy one of her husband's works and introduce her to others who might.[30]

The hitch was that few people wanted to purchase Adolphe's uninspiring canvases. Plenty of them were interested in Meg, however.

She decided to strike a deal with them: buy one of Adolphe's paintings, and she'd make herself available for an affair. In her words, "Every time that my husband did not have the courage to go and sell his paintings, it was me who attempted to sell them among the people who were around me. Among those people who were around me, there were those who became my lovers."[31] It was an unusual form of sex work, one that her husband didn't like but that was service to his career.

We don't know how she indicated to her potential clients just how far she was willing to go to get them to purchase one of Adolphe's paintings. Perhaps she told them explicitly; perhaps she relied on gesture and tone to convey her meaning. Eventually, gossip did the trick, and men would tell one another how to secure a liaison with Meg. At one society gathering, a prominent official pulled aside a newcomer who had expressed an interest in Meg and told him, "You just buy one or two canvasses, for which you pay a lot, because it's bad painting, but you will have Meg on top of that!"[32]

It was an arrangement in which everyone benefited, to one degree or another. Adolphe got a whole host of new commissions. Meg bolstered the household's finances and her position in high society. Her clients got a painting or two and either an encounter with Meg or a full-blown relationship, depending on how things went. What's more, she was rumored to be very, very good in bed. One society gossip noted that she was thought to be "very expert in what [the author] Guy de Maupassant called the 'art of breaking men's backs.'"[33]

Meg offered Adolphe's new patrons more than just the pleasures of the flesh. She gave them the thrill of the chase and the opportunity to play the seducer. Because she didn't straight up offer sex for money, there was an ambiguity to the transaction. A man would have to work to get her to sleep with him, and she often made a client wait a month or so between the purchase of the painting and falling into his arms. In the meantime, he'd need to pay court to her.[34] This, more than just the sexual release, was something that many men who solicited sex workers in this era sought. They wanted to be presented with a woman who might say no but probably wouldn't. When she eventually said yes, they would feel powerful, worldly, and desired.[35]

Some of Meg's relationships lasted months or years. Others were one-off, transactional encounters in hotels.[36] She juggled lovers, with one primary partner and then other affairs on the side.[37]

Her lovers were industrialists, politicians, and important officials—a veritable who's who of the French elite. Unsurprisingly, given her relationship with Bouchez, there were a whole host of judges. Two of her more enduring liaisons in the mid-1890s were with the magistrates Paul Bertulus and Joseph Lemercier, both of whom were socially prominent.[38]

Meg's clients may also have included women. Beginning in the 1890s, she became close to Berthe Lefèvre, the relative of Bouchez and the purported half sister of "Aunt Lily." Lefèvre was unmarried, rich, in her fifties, and known for her "seductive demeanor" and "elegant tastes," in the words of one relative. She gave Meg money and lent her fabulous jewelry to wear at the opera, pieces that were far above anything that Meg could have afforded on her own. At the time, many seemed to think that Meg and Lefèvre were just close friends.[39] Was this the sum total of their relationship? After all, if you swapped Lefèvre's gender, you'd probably think a sexualized, worldly, rich man who rained affection and money on Meg was having an affair with her. And there's a long tradition of observers being unable to see sexual relationships between women as such.[40]

The Parisian police, who kept an eye on the private lives of prominent individuals, also described Meg in a gossipy memo as a "known lesbian."[41] (At the time, the term "lesbian" was used for any woman who had sex with other women, even if she also had relationships with men.)[42]

Yet Meg's affairs with women are a possibility, not a certainty. As is often true for same-sex liaisons, the evidence for them comes from hints and rumors.[43] In the polite but suggestive words of one of Adolphe's relatives, "Obviously we don't know everything about the very close relations between Mme Steinheil and Mlle Lefèvre."[44] And while it's hard to square Meg's horror at Adolphe's same-sex liaisons with the possibility that she might also have been engaging in them herself, she was never known for her moral rigor or consistency.

If Meg did have lesbian affairs, she certainly would not have been the only woman in Parisian high society to have done so. The city had a thriving subculture for women who sought relationships with other women, including bars and restaurants that catered to them; there were also rumors that brothels did, too. All the same, there were reasons why Meg would have taken extra pains to hide her affairs with women. Lesbians coped with considerable stigmas in this era and were seen as excessively mannish and a sign of society's moral decline, hardly a set of associations Meg would want.[45]

For all the questions that remain about the exact parameters of Meg's clientele, we have a clearer sense of what she got out of sex work.

For one, there was the money. Yet Meg wasn't particularly interested in money for the sake of money or even material luxury. Her dresses were relatively plain and never followed the latest fashions.[46] The house on Impasse Ronsin was always a bit drab, the furniture and decor old-fashioned, and the Steinheils' finances were never particularly stable.[47]

Instead, her earnings primarily went to entertain in style and to bolster her position in high society.[48] This is why Meg structured her affairs in such an unusual fashion. In requesting that her lovers buy Adolphe's paintings, Meg was trying to boost her husband's status in society and, by extension, her own. Because she charged for paintings and not, strictly speaking, for sex, her lovers didn't spend that much on her by the standards of the day. Indeed, Meg never earned a great deal, even though she lived in an era when men were willing to bestow fabulous sums on women and bankrupt themselves if need be.[49]

Meg's feelings about her lovers are also complex. Her confidante and servant Mariette Wolff stated that her employer was "cold and calculating" in her relationships and she never had an affair with someone who wasn't paying for her time, affection, and sexual favors.[50] Some of her short-term, transactional relationships were probably devoid of much emotional content. Yet she had an affection for at least some of her clients. Her admiration, gratitude, and warmth toward Bouchez are all apparent in her memoirs. Indeed, Adolphe often fretted that she tended to throw herself into some of her relationships. He wrote a letter telling her, "You judge people in a superficial way," and warned her not to believe the promises that some of her lovers made her. He feared that she had a habit of becoming emotionally overinvested in some of her affairs and suffered intense devastation when they ended.[51] She had done so with Sheffer. Time and experience had not lessened her habit of rushing headlong into relationships.

In any case, her liaisons were very much work. Mariette recounted that she returned from some of her assignations with "her fatigue visible, her eyes exhausted."[52] She had to be bewitching, to make her clients feel special, to be what they wanted her to be. Meg was good at this and Édouard had raised her to be, but that didn't mean it wasn't draining.

For the time being, though, all this work, from the emotional labor to the chores around the house to the visits to drum up business for her and Adolphe, was worth it. Meg had arrived. The truth was that she was only beginning.

CHAPTER 5

IF YOU REALLY WANTED to make it in Parisian high society, you wouldn't just attend the balls and receptions other women organized in their houses. You'd establish yourself as a hostess who received the most illustrious individuals of the day.

Of course, that was what Meg wanted. In one of the more notable instances of her ability to turn her dreams into reality, that was what she got. It required more work and more money she and Adolphe didn't have, but it meant that she'd be less dependent on others to maintain her status and better able to play the role of a society broker.

Still, entertaining at home came with risks, especially since it exposed her wealthier guests to her strained circumstances. Her home wasn't in any of the typical neighborhoods of elite social life. There was no courtyard for carriages and automobiles, no sweeping staircase to ascend. Her guests would have to be dropped off on the corner of Impasse Ronsin and rue de Vaugirard and walk through the metal gates that blocked the Impasse off. They'd pass a factory and ramshackle artist studios before finally arriving at Meg and Adolphe's home. When they entered the large drawing room, they'd see it was decorated with a hodgepodge of pieces from different eras, as the Steinheils had to make do with what they had inherited or could find relatively inexpensively.[1] There were "cabinets filled with cameos, rare china and silver," centuries-old tapestries on the walls, and an organ, a violin, and a piano so that Meg could show off her musical talents.[2] Sometimes, if guests looked very closely, they could see that the artfully arranged flowers hid holes in the tablecloths that the Steinheils didn't have the money to replace.[1]

In this room, Meg hosted Friday afternoon receptions that were sedate, scripted affairs.[3] Guidebooks advised hostesses to park themselves by the chimney and stand up when another woman, a priest, or an elderly person arrived but not when a man did. Men were to remove their hat upon entry and hold it to avoid the monstrous faux pas of showing its lining to another guest. Meg would serve tea and refreshments and make sure conversation stayed light and in the realm of the arts, travel, and society gossip.[4]

Then there were the soirées where Meg and Adolphe's house was packed to the gills.[5] One journalist stated, "It rained generals, diplomats, and important officials. There were so many judges that no one knew where to put all of them; some evenings, they sat on the stairs for lack of space."[6]

All this crowding created an atmosphere that was more intimate and sexualized than at many other high-society gatherings. One of Meg's lovers found her parties "dazzling" but was taken aback to see "the elite of Parisian society, celebrities and magistrates, financiers, artists, politicians, [and] women who were universally respected" revel with such abandon and drop their masks of propriety.[7] This was the advantage to Meg's relatively tenuous status in high society, for it gave her something to offer her most established guests. On the far side of town, in the home of a couple known for all sorts of sexual misbehavior, they might have felt they could indulge in their desires just a bit more freely than they normally could.

Meg also had a set of regular guests with enough star power to draw others in, including the painter Léon Bonnat, the composer Jules Massenet, the poet and novelist François Coppée, and the novelist Émile Zola.[8] The first three were artistic luminaries particularly favored by the establishment and, as such, were a comfortable fit for many of her other guests.

These included judges, of course, as well as politicians and high officials. It was a place where the son of a former president might hobnob with the head of the Parisian police.[9] There were also attorneys, like Antony Aubin, reputed to be the best criminal defender of the day, and André Paisant, an ambitious lawyer known for his eloquence and charm.[10] Then there were wealthy men from the United States, Latin America, and other European countries who either had an interest in the arts or were willing to pretend that they did in order to secure a relationship with Meg.[11] Some of the guests were her lovers. Others, like Bonnat and Paisant, likely were not and instead were close friends of both Meg and Adolphe. And still others, like Aubin or some of the judges she received, were acquaintances who went to Meg's salon in search of entertainment and connections to further their careers.

Meg wasn't lonely like she was when she first arrived in Paris, and she didn't have to work so hard to sell herself and Adolphe's art. Now, her house was filled with a whole slew of potential clients. As a society hostess, she could play a role in Paris's political, artistic, and intellectual establishment. It was a path to renown and influence that, unlike taking up a profession, was seen as entirely respectable and traditional, one that placed her in a centuries-long line of revered icons of French femininity.[12]

———————

Meg, though, wasn't exactly what anyone would call respectable.

Instead, by engaging in sex work, she became what many saw as the lowest of the low, as far away from proper as you could imagine.

Many in her day regarded prostitution as both necessary and a stain on the women who practiced it. Because men were thought to need regular sexual outlets, prostitutes protected society from male desire gone amok. Officials and hygienists described them as functioning a lot like the sewage system: a revolting but indispensable element of urban life. Although the women who sold sex in Paris were typically poor and doing what they could to make their way in a labor market that offered paltry wages and few protections, not everyone could see that. Instead, they were often considered to be utterly immoral social outcasts who were pathways for the vices and diseases of the poor to infect their well-to-do clients.[13]

To protect society from these dangers, prostitutes were subjected to a complex system of regulation. Even though sex work was legal, women who engaged in it had to register with the police and submit to regular gynecological examinations to check for diseases. If they failed to comply, they could be imprisoned in the grim confines of the Parisian women's prison of Saint-Lazare. It was one of the many ways in which the state violated its commitment to liberty and equality and made the lives of vulnerable citizens even harder.[14]

Mixed in with the fear, anxiety, and hostility toward sex workers was an intense fascination and even idolization of them. This was especially the case for the handful of women who jumped from working in the streets or a brothel to living lives of extraordinary luxury as courtesans. These women were the subjects of some of the most noted novels and paintings of the day, and it was a mark of distinction for a man to have a famous courtesan as a mistress.[15]

Despite the wealth that rained down on them, despite the fact that courtesans had been celebrated for centuries in France, they were excluded from polite society. Elite women often shunned them.[16] Because they weren't respectable, some of their clients thought they enjoyed a certain level of vulgarity and lewd behavior, including being pawed and fondled. Accordingly, their clients didn't always think they had to treat courtesans with the courtesy they showed to elite women.[17]

With her high status and her long-term affairs with prominent men, Meg is often regarded as a courtesan. What was undoubtedly more important to her was how different she was from other sex workers. She was born a Japy, not in the slums of Paris. If courtesans married, they typically did so when they retired, not before they took up sex work. Because Meg was so careful to distance herself from any monetary transactions, so insistent that her fees had to go through Adolphe, she could maintain the polite fiction that she wasn't really selling herself. She sold art, and the sex came as a bonus.

This is another reason Meg never really charged that much: it set her apart from courtesans. They had a reputation for being greedy, wearing ultrafashionable clothing, and draping themselves in the fabulous jewels that their lovers gave them. In this, they were seen as emblems of the worst excesses of capitalism.[18] One observer once told

Meg, "Professionals in your place would have made a fortune."[19] That was the whole point: earning less money allowed her to claim that she wasn't a "professional." That was what allowed her to be received by the women of high society and entertain them in turn. It also gave her the protections of respectability. Maybe her clients would respect her more and treat her better, knowing that she was a married lady welcomed in the best circles.

For all that Meg defied the logics of her day, she wasn't necessarily unique. Other elite women were rumored to offer their services in brothels for a night, and novels of the time portrayed bourgeois women who had affairs to pay off their debts.[20]

In some ways, Meg was a perfect representation of the new, more relaxed codes of behavior for denizens of *Tout-Paris*, a milieu where a married woman's infidelity increasingly provoked little more than amused gossip. Indeed, not following the rules was a sign of how much Meg belonged. In her day, many in the bourgeoisie claimed to uphold family, morality, and modesty. But behind closed doors, they might allow themselves license to do the exact opposite.[21]

Elites often assumed that they needed to show everyone else how to behave. In the words of one chronicler of high society, "the upper bourgeoisie" hated "scandal or acquiring a bad reputation."[22] Judges, for instance, typically came from the bourgeoisie and were the (literal) enforcers of rules in an era when lawbreakers were presumed to be poor.[23] Being too open about their transgressions would reflect badly on their station and their state, which cast itself as the guardian of morality and the family in this era.[24] As a result, flagrant bad behavior could have professional consequences. Meg's lover Bertulus, for instance, was a talented investigator, but his womanizing was constantly getting him into trouble. One of his superiors upbraided him for failing to "demonstrate how a good education was united to austere morals," as judges should.[25]

Yet it was more important to appear to behave than to do so. After all, if you couldn't commit to following the rules, you could at least show that you respected them by pretending to follow them.[26]

Meg and her clients also knew that they had plenty of friends in high places who could intervene if anything threatened to become too public. She had full confidence that she would never fall under the state's regulatory system that led to other sex workers feeling humiliated and trapped. Indeed, Louis Lépine, the head of the Parisian police and the man who oversaw this system, was one of the guests in her salon.[27] He had plenty of other secrets to keep, and his men sometimes cleaned up evidence of sexual indiscretions among politicians and important officials.[28]

Fundamentally, since the bourgeoisie thought of themselves as inherently more moral than the poor, it was fine if they didn't always behave as such.

In this atmosphere, being public about your bad behavior was one of the ultimate transgressions. It was a betrayal of your family and might give outsiders the dangerous idea that elites weren't moral exemplars. In contrast, deception wasn't necessarily bad but a courtesy to yourself and others.[29]

Likewise, knowing the hidden, seamy truth was a sign that you belonged. In her memoirs, Meg wrote of a "M[onsieur]. X., an apparently sedate and worthy Minister of State...who did not hesitate to disguise himself, even donning wigs and false moustaches, on his nocturnal expeditions to cheap haunts of so-called pleasure." Or there was "M[onsieur]. T., a famous banker, who had his house so built he could entertain fifty friends to a bacchanalian orgy without his wife knowing, although she was only on the other side of the wall."[30] Did the special orgy wing, the wigs, and the moustaches really exist? Or were they just figments of Meg's vivid imagination? It's impossible to say. But it was a way for her to assert that she had access to the gossip that provided a more accurate picture of reality than the façade of propriety.

For a while in the mid-1890s, Meg's sex work was one of these insider secrets. It helped that her lovers were never particularly famous and that her own behavior was never particularly flagrant.

All that was about to change.

CHAPTER 6

IN THE SUMMER OF 1897, Meg was on vacation in the Alps with her lover Lemercier as well as Adolphe and Marthe.

It was, to say the least, an awkward situation. Adolphe was preparing to paint a canvas that the Alpine Club had commissioned and so could say that he was there for a reason other than following his wife and her lover around.[1]

It was about to get a whole lot more awkward.

One day in August, Meg and Adolphe were near the Italian border, witnessing the maneuvers of French soldiers. Adolphe, compelled by his artist's eye, had climbed as high as he could to "survey the coming scene," while she was taking photographs of the soldiers. Suddenly, a group of men in civilian clothing arrived. "One of them, wearing a red shirt, a brown suit, yellowish gaiters, and a white *béret*, looked up at me" and asked her if she wanted to take his picture.[2] It took her a bit of time to realize why this absurdly dressed man thought he should pose for her. Turns out he was none other than Félix Faure, president of the Republic.

Meg and Faure weren't total strangers. She had gone to official functions at the Élysée Palace, and the two inhabited the twin worlds of Parisian officialdom and Parisian pleasures.[3] Seeing her now, in the fresh Alpine air instead of the stifling atmosphere of formal receptions where everyone was trying to catch his attention, he was thunderstruck, overwhelmed by her magnetism. Meg had practice eliciting desire in powerful men and reeling them in, but Faure was her biggest catch to date.

So he invited Meg and Adolphe to lunch. Meg, probably because she was playing coy, said no, but Adolphe wasn't going to let this opportunity go to waste and went to "ask the President for permission to paint the forthcoming 'distribution of decorations'" in which Faure was going to give medals to soldiers stationed in the Alps.[4]

Later that day, she ran into Faure again when "a group of little girls, wearing the quaint old dresses of Savoy, were offering flowers to him." He "bowed deeply, and afterwards there came an invitation to dinner—which I declined."[5]

He was nothing if not persistent, and the next day, "another invitation came, this time to lunch, near Bourg Saint-Maurice."[6] Even members of his entourage who were well accustomed to his eye for women were surprised by his singular focus on Meg, particularly since he announced that the schedule of his visit to the Alps would have to be rearranged to make sure that he had a chance to cross her path again.[7]

Again Meg said no, while Adolphe went to curry favor with a new potential patron. At the lunch, Faure seemed far more interested in Meg's absence, to which he "repeatedly alluded," than Adolphe's presence or artistic talents.[8]

Why all these refusals? Meg claimed that "the milk, cheese, and brown bread of the mountaineers" was more appealing to her than "all the dainties and wines of the presidential table."[9] Any notion that Meg preferred the simple life to the company of the rich and powerful was laughable. Instead, she was letting the president know that if he wanted to have an affair with her, he would have to become Adolphe's patron.

Faure had no problem with her terms. Once he and the Steinheils were back in Paris, he reached out to Adolphe to commission a portrait, one that required him to pose in the painter's studio, giving him and Meg plenty of opportunities to meet. After Adolphe painted a canvas commemorating Faure's unveiling of an Alpine fort and exhibited it at the Salon of 1898, Faure arranged for the government to purchase it for the astronomical sum of 30,000 francs. This was considerably more than the typical price for Adolphe's works, which usually sold for hundreds of francs.[10] It was even more than clients paid for a full-length portrait by Meg's friend Bonnat, one of the more esteemed and commercially viable artists of the time.[11] The Steinheils got a sudden influx of cash, and Faure got to start an affair with Meg. The only losers were the taxpayers who were footing the bill.

———————

In 1897, Faure was fifty-six, married with two daughters, and very wealthy.[12] Unlike Meg, who was born into the bourgeoisie but was frequently in danger of falling out of it, his social trajectory was decidedly upward. Faure was from a working-class family, but by the 1860s, he had become a successful merchant. In 1870, amid the disaster of the Franco-Prussian War, Faure entered political life by running for a seat on Le Havre's city council. Eleven years later, he was elected to the Chamber of Deputies, the lower house of France's parliament, and sat on the center-right.

Faure was tall, slightly balding, with white hair, a blond handlebar moustache, and a pale, smooth face. Energetic, dapper, and genial, he was always impeccably dressed. He loved luxury, the pleasures of the table, and Paris's parties, theaters, and sexual underbelly.[13]

Félix Faure in 1895

In 1895, Faure became president of the French Republic, and his term was quickly overshadowed by the Dreyfus Affair, an espionage scandal that consumed France. It centered around the case of Alfred Dreyfus, a Jewish army officer who was wrongly convicted of spying for the Germans.[14] The affair whipped up ugly currents of antisemitism, as Dreyfus's opponents, known as anti-Dreyfusards, came to regard Jewish citizens as all-too-powerful individuals who were conspiring with France's enemies. Faure was aligned with this camp and unwilling to use his presidential authority to reopen Dreyfus's legal case.[15]

Much to Faure's frustration, his was largely a symbolic position.[16]

His job was to be above the fray and project the dignity, unity, and majesty of France.[17] As the embodiment of the nation and the government, he represented all the contradictions of his society's attitudes toward the sexuality of powerful men. On the one hand, he was supposed to demonstrate his commitment to the family, the pillar of French society. On the other hand, his ability to seduce pretty women was regarded as proof of his grandeur and virility.[18]

Faure took these elements of the job seriously—a little too seriously, in fact. As president, he continued to indulge his sexual appetites.[19] Despite or perhaps because of his humble origins, he loved luxury and all the formal trappings of the presidency. His nickname was "the Sun President," as if he was an elected version of Louis XIV, the king who had built Versailles and made elaborate ceremonies the center of his reign.[20] One friend lamented that Faure, who was "in former years so friendly and gay, a fine companion," as president "had acquired the habit of confusing his own person with France" and was now "calmly and serenely ridiculous."[21]

His infatuation with Meg, however, overrode his concerns about his dignity. When he exclaimed to his friend Louis Nordheim that Meg was "a jewel…a ravishing creature," Nordheim warned Faure "how ridiculous his comportment was at his age and how little it was in keeping with his functions."[22] Faure gave Meg wildly expensive jewelry, while tongues wagged that the president was so gaga for Meg because of her skills as a lover and that he was "infatuated by the heady philter of her skillful ardors."[23]

In her memoirs, Meg didn't say much about how she felt about Faure, but that is in itself revealing. She wrote that "when he saw that things always 'went well' with him, he became almost irritatingly self-confident" and that he was "dignified to the verge of aloofness. But he had many worthy qualities: he was endowed with much common sense…and he was an ardent—a zealous, patriot…and there can be no doubt that he considerably increased the prestige of France during his Presidency." That "but" says a lot: sometimes she found him a pompous bore. Elsewhere, she said he was "a downright honest and sincere man, and believed he was working for the greatness of the country he loved so ardently."[24] It's all rather impersonal and flat, suggesting that Meg could never really think about him outside the confines of his presidency, or he himself was unwilling to play any other role when he was with her. She admired him as a politician, but his obsession with his position ensured that she could never get close to him. For her, this wasn't love.

What she did love, however, was the access.

Which she had plenty of. The two saw each other almost every day. She would come to the Élysée Palace in the late afternoon, making sure to arrive via a side door to avoid being seen. She would be threaded through the building and finally ushered into a small room just off Faure's presidential office on the first floor. It had high ceilings, over-stuffed furniture, and gilding everywhere—on the chandelier, on the furniture, on the moldings of the walls and the fireplace—and followed the decorating philosophy that too much was never enough.[25] The two would have what the French call a "five to seven," referring to the two hours between work and dinner reserved for an assignation. Afterward, she would return to the Impasse Ronsin, and he'd go to dinner and resume his life as president and a family man.[26]

During their encounters, they'd have sex, of course, and he'd talk about whatever was on his mind, which was often politics. In her account, she was his political confidante and saved France from at least one disaster. In 1898, Faure and the French public learned that the army had forged evidence indicating that Dreyfus was a spy. According to Meg, Faure decided if he went on a weeklong cruise with Meg, one of her sisters, and one of his friends, the crisis would die down. Fortunately, Meg and Faure's friend convinced him to abandon the idea.[27]

The story strains belief. Faure had to have known that going on a sex cruise in the midst of a political firestorm would hardly convince anyone that steady hands were at the helm of the state. Over the years, Meg spun many yarns about her relationships and her role in history. This one, like so many others, reveals her desire to be seen as a woman at the center of events who was always acting in the nation's best interest.

Meg claimed not to have firm political opinions, and she writes that she "never took part in one single political discussion, not even in my own drawing-room."[28] For all that, she sided with anti-Dreyfusards and, like them, believed that Jews were a danger to the nation.[29]

What Meg cared most about, however, was patronage. One journalist wrote that she "made sure that her relatives and friends, magistrates or officials of every kind, benefitted" from her liaison with Faure.[30] Adolphe was one such beneficiary, of course. Alongside the money Faure shoveled his way to secure a relationship with Meg, the president also arranged for Adolphe to receive the Legion of Honor, a prestigious official recognition.[31] Faure also helped Meg's wayward brother, Julien, obtain a transfer to a more favorable location within the Ministry of Finances.[32] Nor did she forget her in-laws; she launched Adolphe's brother-in-law from a rather unremarkable judicial career into a post as chief of staff of the minister of justice.[33] Many civil servants who weren't related to her found that approaching Meg was the easiest path to promotion and preferment and she acquired a whole set of individuals in her debt.[34] She writes, "My salon was now more crowded than ever before. Invitations were showered upon me both from quarters friendly with the Government and from quarters in league with the Opposition."[35] Her guests knew that despite France's claims to be a meritocracy, getting anywhere in the civil service depended on having the right connections.[36]

Meg didn't see this as maintaining a system built on insider access but as almost a form of charity work with the overprivileged: "It was a source of real joy to me to be able to render services to so many people who seemed to need them." She also claimed that the state benefited from her feminine intuition, writing, "How often I was able to warn the President in time against a dangerous mistake" and that she was able to sniff out many "a man without scruples or principles…ready to sell everything and even himself to achieve his ambition."[37]

Meg's dispersal of favors put her in a long tradition that was uniquely French. In the era of the French monarchy, royal mistresses had used their liaisons with kings to benefit themselves and their families and acquire political influence. Louis XV's mistress, Mme de Pompadour, was famous for this, and commentators called Meg the "Pompadour of Vaugirard," a quip that combined a reference to one of her royal antecedents with the name of Meg's humdrum neighborhood.[38] During the Belle Époque, only men could vote or hold office. But many presumed that behind the scenes, women were still pulling the strings. The public was fascinated by politicians' mistresses who were seen as exceptional figures of female power, "these women who rule over the rulers," in the words of one novelist.[39] Many presumed that their seductive capabilities gave them sway over their lovers who would do whatever these women wanted to keep up the steady supply of sexual favors.[40]

As was true for the French kings, Faure's relationship with Meg was an open secret.[41] The couple regularly appeared together in the Bois de Boulogne, the giant park to the west of Paris, which was known as a place for adulterous couples to canoodle and sex workers to solicit clients.[42] He was often seen at the house on Impasse Ronsin and gave Marthe expensive presents. When they couldn't meet in person, he sent letters to Meg via military couriers on horseback, one of the more conspicuous means of communication imaginable.[43] It helped that journalists didn't report on Faure's affair with Meg. They knew about it but presumed that the French president was entitled to a good deal of privacy, a system that allowed him to do what he wanted without too many consequences.[44]

Faure and Meg even traveled together. In the summer of 1898, Meg, Émilie, one of Meg's sisters, and Marthe went to Le Havre, Faure's hometown, to spend the month of August with him. He was at his family home with his wife and daughters, while Meg and her kin rented a house nearby. Faure visited daily for sex, horse rides, and musical afternoons. Adolphe, meanwhile, was in the Vosges on the other side of the country: the official word was that he was pulled away on his painting duties.[45]

All this was a bit much for Faure's long-suffering wife, Berthe. She typically turned a blind eye to his extramarital liaisons, but Meg joining the family's summer vacation was beyond the pale. She disliked how much power Meg had over her husband and begged him to break off the relationship. Berthe also now refused to accompany her husband to dinners at the Impasse Ronsin or receive Meg when she called on her.[46]

As a sign of Faure's commitment to this relationship, he commissioned a portrait of Meg from her friend Bonnat, which was intended for his private collection. In it, she sits in a chair, looking directly at the viewer. Her dress is fashionable but not extravagant, with the pale color and lace suggesting a certain primness. The pose and the clothes are entirely in keeping with other portraits of bourgeois women from the time. But her hands show another story. She's wearing four large rings: a bit much for a respectable woman but not out of place for a courtesan, who were often depicted wearing fabulous jewelry. There's also that smile, with her teeth visible between her parted lips, an expression common in photographs and paintings of courtesans.[47] This and her soft, direct gaze serve to create an intimacy between Meg and the viewer, who could enjoy the play between the proper and the illicit in Meg's self-presentation and think about how they could encounter such an excitingly wanton woman in high society.[48]

Bonnat's portrait of Meg

CHAPTER 7

FEBRUARY 16, 1899, WAS an unusually warm day in Paris. It was cloudy, but there was no rain.[1] With the promise of spring right around the corner, Meg went to see Bonnat, who was working on the portrait of her. After a brief visit, she went off to her daily assignation at the Élysée Palace.[2]

It was the height of the Dreyfus Affair. At the time, Dreyfus was still serving a life sentence in a penal colony off the coast of French Guiana, even though his innocence was crystal clear. Dreyfus and his defenders were hoping for a formal reopening of his legal case (called "revision"), but Faure was blocking this effort.

At the Élysée Palace, Faure was eager for Meg to arrive. According to one chronicler of high society, he prepared for her visit by taking his usual "two strengthening pills" since "the amourous sentiments of the President [were] lacking vigour."[3] The pills were made of Spanish fly, an aphrodisiac derived from beetles. It's a toxic substance that exacerbated the heart problems Faure had been having for years, but he took it to ensure he would have an erection for his encounter with Meg.[4]

For much of the afternoon, duty interrupted pleasure. First, the archbishop of Paris arrived. Faure was impatient and the archbishop reported that he "marched up and down; I soon had the impression that he was hardly listening to what I was saying."[5] Then Faure had to see the Prince of Monaco, who was trying to smooth over diplomatic feathers ruffled by the Dreyfus Affair.[6]

Finally, he was free. He and Meg got down to business in the room next to his office. His chief aide, Louis Le Gall, was two doors down. Although Le Gall didn't much like Meg, he was well used to her visits.

There are two credible versions about what happened next. The first is Le Gall's. In his account, at 6:30 p.m., Faure tentatively stepped out of the room where he was with Meg and moved achingly slowly toward Le Gall. It was instantly clear that Faure was unwell. He put his hand on Le Gall's shoulder and told him that something sudden and painful had happened when he was in the boudoir. He didn't know it at the time, but it was a stroke. Faure implored Le Gall, "Help me sit down on your sofa," as a crazed Meg escaped from behind the president. She fled the building while Le Gall shouted at her, "Run away and don't come back again!" Faure piteously told Le Gall, "I think that death is near," and the devoted aide called for a doctor.[7]

That might be what happened, but it wasn't the story conveyed through circuits of palace gossip, which became the version that stuck in the public's mind. According to the diplomat Maurice Paléologue, who wrote down the rumors he heard, around 6:30, Le Gall heard "strange, stifled cries coming from the boudoir" where Meg and Faure were having their encounter. After he forced the door open, he found a rather indelicate scene: "The President unconscious, in a fit, in the most significant state of undress, and near him, entirely naked, Mme Steinheil, screaming, hysterical, and frantic." She was "twisting and writhing in an uncontrollable manner" and "the President was clutching her hair in his clenched fist."[8] The presumption was always that she was fellating him and that he had wrapped his hands in her hair: as he had his stroke, his grip had only tightened. Rumors swirled that Le Gall had to cut Meg's hair to release her, that she was rushed out of the presidential palace so hurriedly that she did not have time to put her clothes back on, and that she left her corset as she fled.[9] As the story circulated, it got even more sordid: aides couldn't redress Faure for a while because his erection persisted in his agony. They had to wait until he was decent to tell Berthe and the couple's daughters about his condition.[10]

On the surface of it, the second version seems too wild to be true. It's probably the case that some of the more outlandish elements, such as the impromptu haircut and the drive through the streets of Paris in a state of undress, are nothing more than titillating gossip. Yet there are reasons to be doubtful of Le Gall's account. He was close to Faure and wrote his version down to defend the dead president's reputation. In the end, whether Le Gall opened the door or Faure did, whether he found Meg clothed or nearly naked, the essentials are the same: the president had a fatal stroke in the middle of an assignation with his mistress.

Whatever happened in the suite of presidential offices, we do know that Faure continued to suffer for hours and died surrounded by his family later that evening.

Faure's death, with its blend of tragedy and comedy, has become what he is best known for.[11] Not his diplomatic triumphs or his rare and meteoric rise from the slums of Paris to the Élysée Palace. He was a man who combined a devotion to the pleasures of the flesh with an obsession with his status and grandeur. He probably would have hated the fact that the undignified circumstances of his death have lodged themselves in the French public's mind, even if he would have agreed it was a fitting way for him to go.

————

Meg's last trip to the Élysée Palace had an immediate and dramatic impact on French politics. France's parliament elected a new president who came from the Dreyfusard camp. This led anti-Dreyfusard journalists to spread rumors that Faure hadn't died of natural causes but had been murdered by their opponents—and in some cases, they suggested that Meg was the culprit.[12]

With the new president's support, Dreyfus was retried in a military court in Rennes in the summer of 1899. Although convicted a second time, he was quickly pardoned, and after this trial, passions between Dreyfusards and anti-Dreyfusards cooled. Many were eager to put the scandal to rest, particularly since it had damaged France's international reputation.

If Faure's death led to the eventual righting of the moral arc of the universe, it presented a whole host of complications for Meg, Faure, and his allies. None of these individuals wanted to reveal what he had been doing when he had the stroke that killed him. This would have tarnished his name, distressed his grieving family, and compromised the dignity of the French presidency. Thus, the official narrative was entirely without Meg: on the afternoon of February 16, Faure "suddenly found himself feeling ill," continued to get worse throughout the day, and died "after three hours of suffering" and "after having made the most touching goodbyes to his wife, two children, and those around him."[13]

This version was widely disseminated in the press, but Meg's presence was too good a story not to spread like wildfire. There were legions of quips and puns about Faure's death, many of which revolved around the fact that the word "pompes" appears in the term "funerary rites" ("*pompes funèbres*") and also means "fellate." Meg got the unfortunate nickname of "la pompe funèbre," which meant either "the undertaker" or "the deadly fellator."[14]

A few of the Parisian dailies just couldn't help themselves. With its tongue firmly in its cheek, *Gil Blas* reported that Faure "died in good health, and even due to an excess of health. His death without any suffering was just like his happy life."[15] Fittingly, *Gil Blas* was pitched at a society audience and known for its risqué content. It was a joke for those in the know. Unless you'd already heard the rumors about how Faure had died, you would miss the reference, and this newspaper wasn't going to break the codes of discretion that protected Faure's reputation.

However, two papers that opposed the regime displayed far less deference to the unspoken rules about what could and could not be said. On the left, the anarchist *Le Journal du Peuple* wrote that Faure "died because he sacrificed too much to Venus" and claimed, "We know the name and address of the young person who enjoyed [*jouissait*]...presidential favors. We will refer to her, if you like...as Mme. S." *Jouissait* meant both "enjoyed" and "orgasmed," and the ellipses, which were present in the original, made sure that no one missed the pun. Faure was taken as the embodiment of the hypocrisy of the bourgeoisie for preaching values he did not practice. The author went on, "Come on, bourgeois, do the right thing... Admit that your principles do not conform to your practice...that Love...must be free, liberated, unfettered from your Ethics of Slavery and Lies" and told readers to "scrutinize the life of the...highest magistrate in France. And judge!"[16]

The anti-Semitic and anti-Dreyfusard *La Libre Parole* also spoke of a "Mlle. S." who was the cause of Faure's demise. This newspaper had a reputation for scandal mongering, and its publisher maintained that Faure hadn't died of natural causes but was the victim of a Dreyfusard conspiracy. In his words, Meg was a "Delilah in the pay of the Jews."[17]

The jokes, the rumors, and the threats to reveal her name all mortified and scared Meg. She also got "shoals of anonymous letters" suggesting she had murdered Faure. Others "declared that if I had not killed the President, at least I knew when he died and who had killed him, and that dire calamities would befall me unless I revealed the name."[18] What had been an open secret when Faure was alive was all too close to becoming fully public in the wake of his death.

The fears about public exposure were on top of her sorrow at Faure's passing. As she said, "I had lost a great friend, and France a great patriot."[19] Her status and financial security had evaporated almost overnight. Then there were the painful echoes of her father's demise: the sudden cardiac event and the association between her sexual activity and the loss of a protector who seemed thrilled by her very existence.

Characteristically, though, the line about the death of her "great friend" was pretty much all she said about her grief. Perhaps Faure didn't mean that much to her, or perhaps her fears about her reputation didn't leave her space to mourn.

Meg considered suing the newspapers that came close to naming her but was told she couldn't, since they had only ever used an initial to refer to her. Instead, she resorted to informal efforts to deny her involvement in his death. She had a woman who had worked for her as a nurse state that she had been taking care of Meg on February 16.[20] She also wrote Bonnat and told him that after she left his studio that afternoon, she had suddenly felt ill and skipped her visit to the Élysée Palace.[21] The lady was protesting entirely too much, and it's doubtful that anyone believed her.

Instead, another woman gladly took some of the heat. Cécile Sorel, a celebrated courtesan who had also been linked to Faure, went to his funeral to attract attention and whip up some notoriety, while Meg stayed away from the funeral to avoid any such set of associations.[22] Rumors swirled that state officials paid Sorel to take the blame for precipitating the stroke that killed Faure.[23]

Sorel was an actress—a not entirely respectable profession at the time—and her career as a courtesan could only benefit from a whiff of scandal.[24] In contrast, Meg needed to stay out of the limelight to retain her status.[25] In the coming months and years, she'd learn how Faure's death both closed down and opened up possibilities for her.

CHAPTER 8

MEG HAD A CHOICE. She could slink away and leave high society, perhaps going to live with her mother in Beaucourt or retreating to the Impasse Ronsin with Adolphe and Marthe. Either would mean giving up all that she had worked for over the years: her position, her salon, her connections. Furthermore, it would be to accept the disgrace that Faure's death brought.

As ever, giving up was impossible for Meg. She was a gambler, willing to take huge risks, and so decided to reopen the doors to her salon. Now it was full of "amiable persons of both sexes, who gazed at me, looked me up and down, and studied me as if I were an object of great curiosity." It was uncomfortable and invasive as they searched her body for any signs of promiscuity and stared at her hair to see if they could spy a patch that was shorter than the rest peeking out from her updo. Any acknowledgment was an admission of defeat. She had to plow through with no indication that anything had happened or that she knew why her guests were so interested in coming to her salon. So

"I smiled on them all, as I had in the past, and sang and played to them in the old way."[1]

It could have ended horribly. If Meg had looked distressed or snapped at one of her guests or given any hint that the rumors were true and bothered her, she would have to retreat, her dignity in shreds. But Meg had triumphed before and would do so again. She recounted that by the end of 1899, "my receptions were more largely attended than ever. I had tested all those who claimed to be my friends, and found they were sincere. In official circles my influence had not waned, and I was able to render service to many as in the past."[2]

Meg credited her mother and Marthe with helping her recover from both the emotional and reputational shock of Faure's death. Ironically, her mother's immaturity was just what she needed now: "My mother looked after me in that pretty way that children often have; and, on the other hand, my little daughter, now a tiny mite of eight, was almost maternal in her solicitude for me."[3] It's a statement that reveals that Meg may have come to expect that Marthe play a parental role for her, just as she had done for Émilie.

Meg's boldness was also a gift. In an earlier era, when the rules were more strictly applied, the rich and prominent might have refused to come to her salon or receive her at their receptions lest her bad reputation rub off on theirs. In the years around 1900, the prospect of a beautiful, notorious woman showing up at high society events was thrilling. It added a frisson of excitement in a milieu defined by its commitment to sensuality and somewhat discreet rule breaking.

Still, not everyone could stomach Meg's infamy. Adolphe's kin decided that they could not countenance a relationship with her.[4] There was no small amount of hypocrisy in this. Adolphe's brother-in-law had benefited greatly from Meg's relationship with Faure but now was trying to distance himself from her because of that very same connection.

Faure's death was also the last straw for the ever-disapproving Japy kin. They refused to go to family gatherings if they thought Meg would be in attendance, and one cut off relations with Émilie because she "ignored his warnings about the notorious misconduct" of her daughter.[5] Any continued association with Meg would threaten their own moral standing.[6]

Then there was Adolphe. His wife's infamy was entirely too great a burden.[7] Finally, he and Meg accepted that their marriage was at an end and started divorce proceedings.[8]

Only it wasn't the end. Once again, a divorce threatened to air too much dirty laundry. This time, the laundry wasn't Adolphe's but Faure's. According to rumors that circulated at the time, "on the insistence of very highly placed individuals," Meg and Adolphe were persuaded to remain married. These prominent officials "appealed to their adherence to the Third Republic, to the inevitable scandal that their divorce... would cause. They spoke about the grieving widow and daughters."[9] The unhappy couple decided that staying together and maintaining the façade of respectability would be their civic duty.

———

For Meg, notoriety also came with benefits. With her name now on everyone's lips, she didn't have to hustle as much as she had in the past. In the words of one observer, "Fame proclaimed her name as a lover throughout the universe. She rapidly took advantage of the situation, accumulated profitable lovers, and directed them to the best of her interest."[10] Another stated that after this point, "she wanted to acquire and maintain her society relations, and henceforth she sought to put prudence, circumspection, and choice into her affairs."[11] In other words, she could now be a lot choosier about who she slept with.

Even the circumstances of Faure's death could be turned into an asset. Meg acquired a reputation as a lover capable of providing exquisite pleasures. Among them was fellatio. At the time, it was regarded as a degrading act, not the sort of thing that respectable women did. For that very reason, sex workers who specialized in it were especially sought after.[12] Meg was appealing because clients could enjoy the play between her semblance of propriety and her willingness to be disreputable in private.

Meg lived in an era that had elaborate rules about who did what and to whom. What she offered her clients was the chance to violate these cultural scripts of status—to experience the special pleasures of a bourgeois woman who didn't act like one, to take a break from the codes of gallantry that required elite men to treat the women they met in high society with painstaking consideration.[13]

Fundamentally, Meg managed to eroticize the idea that bourgeois women were uninterested in sex. Even her matronly face and physique, which was so different from the wasp-waisted one typical of courtesans, was an asset. It could be read as a sign of her elite status and, by the standards of the day, as proof of her carnality.[14] She gave lovers the sense that underneath it all, high society women were roiling with currents of raw sexuality.

Also appealing: the risk. Was Meg so good that she had killed a man? This was an era when the figure of the femme fatale held a powerful appeal as an object of desire, fascination, and fear.[15] What could be more exciting than a romp with a woman who was so sexy that she just might kill you? If you lived, you were guaranteed to have memories of a great time, a story to tell, and the relief of having survived.

As a result of her newfound fame, she was able to attract a more elevated clientele: not so much judges as royals, including the Prince of Wales, the future Edward VII, and the Russian Grand Duke Vladimir Alexandrovich, the tsar's uncle. Both were in the habit of coming to Paris to enjoy its many pleasures, including its beautiful women. To court Meg, they duly went to her salon.[16] Unlike her relationships with Bouchez or Faure, these liaisons were likely brief and relatively transactional.

Meg was now more willing to play with infamy than she had been in the past—even as she did so in ways that allowed her to keep her misbehavior hidden from the public's gaze. She and a lover spent a few weeks in a house outside Paris, and while they were there, she called herself "Cécile Sorel."[17] It was both an open acknowledgment that she was akin to a scandalous courtesan and ensured that the neighbors had no idea who she was.

Alongside her affairs, Meg may have had another way of capitalizing on her notoriety: blackmail. Faure's death had given his wife no relief from hearing about Meg. Someone close to the Faure family recounted that "after the death [of Faure], Mme Félix Faure had only one concern: to prevent the public from knowing the exact conditions of the former president's death." When Meg considered suing newspapers for implying that she was the cause of Faure's demise, his widow panicked. "If there was a trial, there would be a scandal. Naturally the newspaper would defend itself" by revealing what it knew about Faure's death. A terrified Berthe went to see Adolphe, who agreed to give up the suit after a payoff.[18] The lesson for Meg? There were others who were far more anxious about the truth coming out and who were willing to pay for her silence. Accordingly, there were rumors that she repeatedly went back for more.[19]

Meg was a virtuoso of making the best out of a bad situation. It was a talent she demonstrated again and again—and nowhere was this truer than in the aftermath of a sudden loss that she turned into an opportunity for money and status.

————

Not everyone was a fan, though. Meg could be calculating and manipulative, traits that wore on those around her. She was both more famous than ever before and had a more tenuous position in high society. Her anxieties about losing her status may have brought out an unpleasant side. Or if she was indeed blackmailing her dead lover's family about how he died, she may have learned just how far she was willing to go.

Some of those around her felt used by her. One rich and prominent society figure described her as shamelessly knowing "how to use her connections": he met Meg at a dinner and found that this brief acquaintanceship led her to ask him for favor after favor, much to his annoyance.[20] Meg also relied on her female friends to facilitate her affairs to a degree that exasperated them. One, a neighbor named Mme Prévôst, allowed Meg to rent a house in her name so Meg could meet lovers in it with some amount of discretion. Meg had also arranged for some of her lovers to send letters to her via Mme Prévôst. Eventually, the poor woman became so tired of Meg's incessant demands that she considered moving to another part of Paris.[21]

Other friends feared her. One, a woman named Mme Deteure, decided that Meg was too much to handle and stopped coming to

Meg's salon. Soon after, she started getting mocking anonymous letters in the mail that she knew were from Meg. Around the same time, Mme Deteure received a mysterious box of chocolates that lacked a return address. She became convinced that Meg sent them to her after slipping a purgative into the chocolates. Eventually she figured out that the chocolates weren't poisoned or even from Meg at all.[22] Still, the fact that Mme Deteure's first instinct was to think that Meg was plotting against her reveals that her friends saw her as vindictive and capable of cruelty if they crossed her.

Then there was the consensual revenge incest. In the 1900s, Meg had an affair with one of her cousins on her father's side who spent huge sums on her. The Japys were horrified. One of their promising scions was ruining himself financially for a woman who was a source of great shame. Eventually, they sent him off to Russia to end the relationship.[23] For Meg, this affair might have been true love or a chance to earn a great deal of money. It was also a terrific way to get back at the Japy cousinage who so disdained her. They couldn't ignore her power and magnetism. Try as they might to distance themselves from her, she could always hit them where it hurt: their pocketbooks and their attitudes of moral superiority.

CHAPTER 9

FOUR YEARS AFTER FAURE'S death, something shifted for Meg. Celebrity, revenge, and money weren't enough. Now she wanted romance, stability, and an escape from her increasingly miserable marriage to Adolphe. Her cook called this period "the era of great loves." Her lovers still paid her, but they were now doing so for "liaisons that were more serious" than the brief, transactional ones she had been having.[1]

The greatest of those loves was a man named Émile Chouanard, a wealthy industrialist. Meg rented a villa called Vert-Logis in Meudon, just outside Paris, for their affair. There would be no more quick encounters in hotels. Instead, the two met there three or four times a week to spend time with each other.[2] She even went so far as to cook for him, creating a version of domestic life together that was happier than what either one of them had with their spouses.[3]

There were many things that she appreciated about Chouanard. For one, he brought some stability into Meg's life after the turbulence caused by Faure's death. He promised her they'd be together for a long time and may even have given her some indication that he would marry her once he finally divorced his wife.[4]

He was also exceedingly generous and knew how to give Meg what she wanted in the way that she wanted it. He paid for the food at her dinner parties at Impasse Ronsin so that she could entertain in style. She was relieved that she never had to ask him directly for money like a common prostitute might have done.[5] As she put it, he, "as a gallant gentleman, anticipated my concerns. One day I found six bills of a thousand francs in a bouquet of flowers that was delicately offered."[6] A man could not simply hand a woman of her status a wad of cash without challenging that status, but what woman would refuse flowers from her lover? If she found a good chunk of her household's yearly income hidden in them, maybe this was payment for services rendered, or maybe it was just him taking care of her emotionally by alleviating her financial concerns.

In return, Meg made sure that Chouanard benefited from all her connections. She navigated the labyrinths of French bureaucracy for him and got him permission to get a new factory up and running in a mere twenty-four hours, an astonishing feat for the day.[7] In her estimation, "Chouanard earned fifty to sixty thousand francs with me."[8] Many a courtesan took it as a matter of pride to ruin rich men.[9] Meg made sure that Chouanard knew that she was different from those other women, that she'd make his fortune, not break it. When it came to his family, Meg also played a wifely role. She brokered a mutually advantageous marriage between his daughter Lucie and her new husband.[10] It was another way that she acted a whole lot like his wife and worked hard to further his economic interests.

The problem was that the stain of Faure's death lingered. Once Lucie was engaged, her future mother-in-law, Mme Goiran, "wrote to

M. Chouanard to make him choose between his mistress and his daughter."[11] Meg and Mme Goiran had been friends up to that point, so it's safe to say that the latter did not object on principle to Meg's behavior, past or present. Now that the families were about to tie themselves to each other, Meg's infamy threatened to tarnish the Goiran family reputation.

Here was one of the many cruelties of the elaborate calculations about status and reputation that individuals in high society made. Mme Goiran was perfectly willing to benefit from the connections that Meg's sex work gave her as long as no one really knew too much about her relationship with Meg. But a public association with Meg was another matter. Had Chouanard's mistress been a typical courtesan—someone who didn't circulate in the same salons as Mme Goiran, someone she never would have met—she likely wouldn't have objected to Meg's presence in his life. In that case, his affair would be his business and entirely separate from his family life.

For over a decade, Meg had tried to walk a narrow path between the poles of respectability and scandal. Follow the rules too closely and she wouldn't have enough money to stay in high society. Break them too openly and she might not be received in elite circles. She'd succeeded through her charm, force of will, and the relatively lax moral standards of the day. There were limits to what even she could do, however, and her balancing act might be at an end.

———

In December 1907, Chouanard ceded to Mme Goiran's demands and abruptly ended his relationship with Meg.[12]

It was a terrible blow.

She had lost a lover who served her well as both a client and companion. In the wake of the breakup, she had a mental collapse and spent months in bed. When she finally emerged from her breakdown, she lacked her usual vigor and had lost thirty pounds.[13]

Chouanard's desertion also sent the household's finances into chaos. Adolphe's income from restoring stained glass was drying up, thanks to a 1905 law separating church and state.[14] At the same time, the Steinheils' obligations were only mounting. Marthe was engaged to a young man named Pierre Buisson, the son of family friends, and she would need money for her dowry.[15] Meanwhile, time had done nothing to abate Émilie's building mania, and Meg often had to bail her out.[16]

By early 1908, the Steinheils were behind on payments to their provisioners, weren't paying their servants regularly, and even occasionally borrowed money from the ever-loyal Mariette.[17] A humiliated and dejected Adolphe went to one of his brothers-in-law to borrow fifty francs to pay for basics.[18] Meg and Adolphe also asked friends to take their valuables to the pawn shop on their behalf to keep information about their financial difficulties from becoming an irresistible piece of high-society gossip.[19] Even if they could barely put food on the table, the Steinheils still insisted on maintaining appearances.

Meg's misery and stress turned into fury at Adolphe. Their valet Rémy Couillard recounted, "M. Steinheil didn't count for anything in the house. He was nothing. We never heard him, he would not have been able to give an order to Mariette or me; Mme. Steinheil would not have accepted it!... For us he did not exist, for madame even less." When Adolphe spoke, Meg thundered at him: "You know well that you have nothing to do here... Be quiet, you are nothing... You only have the right to be silent."[20]

Heartbreakingly, Meg used Adolphe's unchanging love for her to humiliate him. She took carriage rides with him and her lovers—and told him to sit with the driver while she sat with the other man. Or she would spend time with him and Marthe at Vert-Logis and then tell them to leave when a client was about to arrive.[21] In every way that she could, she wanted him to know that he didn't matter.

Adolphe now saw his life as string of failures. He mournfully told a fellow artist, "Can you imagine what it was to throw your wife, your wife that you loved, in the arms of others in order not to die of starvation?"[22] Alongside the disaster of his marriage, he was completely out of step with the artistic currents of the time, still painting an academic style in the era of cubism.[23] In his depression, he retreated into passivity and possibly into an opium addiction.[24] While Meg was determined to maintain her position in elite circles, Adolphe was drawn to the low and not the high; he vastly preferred the company of the down-and-out models he recruited to Meg's high-society connections.[25]

In early 1908, Meg decided she just couldn't take it anymore and that it was time to resort to the solution she and Adolphe had both avoided for so long: they needed a divorce.[26] Sure, gossips would run riot with the news. It might also lead Marthe's fiancé's parents to pull their support for the engagement. For Meg, though, the hopes of attaching herself to a man who could offer her more security and stability would be worth it. She was approaching forty and by the standards of the day becoming less desirable.[27] If she wanted to find a new husband, it needed to happen fast.

But Adolphe said no. He had wanted a divorce after Faure's death but now was adamantly opposed to it. Perhaps he had grown accustomed to Meg's infamy, or perhaps he didn't want to damage Marthe's marital prospects. Perhaps he had bent to Meg's will so often over the years that he felt this was his one chance to have the upper hand and have some control over their relationship. Or perhaps, even though he was miserable and Meg was cruel, he couldn't imagine living without her.[28]

With an eye to the state of her bank account and her romantic prospects, Meg returned to the sexual marketplace in early 1908.

She was eager to expand beyond the circles of those she already knew and turned to the city itself. In this era, all of Paris seemed to give itself over to flirtation and solicitation. Its parks, its theaters, its boulevards, and its restaurants were all considered locations to look for a sexual partner.[29] One author described Paris's streets as a "magical Eden of unexpected desires, sudden admiration, and strange adventures."[30]

In February 1908, Meg set off on her own strange adventure. One afternoon, she was traveling in a crowded metro car and fainted. Or, at least, she appeared to faint—this and pretending to twist her ankle were tricks she used when she saw someone who interested her.[31] This time, her target turned out to be a man named Dominique-Marie-Joseph de Balincourt. When she learned that he was a count, Meg might have saluted herself for choosing so well.

After Balincourt rescued Meg, he accompanied her to the Impasse Ronsin. It would be ungallant to leave a woman in such distress on her own, just as it would have been rude for her not to offer him an invitation to call on her after he had so heroically come to her aid.

In the coming weeks, Balincourt followed the script Meg laid out for him. He called on her to see Adolphe's paintings. Soon, he started attending her salon regularly and commissioned a portrait from

Adolphe. He agreed with Meg that her husband deserved to be better known. Perhaps he could help her organize an exposition of her husband's paintings in the Steinheils' house in exchange for a commission on anything he helped sell.[32]

In what sounds like the world's worst group project, it ultimately fell to Meg to do everything for the exposition, which was far less successful than Balincourt, Meg, and Adolphe had anticipated. Still, though, he had plenty of opportunities to see Meg.[33] She started to hope that he might be the next lover who was wealthy, generous, and in it for the long haul.

Unfortunately, he was none of those things. His aristocratic title was real, but whatever aura of wealth he had was an illusion. He was grossly in debt and on the verge of being evicted from his apartment in the slums of Paris. The Parisian police stated that he "comes from a shady world," and they suspected him of having robbed his ex-wife's grandmother.[34] They noted that he had dipped into right-wing nationalist politics "in the hope that this could open the door to certain aristocratic mansions. He tried to use his name and his title to make money."[35] Undoubtedly, he thought that Meg could facilitate his entry into the worlds of politics and high officialdom.

Essentially, he and Meg were birds of a feather. He was trading on his aristocratic title in the way that she traded on her beauty and charm. Both were using the assets they had to carve a place for themselves in high society and avoid falling down the social ladder even further.

Balincourt courted Meg for a month and as he stated, "The adventure...took place according to the rules." After going to a Parisian teahouse and taking a stroll in the park, there was "finally, an evening spent at Vert-Logis." This was their one and only sexual encounter, and he found it a "charming evening, a little...faked, perhaps... She visibly exaggerated her joy; I know that... She was always absolutely uninterested."[36] Even if he didn't feel anything for her, he wanted her to make him feel special and desired.

The disappointment was mutual. Meg was incensed that he broke the script of male gallantry that he had been following up to that point. As Mariette Wolff recounted, "He arrived for the evening without even a flower. The next day, he left without leaving anything."[37] He had treated her like a street walker instead of a high-society lady.[38]

In the harsh light of the morning, they saw each other for who they really were. She traded sex for money while clinging to the pretense that she didn't. She had once reigned as mistress to the president. Now she was essentially soliciting strangers on the streets of Paris. He was a broke grifter who was along for the ride of feigned passion and a good story. Meg invested so much in maintaining the appearance of respectability that she may have thought that anyone who could do the same was worthy of her time and attention. It took her a while to understand that a man who could master the codes of high society wasn't necessarily a gentleman.

———

Meg's next liaison was a return to type. Now it was back to introductions arranged by mutual friends, a series of high-society settings, and money flowing into her hands from a man who saw it as his pleasure to pay for her company.

His name was Maurice Borderel. He was a wealthy, widowed landowner from the Ardennes, in northeastern France, and mayor of his tiny town of Balaives-et-Butz. They met at a soirée in March, and when Borderel saw her across the room, he exclaimed, "Good god, she is charming, this woman. What a pleasure it would be to have this woman! That Steinheil is a lucky devil! Only artists can find such perfectly beautiful creatures!"[39]

Not true, one of his companions told him: all Borderel had to do was buy a painting from Adolphe and he could have her. When he was introduced to Meg, he made sure she knew about his interest in art, and she suggested that he see her husband's studio. He bought two paintings for the handsome sum of eight thousand francs, more than enough to secure him an invitation to her salon. There, she showered him with attention. He was flattered that she preferred him to "the judges—all the judiciary—the officials, the former aides to the president of the Republic, the very rich industrialists."[40]

A month later, she took him aside and said, "We are now good friends and for my part it seems as if I have known you forever, and if you leave, I will feel a great sense of loss. You are my true friend. Come to Vert-Logis, my house in the countryside in Bellevue; Spring is coming and it will be beautiful there."[41]

Borderel was overjoyed. He and Meg took long walks in the woods and kissed under the moonlight. In the indelicate words of one newspaper, that first night, "Monsieur the mayor voluptuously savored his pleasure and every day it was stronger and more intense for him as it was for her."[42]

She told him the lies that she thought he wanted to hear: that he was her first lover, that the whole thing about Faure was malicious gossip.[43] He knew that these statements were fabrications. And she probably didn't expect him to believe her. But it was nice that she wanted him to think that he was special. In return, he humored her in a gesture toward her feelings. These lies allowed the two to shut out the rest of the world and imagine themselves as totally and completely smitten with each other.

Unlike Balincourt, Borderel treated her like she wanted. He didn't balk at paying inflated prices for Adolphe's paintings. Once at Vert-Logis, Meg discreetly let it slip that she didn't own the villa but was renting it. In what seemed like an act of unprompted gallantry, Borderel leapt to give her money to cover the rent. He couldn't have a woman bear the expenses of their romance. Every day, Mariette presented him with a bill for the food that she had cooked. Her accounting was generous, to say the least, but Borderel had no quibble with it.[44] One journalist recounted that "bills of a thousand francs flew all around like letters sent in the post."[45]

This was a system of payment that Meg and Mariette had worked out long before to use with other lovers. By charging inflated prices for food instead of for sex, it fell to Mariette, a working-class woman, to ask for money, while Meg could keep her distance from squalid financial transactions that would have put her awfully close to open prostitution.

Once again, Meg rushed into the relationship. On their rambles through the woods and in the privacy of Vert-Logis, they confessed their feelings for one another.[46] Meg then revealed how miserable she was in her marriage, telling Borderel that Adolphe had confined her to a life of domestic drudgery and that "my husband leads an infamous life [i.e., has sex with men]. I will ask him for a divorce, and you will marry me. I will leave with you for your château in the Ardennes… And there, we will live happily, in the wild solitude, in total comfort, without having to fear any slander."[47] Would the ultimate act of courtesy be for Borderel to rescue her from her marriage?

Borderel was more reticent to come to her aid this time. He still had young children at home and did not want to impose a stepmother on them. A long-term affair wasn't out of the question, though, and he agreed to pay the rent for Vert-Logis for the next nine years.[48] He hinted that once his children were out of the house, marriage might be a possibility.[49]

After a few weeks, Borderel reemerged into the real world. His children and his life in the Ardennes were calling him. With a little bit of distance from Meg, he started to feel uneasy about this relationship. He remembered "certain scenes that were too intimate, perceived in the shadow of Adolphe's studio" among Meg's guests and stated that with "the old country gentleman in me regaining the upper hand, I understood that the world that I had joined was not made for me, that I had neither the heart nor the spirit to become acclimated to it."[50]

Borderel was not exactly an upstanding provincial. He was a long-time habitué of the capital's sexual underbelly, and the police described him as "a partier who for years has led a life of debauchery in Paris." He haunted bars in seedy neighborhoods where he drank heavily and sought out paid encounters with men. He also had another mistress, a madam, and he and Meg even had sex in her brothel. The many transgressions that involved—bringing a bourgeois woman to a house of prostitution, conducting his affair with one mistress in the establishment of the other—were no doubt part of the appeal for him.[51]

But while he could manage these other affairs discreetly, Meg expected more from him. She'd want him to come to her salon and accompany her to society events. It seemed that he preferred to keep the seamy and the respectable separate, or at least he didn't want to be the subject of gossip. In a replay of her relationship with Chouanard, the problem was that Meg was at once too notorious and too embedded in high society.

Borderel thus told Meg that they would need to cool things off once he was home in the Ardennes.[52] He didn't back out of his financial commitments to her, but for him, the relationship was now about fulfilling his obligations and letting her down gently.[53]

———————

Meg's dilemma was becoming increasingly clear. Remaining in her marriage meant years, even decades, of misery and increasing financial strain. Divorcing meant a scandal. She was also running out of time to find a wealthy lover who did not mind marrying an infamous woman, even as she had learned from Chouanard and Borderel how hard this would be.

Yet for all that spring 1908 was a difficult time for Meg, things were about to get far, far worse.

PART 2
CRIME FICTIONS

"It's a sham!"[1]

CHAPTER 10

IN MID-MAY 1908, MEG, Adolphe, and Marthe went to spend a few weeks at Vert-Logis. There, they could enjoy some calm outside the hustle and bustle of Paris and host their friends, M. and Mme Buisson. On May 29, Meg and Adolphe came to Paris to pick Émilie up from the train station. She was in town to visit the Steinheils as well as her other Parisian daughter, Juliette, and her family.

Émilie often came to Paris. There was shopping to do, a city to enjoy, and family to see. This time, she was there to sort out her son's chaotic life. Juliette was tasked with finding him a second wife after the first divorced him for horrific abuse, while Émilie and Meg focused on advancing his career in the Ministry of Finances. To help the son and brother they loved deeply but whose troubles they could do little to alleviate, they paid a call to one of Meg's government contacts in the hopes that he could do something for Julien.[1]

Initially, Meg, Adolphe, and Émilie had planned to stay in the house on the Impasse Ronsin on the night of May 29 and then take the forty-five-minute trip to Vert-Logis the next day. Yet on May 30, Émilie declared that her rheumatism was acting up, and the three decided to stay in Paris for another night. Marthe would remain at Vert-Logis, where she had Mariette and the Buissons to look after her.

That evening, the household's valet, Rémy, served a lobster dinner to Meg, Adolphe, and Émilie. Husband and wife were in an unusually good mood. His gloom temporarily lifted, she stopped yelling at him, and they had a sweet-tempered guest to entertain. Months later, Meg recalled that "we even danced around the table and he treated me like his daughter. He said that he had two daughters, one who was reasonable and one who was not."[2] Marthe was the sensible daughter and Meg the wild one.

After dinner, Meg prepared a rum toddy for Adolphe and Émilie to help them sleep and then wrapped her mother's aching limbs in cotton wadding. Adolphe went back to his bedroom. Émilie retired to Meg's room, where she would be most comfortable, and Meg would sleep in Marthe's bed. Husband and wife had stopped sharing a bedroom long ago.[3]

Sometime around 5:30 the next morning, Rémy woke up in his attic quarters above Adolphe's third-floor studio. As he descended the staircase to start his tasks for the day, he heard Meg calling out to him from Marthe's room on the second floor of the house.[4]

The young valet was plenty used to seeing strange things in the Steinheil household, but nothing could have prepared him for what he found that morning. Meg was tied to the bed, a gag by her side. Rémy ran to the nearest window, threw it open, and called for help.

The first to arrive was a neighbor, an engineer named Lecoq, who found the door to the house unlocked and pushed it open. Lecoq and Rémy untied Meg, a task that took a long time since her arms were tied to the bed, as was each toe individually. Meg piteously asked him where her husband was, where her mother was, where her doctor was. She also told him how afraid she was of "that fierce woman, and those men, and those two lanterns."[5] Lecoq didn't quite know what she was talking about, but he knew that the police would arrive soon and figure it all out.

Within minutes, the house was swarming with police officers. First, two neighborhood watchmen came after residents of Impasse Ronsin told them about Rémy's cries. They saw Meg and the lifeless bodies of Adolphe and Émilie, who had been murdered in the adjoining rooms.[6] Then, members of the Security Brigade, the detective branch of the Parisian police, showed up to hunt for clues and listen to Meg and Rémy's accounts.[7] There were also doctors, some to tend to Meg, others to examine the corpses.[8]

One of the men on hand was Alphonse Bertillon, one of the most famous criminologists of the era. He was a pioneer in techniques of criminal identification and is often regarded as the inventor of the mug-shot.[9] That day, he collected fingerprints and took photographs.[10]

These are the most remarkable records from that terrible morning. One of Émilie's corpse, taken from above, shows her eyes open, a gag in her mouth and a cord around her neck. The expression on her face is peaceful but the perspective entirely unsettling. Another shows Adolphe's body on the floor between his bedroom and the bathroom, his bare legs exposed and his knees bent. There is a rope around his neck and a cane to his left. If he had grabbed it in self-defense, it was obviously of little use.

Even over a century later, the photographs have the ability to shock and chill the viewer. For all that Meg's story and personality came to overwhelm the investigation, they are a reminder of the two murdered individuals at the heart of the case. This was one of Bertillon's goals in photographing crime scenes. He wanted his images to convey the full horror of a murder and sway jurors away from leniency.[11]

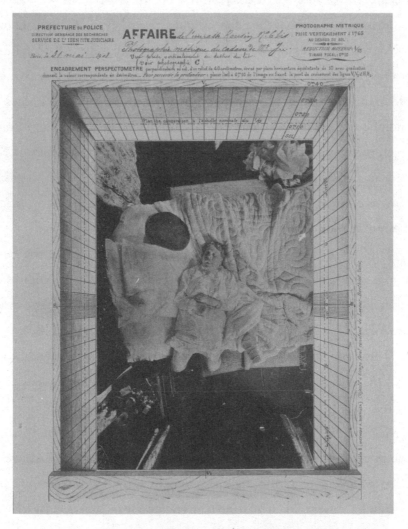

Bertillon's photograph of Émilie's corpse

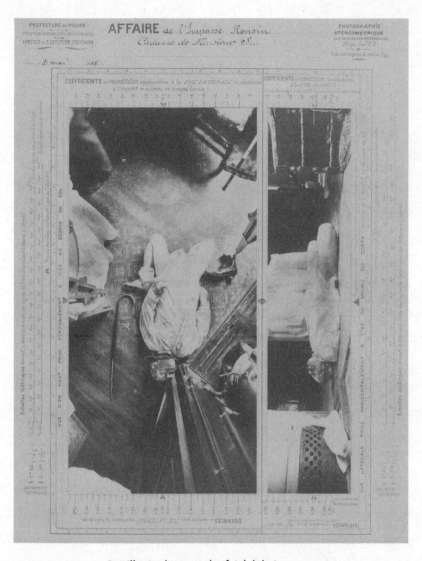

Bertillon's photograph of Adolphe's corpse

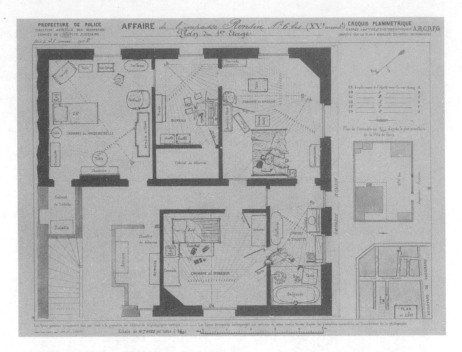

The police floor plan of the second floor of the Steinheils' house, which includes images of Émilie's corpse in the room on the upper right of the floor plan and Adolphe's corpse on the threshold between the two rooms on the lower right

Other detectives asked Meg to tell what she remembered of that night. Although she was, in her words, "in a terrible state of mind, and even on the verge of utter collapse" that morning, she was able to recount what she had seen just a few hours before.[12]

She said, "It was around midnight, I was half asleep...when I felt someone suddenly and violently seize my wrists. I opened my eyes. I saw three men around my bed who seemed to be astoundingly tall. A woman who had red hair stood near them. The men seemed to obey her orders."[13] She recognized one of these men as one of Adolphe's Italian models.[14]

All four intruders were dressed in long, uncollared black robes with flat sleeves. The men were bearded and carried lanterns whose shutters hid the light, while the woman had a revolver. She was the most ferocious of the bunch and said to Meg, "Be a good girl, tell us where the money is. We won't kill your father or your mother. We know that your father sold some paintings and that he's got money. Your father sold his paintings. Where is the money?"[15] Clearly, they had mistaken her for Marthe, in whose bed she had been sleeping. Meg was thirty-nine but looked young for her age. During her collapse after her lover Chouanard left her, she had lost a lot of weight, which made it even easier for her to pass as her daughter.

When Meg told them where to look for the household's cash, the woman yelled at her, "No lying or we'll kill you, bitch!" One of the men, though, came to her aid, declaring, "We don't kill kids!" Then the intruders tied Meg's hands, toes, and neck to the wrought-iron bed, shoved cotton wadding in her mouth to gag her, and threw a cloth over her head. Although she was out of her mind with terror, she soon realized that the cords were not very tight and the cloth protected her neck from the cord around it. For the next few hours, she drifted in and out of consciousness, unable to move and gasping for breath through the gag. Sometime early in the morning, she fully came to and found that with great difficulty, she could work the cotton wadding out of her mouth. Once freed, she started calling for Rémy. She had believed the redheaded woman who said that Adolphe's and Émilie's lives would be spared and hoped that once her valet untied her, she could come to their aid and piece their lives back together.[16]

As the police looked for physical evidence, they found a great deal that helped confirm Meg's story. There was a grandfather clock on the ground floor of the house whose hands were stuck at 12:10. Perhaps the criminals had stopped the clock when they entered to prevent anyone from waking up to its chimes and realizing that there were intruders in the house. Then there was a pair of gloves on the floor of Meg's study, a small room that connected her bedroom with Marthe's. Rémy did not recognize the gloves as belonging to anyone in the house. The perpetrators might have brought them to avoid leaving fingerprints.[17] Meg stated that she and Adolphe had had around 7,500 francs in cash in their house, largely from Adolphe's recent exposition. All of that was gone, as was much of Meg's jewelry.[18]

There was also an ink stain on Meg's left leg. The ink probably came from an inkstand that had fallen off the desk in the study where the gloves were. There was a pool of ink on the floor of the study and drops of ink leading from the desk to the bed Meg had been tied to. It seemed likely that one of the murderers had overturned the inkstand as they ran through the house, gotten ink on their hand, and then transferred some of it to Meg as they tied her up. Strangely, though, the stain on her leg looked more like a splash than a handprint.[19]

The authorities could combine Meg's account with details of the crime scene to piece together a rough outline of what had happened. One of Adolphe's models had realized the painter had a lot of cash from his exhibition and rounded up accomplices to rob the house. Maybe Adolphe had told him that he planned to be at Vert-Logis that night and the model expected the house to be empty. Once they arrived and realized that the family was still there, they decided to go through with the robbery anyway and stopped the clock on the ground floor so that no one would wake up with its chimes and hear the intruders. They killed Adolphe and Émilie to silence any witnesses but had flinched when it came to murdering someone they thought was an adolescent. As they ran through the house looking for valuables, they opened drawers, rifled through the inhabitants' belongings, and threw some of them on the floor. In their haste, they knocked over an inkstand on Meg's desk and dropped a pair of gloves in her study.

Meg was the sole survivor of a horrific attack, lucky to be alive and unharmed. And she had given the authorities a lot to go on: they could start by tracking down Adolphe's Italian models.

————————

Or not.

Any detective could see that Meg's account was a work of fiction.

Most obviously, the house didn't appear to have been robbed. There were no signs of forced entry. The Steinheils' neighbor Lecoq—the first person to enter the house on the morning of May 31—had found the door unlocked, even though Rémy swore he had locked it before he went to bed. Despite the fact that there had been a storm that night, there were no traces of mud inside the house.[20] Moreover, if the criminals' intention was to steal from the Steinheils, they did a poor job of it. The murderers didn't take all Meg's jewelry and left a fifty-franc note lying in plain sight on a table. Indeed, the entire ground floor was untouched, including the household's silver.[21] Once investigators looked into the Steinheil's finances, Meg's claim that there had been 7,500 francs in the house strained belief. Meg and Adolphe had been borrowing ten francs here and there from servants and relatives in order to make ends meet. They had nowhere near that amount on hand.

The crime scene photographs also show that the house had not been fully ransacked. Marthe's bedroom hadn't been touched. In Adolphe's, the contents of his wallet had been strewn around the floor and the top drawer of his bureau had been opened, but many of his clothes were still lying neatly in them. Neither his armoire nor the other drawers in his bureau had been disturbed. The armoire in Meg's bedroom had been opened and some items had been thrown on the floor, but for the most part, it was still in order and her clothes were carefully folded on its shelves.[22] Her study was in the worst shape out of all the rooms in the house. Her desk drawers had been thrown onto the floor, along with the overturned inkstand and the mysterious gloves. Once the police investigated, they found that the gloves weren't mysterious at all: they had been a gift from Meg's ex-lover Chouanard.[23] What's more, there was a small bureau in this room whose drawers were firmly closed. All in all, it might have taken Meg, Mariette, or Rémy ten minutes or so to put everything back. In other words, it seems unlikely that Meg's story about a robbery gone wrong was anything close to the truth.

The crime scene photograph of Meg's study. The untouched bureau is to the left of the door, its drawer pulls still neatly lined up.

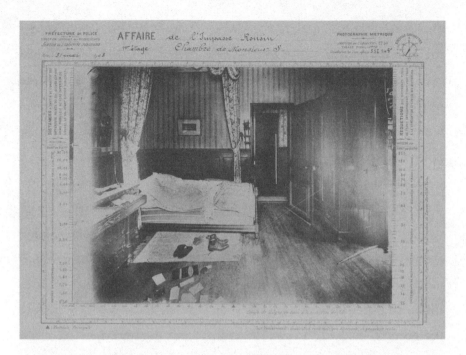

The crime scene photograph of Adolphe's room. The cane found near his body is on the right, close to the armoire, which was undisturbed. The contents of his wallet are on the floor on the left, not far from the bureau whose top drawer is opened.

Even more perplexing was the state of Meg's, Adolphe's, and Émilie's bodies.

For such dastardly criminals, the intruders had been remarkably considerate toward Meg's person. She had been tied to the bed so gently that she bore no marks on her body or any other signs of struggle. And why tie individual toes to the bed when throwing the cord around her ankle would have been a faster and easier way to secure her feet? Rémy also stated that the bonds were so loose that she probably could have untied herself. Doctors would later conclude that the gag she claimed to have worked out of her mouth had no traces of saliva on it, indicating that it may have been no more than a prop.[24]

Additionally, the cords that bound Meg's body to the bed and the one around Émilie's neck had come from within the household, as did the material for the gag in Émilie's mouth and the one Meg said had been in hers. In fact, it was the same cotton wadding that Meg had used to treat her mother's aching joints.[25] The murderers had come armed with a revolver but apparently not the material they used to attack the household's residents.

Once the autopsy report came in, it became clear that the circumstances of Adolphe's and Émilie's deaths were not what they seemed. Adolphe had probably died when he was awake. The best explanation for why his corpse was on the bathroom floor with his legs bent underneath him was that he had gotten out of bed, walked toward the bathroom, and been strangled on the spot. As he fell (or was dropped) to the ground, his body awkwardly crumpled. However, there were few signs of struggle on his corpse. Doctors only found two small, relatively light bruises on his arms during the autopsy. The cane by his side was thus not something he had grabbed to defend himself but likely had been placed there after the murders to make it look like Adolphe had tried to fight his assailant off. And although there was a rope around his neck, he had actually been strangled by someone's bare hands, another indication that the crime scene had been staged.[26]

Émilie had a cord around her neck and a gag in her mouth. However, the authorities announced that she died of asphyxiation, not strangulation. They claimed that the cotton wadding had been forced into her mouth with such ferocity that her dentures had slipped back into her throat and choked her.[27] Even this might not have been the real story. Years later, a doctor who was present at her autopsy reported that Émilie had actually died of a heart attack, presumably brought on by the horror of what she saw that night.[28] Whichever version is true, it seems that Émilie's death was accidental and the cord—and possibly the gag—were just more props.*

Last but not least, there was the sheer preposterousness of Meg's description of what the murderers were wearing. The hats she described looked more like sombreros than any headwear worn in France at the time.[29] Meg also said that the robes were like those of "Russian Orthodox priests."[30] This garb was hardly the most common sight in Paris and would have been cumbersome in the midst of a robbery/ murder.

All these details and inconsistencies led one doctor who was at the crime scene on the morning of May 31 to exclaim, "It's a sham!"[31]

In many ways, it seemed that Meg's account was just another one of her elaborate stories. Like so many others, it was designed to hide a truth that she did not want to reveal—or perhaps could not.

---

* Although Émilie's death was probably accidental and not a murder, I refer to the crime as "the double murder" or "the murders" for the sake of simplicity.

CHAPTER 11

WHAT REALLY HAPPENED?

This question has perplexed observers since the double murder itself. There is the strangeness of what happened, from the staged elements of the crime scene to Meg's odd method of being tied to the bed. And there is the strangeness of what Meg said had happened, from the robes to the mysterious lanterns.

Sadly, the crime remains as unsolved as it was on the morning of May 31. Nevertheless, there are two basic theories of what happened. Both have existed, in some form or another, since the murders.[1]

The first on the surface is the simplest: Meg did it. She was desperate to be free of her husband and marry another man, but he wouldn't divorce her. Murder it was. She would have needed help, especially since strangling Adolphe would have required more strength than she had. She would also have needed someone to tie her to the bed. Rémy, who was already in the house that night, was one possible accomplice. Another was Mariette, whose loyalty to Meg knew few bounds. For almost fifteen years, she had cooked for Meg, facilitated her affairs, kept her secrets, and refused to say a word to anyone.[2] She could easily have come in from Vert-Logis to help her employer dispose of Adolphe.

This theory is not outside the realm of possibility, but it poses more problems than it solves. For one, if Meg had planned the murder, she would have had time to come up with a better story of what she had witnessed and would have been able to fake the crime scene more convincingly. She was an impulsive gambler and a sloppy liar, but even she had to have known that her account of what she had seen would strain belief.

There is also the issue of Émilie's presence, even if we assume that her death was accidental. Meg was protective of her mother and typically regarded her as someone who needed to be sheltered and cared for. This is true in the days after Édouard's death, when Meg took on the role of the head of the family. Just before the murders, Meg defended her mother after her sister Juliette flew into a rage over Émilie's over-spending.[3] Given all this, it seems improbable that Meg would have chosen to murder Adolphe on a night when her mother would have been a witness to such a horrifying scene.

If Meg had decided to commit premeditated murder, it seems more likely that she would have come up with a scheme that was more discreet. After all, husband and wife had plenty of opportunities to be alone together, and there were numerous other ways she could have killed him, from a slow poisoning to staging an accident, that wouldn't have raised as many questions. Adolphe wasn't young, might have had a substance abuse problem, and was hardly full of pep. If he "fell" down the stairs one day, many might have thought that it was sad but hardly shocking.

The second main hypothesis about the crime is more complicated but fits more closely with the facts. In this version, the murderer was one of Meg's prominent lovers, and the crime wasn't a robbery gone wrong but an assignation gone wrong.

This theory gained particular prominence due to the work of Edmond Locard, who wrote about the murders as a hobby. During his day job, he was the most renowned forensic scientist in twentieth-century France. It was he, for instance, who first proposed that crime scene investigators should look for trace evidence to track down perpetrators. He also worked with many of the investigators of the double murder, including Bertillon and the head of the Parisian detective bureau.[4] It is quite possible that one or both knew the real story of what happened on the Impasse Ronsin and told Locard the truth about the murders. Maybe there were whispers in a corridor of the police's headquarters, or maybe there were secrets spilled during a long, wine-soaked evening.

According to Locard, Meg had a rich and powerful lover who had paid her handsomely for a few encounters. These assignations were long past, but the two remained "on excellent terms."[5] Although Locard never provided a name for this lover, he told a Parisian newspaper in 1955 that the man was a "boyar—MUCH MORE THAN A BOYAR— (attention here, every word counts)."[6] "Boyar" is a term for a member of the Russian aristocracy, and Locard's phrasing and use of all caps suggest that the lover was a member of the tsar's family. One strong possibility is Grand Duke Vladimir Alexandrovich, Tsar Nicolas II's uncle, a man known for his pursuit of Parisian pleasures and his fierce temper.[7] He had been one of Meg's clients and had been spotted dining in Paris a few days before the crime, only to leave the capital on June 1 in great haste, perhaps to put distance between himself and the murders.[8]

In May 1908, Meg, desperate for cash, asked her old lover to come to the house. She might have slipped something in the toddies she so lovingly prepared for Adolphe and Émilie to ensure that she and the Russian wouldn't be interrupted. He arrived excited for their assignation, only to have Meg tell him that she wanted to postpone the sex. Perhaps she had her period. When she asked for the money in advance, her lover became incensed at her presumption. The two started arguing so loudly that they woke Adolphe up. As the drugged painter lumbered around, the Russian feared a trap. In Locard's words, he "jumped at the intruder's [i.e., Adolphe's] throat. His strong hand gripped the neck of the painter, killed him while he was standing, and then let him fall." Émilie also woke up and went to see what the commotion was. The sight of a well-dressed man standing over the corpse of her son-in-law was enough to send her into a heart attack.[9]

Others in the know provided additional support for this version, although there is some question about the nationality of the lover. A doctor who witnessed the autopsies claimed that the murderer was a powerful foreigner with diplomatic immunity and guessed the lover was British, not Russian. Although the perpetrator's status and nationality are not the type of evidence that would have surfaced during the autopsies, it's possible that someone in the Parisian police who knew the real story told the doctor what had happened. Roger de Chateleux, who was Meg's lover in the 1910s and ghostwrote her memoirs, also confirmed the essentials of Locard's account without attributing a specific nationality to the murderer.[10]

Two further bits of information support the notion that the murderer was someone of considerable wealth. Around 12:00 a.m. on the night of the crime, multiple witnesses saw an automobile idling outside the Impasse Ronsin. This could be a coincidence or an indication that Meg had a wealthy visitor.[11] Additionally, in November 1908, Mariette, Meg's cook and secret keeper, told journalists that they should "look among the greats" to find the perpetrator, a phrasing that indicates that she believed the murderer was someone from the top of the social hierarchy.[12] This was the only time she spoke publicly about the identity of the murderer, as she typically refused to say a word about the crime. Yet it is clear that she knew something about who committed the murders and either helped Meg plan the events that night or hide what had happened.[13]

One merit of this theory is that it can help explain many of the more confusing elements of the crime. If it is true, then we know why Meg was in such a good mood on the evening of May 30: she saw her financial difficulties lifting. Same with the stopped clock: she did it to keep Adolphe and Émilie from waking up. The door to the house was unlocked even though Rémy remembered locking it because she opened it to let her lover in. The murderer was polite enough not to track mud in the house, though not so polite that he refrained from murdering Adolphe.

Following this theory, we could also imagine that as Meg and the Russian looked at the two dead bodies on their hands, they decided to stage a break-in. They put a cane by Adolphe and rope around his neck. A cord went around Émilie's neck and a gag in her mouth. They dragged Émilie from the spot she had died to her bed out of consideration for Meg's beloved mother. But they left Adolphe where he was, with his legs exposed in an undignified fashion, either because they didn't care to make him comfortable after his death or because he was too heavy for them to move. Meg and the murderer rifled through the household's

belongings in a perfunctory fashion. In her haste, she probably overturned the inkstand in her study and splattered ink on her leg. As she
was tearing through her desk drawers, she pulled out a pair of gloves
that her ex Chouanard had given her. The lover took some valuables,
tied Meg up, and put a gag next to her. He didn't want to make her too
uncomfortable. Still, there was a thrill in tying a beautiful, sexy woman
to a bed, hence his decision to tie her toe by toe. We can imagine that
this was a moment when he slowed down after rushing through the
house to help stage a break-in. It might have given him a sense of power
and control after a night that had gone so horribly wrong and had been
far from the fun romp he had imagined.

All this staging was for Meg's benefit, not his. He didn't really care
how fake it looked. Thanks to the gift of diplomatic immunity, he'd
never be arrested. The crime would never be solved because the authorities would essentially refuse to solve it, lest they damage the reputation of someone so powerful and compromise diplomatic ties between
France and Russia. Likewise, it also didn't matter to him whether Meg
had a plausible story of what happened. He just wanted to put the
whole disaster of a night behind him.

Meg would be left to deal with the consequences and to explain
what had happened. Panicked, she came up with the tale of the robed
intruders.

As she did so, she may have drawn on two sources for her story. One
was a crime that had occurred in Montbéliard, a city close to Beaucourt,
in 1885, when Meg was sixteen. A tax collector named Brévard claimed
that two men with blackened faces who were wearing long black blouses
had entered his home, attacked him, and tied his pregnant wife to the
bed. The robbers forced her to reveal the combination to the safe where

her husband kept the tax revenue he had collected. Turns out, though, that Brévard had staged the whole thing to cover up the fact that he had spent all the money on alcohol and women.[14]

The other possible origin was an 1875 potboiler titled *The Five Fingers of Birouk* by Louis Ulbach. In it, a Russian soldier named Birouk schemed with a woman to kill a wealthy relative for his inheritance. To make it look like a robbery gone wrong, Birouk teamed up with two other men to break into the man's house during the night. All three attackers were bearded and wore long robes. Birouk strangled the rich man with his bare hands and sliced a servant in half with a saber. The sole survivor was another servant who was found tied to her bed. The Steinheils had other books by Ulbach on their shelves, but not this one.[15] Still, it's quite possible that Meg had read it at some point.

In the early hours of May 31, Meg may have woven together these two tales to come up with something to tell the authorities. To explain why she had been spared, she claimed that the redheaded woman and the intruders had mistaken her for her daughter. Blaming the crime on one of Adolphe's models conveniently fit many prejudices of the day about Italians, those who belonged to the world of the arts, and the type of men who were interested in modeling for Adolphe. Italian immigrants were regarded as particularly prone to violence, although this was not actually the case.[16] Artists and the people who surrounded them were known to be on the eccentric side. They would be exactly the type of individuals who would wear strange outfits and fail to follow society's rules, maybe even to the point of committing murder.[17] Many in this era also associated male homosexuality with criminality.[18] This was another group of people who didn't behave as they should. It was well known in high-society circles and the Steinheils' neighborhood that Adolphe had sex with men, including his models.[19]

According to Meg's version of the double murder, Adolphe was the victim of a terrible crime. But he had acted recklessly by inviting dangerous men into his house who had given in to their worst inclinations toward violence. Homosexuality was also regarded as a symptom of France's decline that would lead the nation to an early demise: Adolphe's death was a warning about the perils of desire run amok.[20] From a certain angle, he was responsible for the fate that befell him, just as France would be if its citizens gave in to the wrong types of sex. For Meg, this version of the murder may have been one last act of revenge against the husband she so hated.

If the killer was one of Meg's royal lovers, she would have known that she didn't have the backing of a powerful family or the protection of diplomatic immunity. She would also have guessed that she would face some level of scrutiny by virtue of being the sole survivor. But she also knew that she had a lot of sway in the halls of power. The authorities didn't want a scandal, didn't want the public to think the mistress of a deceased president had been involved in two murders. She knew they would do their best to protect her reputation and that it wouldn't matter how believable her story was.

Or, at least, that was what she thought.

CHAPTER 12

ALTHOUGH THERE IS NO good time for a double murder to occur, 1908 was a particularly bad one. Parisians were terrified of what seemed like a rising tide of violent crime drowning their city. Some of this fear was due to the fact that murder rates started going up in 1905 after many years of decline. But it's also the case that many felt unsafe because the press had turned to printing stories about crime and the dangers of urban life to sell copies in a fiercely competitive market.[1]

Here was a crime that would send newspapers flying out of the kiosks that lined the capital's streets. It wasn't every day that journalists could report on the murders of a woman who had married into one of France's great industrial dynasties and an award-winning painter—to say nothing of the fact that the only surviving witness had played a starring role in French history. Still, the press was largely respectful of Meg's privacy and her past. They didn't talk about her sex work or how Faure had died. Instead, they referred to Faure as a friend of the Steinheils, or even of Adolphe, and largely maintained the silence and protection for Faure and Meg that they always had.[2]

In the coming weeks and months, the authorities would have to navigate the problems that the murders posed. They needed to give every appearance of trying to find the perpetrators. Otherwise, the public might think that the government wasn't serious about addressing the crime wave. But if the perpetrator was a powerful foreigner who had already fled the country, they couldn't exactly bring him to justice. They also wanted to protect Meg, both for her own sake as a well-connected woman and for the sake of the president who was her most famous connection.

This job fell to two men: Octave Hamard, the head of the detective branch of the Parisian police, and Joseph Leydet, the examining magistrate for the case. Both were at the villa on Impasse Ronsin on the morning of May 31 because they were well accustomed to balancing the need to find the truth with the task of protecting the reputations of the powerful.

Of the two, Hamard was more famous, even a bit of a celebrity. Detective fiction was wildly popular in the Belle Époque, and police officers were seen as figures who used reason, deduction, and science to unravel society's greatest secrets.[3] Hamard, as Paris's top detective, fully played into this mystique. He had piercing eyes and a carefully trimmed goatee and was always impeccably dressed. A former artillery officer, he was known for his personal bravery and often showed up at crime scenes to search for evidence with his men, as he did with the murders on the Impasse Ronsin. But there was another side to his career, one that was less well known. He had a talent for remaining on the right side of power and going to great lengths to conceal the truth when he deemed it necessary.[4] While he might have taken this further than other men in his position, he was the rule, not the exception, and the police often understood that helping prominent individuals maintain their reputations was part of their job.[5] (Ernest Raynaud, an author and police official, recounted that "two adulterers, both prominent, were trysting at the woman's house when the man suffered a fatal heart attack. The inspecteur arranged for the body to be removed and filed a report that the man died elsewhere.")

That morning, though, it was Leydet's show. As examining magistrate (*juge d'instruction*), it was he who ordered searches, issued arrest warrants, and interrogated suspects and witnesses. It's a function that has no equivalent in Anglo-American judicial systems; as a judge, his role was not to act as a neutral arbiter between the prosecution and the defense in the courtroom but to ferret out the truth through an extensive pretrial investigation. Examining magistrates were much feared at the time, in part because there wasn't much that was off-limits during their investigations.[6]

Leydet was a rising star in the judiciary and had a reputation as among the best examining magistrates.[7] His superiors praised him for his tenacity, diligence, and knowledge of both the law and his fellow human beings. Prior to the double murder, he had investigated two of the era's biggest cases: the Humbert Affair, an elaborate confidence scheme perpetrated by elites of the Third Republic, and the Ullmo Affair, a sex, drugs, and espionage scandal in the navy.[8] This last case had just wrapped up, and Leydet's work had helped the government secure a conviction. When he arrived at the Steinheils' house on the morning of May 31, he was riding high as a talented investigator who could protect the country from the dangers that threatened it.

However, as was the case for Hamard, Leydet may not have been at the Impasse Ronsin to find out what happened. One of the reasons that he was assigned high-profile, politically sensitive cases was that he was regarded as someone who could make sure that the regime's reputation remained intact, even if that meant that the truth never fully came to light.[9] For instance, at the end of the investigation into the Ullmo Affair, Gaston Thomson, the minister of the navy, sent a letter to the minister of justice, Leydet's ultimate superior, praising the judge for "avoiding anything indiscreet and focusing on the essential facts" and keeping him informed on the course of the investigation.[10] That Thomson took the time to write such a letter suggested that Leydet's efforts to shield the navy from scrutiny were indeed noteworthy—and perhaps that there had been a great deal to hide.

These two men perfectly represent the criminal justice system's complex relationship to the truth in this era. The nationalist journalist Léon Daudet summed it up best when he wrote, "The narrow duty" of the examining magistrate "is to plunge to the bottom of a crime and bring its bloody origins to light, whatever they may be." But, Daudet suggested, "Isn't his larger duty to respect the mysteries of the regime, to deny what must be denied, to keep its secrets hidden?"[11] In theory, the authorities were supposed to pursue the truth, no matter the cost. In practice, they worked hard to keep the reputation of the government and those in its inner circle intact. It's hardly a coincidence that this attitude was similar to the regime's elites' notions regarding their own transgressions. In both cases, preserving the façade of propriety trumped honesty.

Meg knew how the system worked better than anyone. She knew the lengths officials had gone to to hide her involvement in Faure's death. And she was connected, to put it mildly—and nowhere more so than in the world of the Parisian judiciary. After all, one of the guests to her salon (and thus perhaps one of her lovers) was Louis Lépine, Hamard's superior.

What's more, she was also close to Leydet, although just how close is hard to determine. In her memoirs, she called him "a great friend of both my husband and myself" and recounted that he "came frequently to the house."[12] Often, the term "great friend" was Meg's euphemism for a lover, and many suspected that the two were having an affair. What is known is that he asked to be assigned to this case out of a desire to be of service to Meg during a moment of crisis and was, at the very least, an admirer, even if the two had never sealed the deal.[13]

When Hamard and Leydet arrived at the house on Impasse Ronsin, they knew they had a mess to clean up. Their job was to look busy, to order Hamard's men around as they hunted for clues, all while shielding the perpetrators from scrutiny.

———

So Leydet and Hamard would have patiently listened to Meg's account on the morning of May 31. They would have given her every outward indication that they believed her, no matter how wild her story was. We can also guess that they would have told her what they would have told any victim of a horrific crime: that they were on her side in the search for justice.

Which, in a sense, they were—just in a very particular way.

Their work to protect her began with a series of inactions. They didn't have the doctors who autopsied Adolphe's and Émilie's corpses examine whether the two had been drugged. In what was either an act of spectacularly shoddy police work or an effort to cover up Meg's involvement, a police officer broke the glasses from which Adolphe and Émilie had drunk the toddies that Meg had prepared for them. As a result, they could not be tested to see if Meg had laced them with something intended to knock out her husband and mother.[14] Leydet didn't order a search of Vert-Logis, either. Had he done so, the police would have found that much of the jewelry that Meg claimed had been stolen was there.

There was also their decision not to inform Meg that Adolphe and Émilie were dead until after their bodies had been taken to the morgue. Meg saw this as an act of consideration for her fragile psyche. She wrote, "I wanted to rush to my dear dead, to look upon them, guard them, close their eyes—but they would not let me… They said I was too weak, too ill… They said it was impossible."[15] This was an act of protection in another sense: at the time, investigators thought that if a murderer saw their victim's corpse, they might suddenly reveal their misdeeds.[16] Neither Leydet nor Hamard wanted Meg to come out with a spontaneous revelation of what she had actually seen and done.

Instead, they pressed Meg to identify which of Adolphe's models she had seen. Even if they knew her story was a cover-up—even if they knew who had committed the murders—they may still have felt that they had to go through the motions to reassure the public that they were doing everything they could to find the perpetrators. At this point, she was reluctant to send the authorities chasing after any one individual. Accordingly, she quickly altered her story to say that she hadn't recognized any of the murderers.[17]

It was the first time Meg's account would change, but certainly not the last.

Meg's retraction was inconvenient for Hamard, who was in charge of updating the press on the course of the investigation. Yet if Meg wasn't keeping her story straight, well, it was understandable: she had been through a lot. Besides, everyone knew that women tended to be mentally unstable and couldn't really be trusted to tell the truth.[18]

Still, he'd need to give the press something to go on, some theory of the crime that was not one of Meg's powerful lovers committing murder. He thus turned to the usual suspects of the day, saying, "We are in the presence of criminals from the lowest walk of life."[19] Hamard was here referring to what was known as the underclass or underworld in English. (This is the origins of the term "criminal underworld.") Its realm was made up of the poorest of the poor whose inhabitants were thought to be prone to all sorts of immoral and violent behavior.[20]

Undergirding the idea that those at the very bottom of the social ladder were prone to criminality was a set of prejudices about status and behavior. The poor were the problem, while the middle classes and wealthy needed to be in charge, lest the dangerous elements lurking below run free and destroy society.[21] (In the words of one criminologist of the mid-nineteenth century, "If the well-to-do rarely commit crimes, it is because they have the money to meet their needs, and even their passions, something that others can only afford through crime; it is also because they can obtain a moral sense from their education.")

In the 1900s, the particular threat from the lower depths came from gangs of youths called "*apaches*." The men had their own dress (bell-bottoms; short, belted jackets; colorful scarfs; and striped shirts) and their own customs (including a unique slang, tattoos, and a strict code of silence) and often lived on the periphery of Paris. Hence, in another interview the day after the murders were discovered, Hamard said that the redheaded woman was "quite the ignoble *apache* from the exterior boulevards."[22]

The name "*apaches*" added racism into the swirl of elitist ideas about the composition of the underclass. For decades, the French reading public had devoured racist stories about Native Americans that painted Apaches from the American Southwest as savage and resistant to white settlement.* When this term migrated into the French context to describe gangsters, it indicated that these individuals were in an "insurrectional state against society," in the words of one newspaper. They didn't go to school, refused to do honest labor, and hated the police.[23] These individuals refused to follow the rules of conventional morality. Of course, many elites did, too. The difference was that those at the bottom of the social ladder did so openly, flagrantly, and without any sense that they should follow the rules or at least appear to do so. It was as if these men and women had somehow fallen out of whiteness and the good behavior and moral sense that were assumed to come along with it.[24]

The advantages of blaming the double murder on individuals from Paris's underworld were many. If these particular perpetrators were never found, that just proved how dangerous and secretive they were. Above all, if common criminals did it, then the crime was totally ordinary and unrelated to Meg's life or loves before the murders.

This was Hamard's line, again and again. A week after the murders, he told reporters, "This case is infinitely less complicated than some seem to suppose. This is not something out of a novel. If it is a novel, it's just

---

* To avoid confusion and differentiate between Native Americans and members of the Parisian underworld, I use italics but don't capitalize the latter.

the ordinary story of the work of burglars that always unfolds in the same way." At other times, he and Leydet worked together to declare that Meg could not possibly have been involved in the crime. Readers of the June 6 issue of the Parisian newspaper *Le Matin* were thus treated to an interview with Hamard in which he stated, "The more this investigation advances, the more I find it abominable that anyone could have suspected Mme Steinheil for an instant." At that moment, Leydet popped into Hamard's office to affirm that he was "totally in agreement with" the detective.[25]

The only problem? Few believed them.

———

In the first few weeks of June 1908, you could go to any café, any gathering among friends, or any shop on the capital's wide boulevards and hear a variety of pet theories about what had really happened in the villa on Impasse Ronsin. Maybe Meg was the murderer, maybe it was one of her lovers, or maybe it was somehow connected to Faure's death.[26] At the very least, everyone was sure that there was more to the story than Hamard, Leydet, and Meg were saying.

Parisians talked endlessly about the details of the crime scene that didn't make sense, from the lack of signs of forced entry to the absence of any indications of struggle on Meg's and Émilie's bodies. Many speculated that Émilie and Adolphe had been drugged before they were murdered. They laughed about Meg's tale of the robed men and the redheaded woman while pointing out that the intruders spoke "the outdated slang of *Les Misérables*" from the 1830s, not the slang that the Parisian *apaches* of the 1900s used.[27] (The equivalent would be if today, someone said an intruder broke in and threatened to give them a knuckle sandwich.)

It became a vicious cycle. Hamard's and Leydet's statements were meant to quell all the rumors, but they only added fuel to the fires of disbelief. The interview in which Leydet popped in to Hamard's office to declare Meg's innocence was so obviously staged. And Hamard also spoke much more about this case than others in the news, which drew attention to his personal investment in keeping suspicion away from Meg.[28]

Then there was the problem of Meg. She was under pressure from investigators who were working independently from Hamard and Leydet and from journalists who wanted her to clarify the inconsistencies in her story.[29] As she elaborated on her tale of what she had seen, she rejected Hamard's implication that she had been the victim of a garden-variety crime. After all, any drama in which she was involved had to be something exciting, mysterious, and proof of her importance.

Two weeks after the murder, she told the police that she thought that one of the men had a "Bedouin, Egyptian, Algerian or Brazilian complexion" and "his appearance was distinguished."[30] Meg was resorting to a set of prejudices about the association between good behavior and race, one that was used as a justification for imperial conquest, including in North Africa.[31]

As for the redheaded woman, Meg recounted that her hands were "soft and indicated a life of leisure" and she had only been imitating the speech of someone from the Parisian underworld.[32] If this intruder was a well-to-do woman pretending to be an *apache*, it could explain why the slang she spoke wasn't quite right.

After that, the different versions just kept coming. A few weeks later, Meg told *Le Matin* that she thought that a family member had killed her mother and husband out of a desire for revenge. Soon after, she suggested that it was one of Adolphe's German clients. At other times, she would add fanciful details that pushed the case even further into the realm of the absurd, as when she claimed that the murderers were wearing elbow-length gloves that flared out like those worn by musketeers.[33]

Not for the last time, we are confronted with the question of what Meg thought she was doing. If she had just gone along with Hamard's version and maintained the consistent story that the murders were a run-of-the-mill break-in gone wrong, the press and the public would have had fewer questions. But by giving interviews, she kept the case—with all its mysteries—in the headlines.

It was her old demons and drives that undid her. In the wake of the murders, her mental state took a turn for the worse. As was true in the aftermath of Faure's death, the stress pulled at the already loose seams of her relationship with the truth. Keeping her story straight proved to be too much of a burden. Each new version and every attempt to explain one element of the account, such as the outdated slang of the intruders, made her look more and more like the fabulist that she was.

Her go-to pattern of lying was to envelop herself in an air of intrigue. It was a way to create the world she wanted to live in, one where she was a celebrity at the heart of international events. So there had to be some sort of complicated drama behind the murders. The suggestion that the perpetrator was German, for instance, hinted that there might be ties between this crime and her relationship with Faure, who had cemented a Franco-Russian alliance out of a concern with Germany's rising power in the world. Or maybe it was a vicious feud with a family member. Or maybe it was an international drama that revolved around a hidden connection between Adolphe and a wealthy Brazilian or North African.

The irony, of course, was that there probably *was* a fascinating drama at the heart of the murders, one that combined sex and international intrigue. But it wasn't one that Meg could relay to the press.

Unsurprisingly, Meg's obvious lies and Hamard's somewhat less apparent ones led ordinary Parisians to investigate the murders on their own. They went to Impasse Ronsin to hunt for clues, followed someone they saw on the street who looked suspicious, or strained to overhear a conversation at the next table in a café that they decided was connected to the murders.[34]

No one went further than a man named Martin who claimed he had seen a car outside Impasse Ronsin on the night of the murders. He hired friends to help him track down the car's owner and rented an apartment under an assumed name to receive mail about the case. He also constructed an elaborate ruse involving a sudden, mysterious inheritance to lure the mistress of one of Meg's neighbors in case she knew something about the household's secrets.[35] None of his efforts panned out.

Others just gossiped and guessed about the case. Newspapers made fun of the "Sherlock Holmes of the café"—the person who thought they were such a genius that they could solve perplexing crimes by reading the newspaper and noticing the one detail that unlocked the whole mystery.[36] It was an opportunity for voyeurism and to try to make sense of a very messy criminal case.

But behind the fun of being an amateur detective was a sense of frustration. Observers knew that the criminal justice system could buckle when the perpetrators were rich and powerful, just as it reacted too harshly when it came to those who lacked the protections of money. Indeed, much of the Sherlock Holmes-ing of the double murder was shot through with a strain of antiauthoritarianism. Private citizens felt they had to investigate the crime because it was so clear that the police weren't going to. The socialist daily *L'Humanité* spoke of all the "journalists, waiters, cab drivers, clergymen, soldiers" who considered themselves to be the next great detective of the day and who "suddenly discovered amazing powers of analysis and intuition" thanks to the double murder. For some, it was a fun pastime. Others were outraged that "Hamard takes us for suckers," as one pastry chef was overheard bitterly declaiming on the streets of Paris.[37]

These were people who knew that the police weren't necessarily there to find perpetrators but to keep the rich in their place and the poor in theirs. And they knew that the only way the crime would be solved was if the press or the public intervened.

For the moment, this would not be the case. Instead, the murders faded from view within a few weeks. Without any indications of new leads, there simply was not enough to keep the events in the news. In mid-July, newspapers reported that the investigation was at an end.[38]

As the French proverb states, truth lay at the bottom of a well.

CHAPTER 13

IN FACT, IN THE summer and fall of 1908, the police were still hard at work on the case, only doing nothing to solve it.

Detectives looked into almost anyone who was connected to the Steinheil household—as long as they lacked money or connections. Following Meg's statements on May 31, they tracked down Adolphe's models. All had alibis or were deemed too respectable to have committed murder.[1] The police questioned the Steinheils' former servants on the theory that one of them might have had a grudge against Adolphe. No dice there. They also went to the heart of avant-garde Paris, the Lapin Agile Cabaret in Montmartre, to see if there were "any painters, models or artists without work" "whose means of existence were problematic, in a word what we call 'bohemian'" and who knew something about the murder.[2] This was where Picasso, Apollinaire, and Modigliani rubbed elbows with prostitutes, anarchists, criminals, and slumming elites.[3] It's hard to imagine that the antiauthoritarian patrons and employees of the Lapin Agile were welcoming to the police, and they ended up with no leads after their excursion.[4]

By the same token, the police avoided looking into any of Meg's lovers, with the exception of the disreputable Balincourt.[5] According to Meg, they didn't want to touch her relationships with Bouchez or Faure with a ten-foot investigative pole. She recounted that when she was staying at Vert-Logis, the authorities sent her letters from Bouchez and Faure that she had kept in the house on Impasse Ronsin. She writes, "If these objects are returned to me, I thought, it is evidently because it is not desired that anything concerning the late President of the Republic and the Attorney-General be brought up in the 'Affair of the Impasse Ronsin.'"[6]

Meanwhile, Meg received regular visits from the investigators. Sometimes they had more questions for her, and sometimes they were there to reassure her. According to Meg, a few days after the murders, Leydet called on her and said, "Hamard is coming… It is not the judge in charge of the Impasse Ronsin case who stands before you, but your old friend… It is dreadful. The whole population is against you… You must collect yourself, you must be calm…and help us to find the murderers." And then, as Hamard strode in, he announced to her, "We promise to find the murderers… Have courage, we will find them." After that, one of his men entered wearing "a black gaberdine and a large hat with a turned-down brim." He put on a fake beard while the investigators asked Meg about his getup. She writes that she told the police that "there was a great similarity between the detective's attire and that of the murderers" and that she "gave [the police] various details about the gowns and hats of those murderers."[7]

Behind these absurd theatrics, it's possible to see that these two men were revealing their positions to her in this encounter. Leydet was there because he loved her and wanted to help her however he could. Hamard was there because his job required him to humor her, but he would always maintain a personal and professional distance from Meg.

Not every magistrate was on her side, however. At the end of June, Victor Fabre, a highly placed member of the Parisian judiciary, hauled Leydet and Hamard into his office and urged them to investigate Meg. It was a waste of his time. In his words, "I was listened to with defer-ence, but that was all."[8] According to Meg, a deputy public prosecutor named Grandjean also subjected her to a hostile interrogation in June, asking her to explain how the cords that bound her to the bed came from inside the house and how the perpetrators could have mistaken her for her daughter. It was more than a little awkward for them both, since Grandjean was close to her friends the Buissons, the parents of Marthe's fiancé.[9]

The fact that there were two members of the judiciary who were skeptical of Meg suggests there was no orchestrated conspiracy that per-meated the entire judicial system to protect her. Instead, it's more likely Leydet firmly committed himself to Meg's cause and that Hamard was willing to go along with him. Perhaps his superior Lépine, a habitué of Meg's salon, had told him to do so. Perhaps it was simply that Hamard saw this as Leydet's investigation and that it was the police's job to follow the judge's orders.

Whatever Hamard's and Leydet's motives were and whatever opposition they faced from other authorities, it is also true that they would not have been able to pursue such a high-profile case in the way they did without at least tacit permission of their superiors and maybe explicit instructions to help Meg out.

The problem was that Meg needed more than a discreet cover-up, more than Hamard's and Leydet's statements saying that she could not possibly have been involved in the murders. She needed a resolution to the affair, one that pinned the crime on someone else. Otherwise, her life as she knew it was over.

Because so many were suspicious about her involvement in the crime, she became socially radioactive. In her words, "The circle of my friends was daily growing smaller, which was perhaps only human, since I was in trouble. I still received many letters from friends and acquaintances, but they were every day fewer in number. And their tone grew less sympathetic, their style more formal... Soon no letters reached me at all."[10] Some of her lovers, including Borderel, told her that they couldn't see her again until her name was cleared.[11] Similarly, the Buissons indicated that they "thought it wise that the engagement between their son and my daughter should not be insisted upon until the murderers were arrested, and the 'Impasse Ronsin Mystery' solved and forgotten."[12]

She had survived considerable infamy after Faure's death, but this was a different level. It was one thing to have had an affair. It was quite another to be involved in the murder of your husband and mother. And if the press had avoided mentioning her name in 1899, newspapers were now clear that her account of the crime didn't add up.

Retreating from her life among the elite would mean loneliness and a bitter end to years of work to turn herself into a grande dame of high society. Marthe's marriage prospects would suffer a terrible blow. Last but certainly not least, Meg was cash-strapped. No affairs meant no money.

One option was to commit to living modestly, although she'd never shown any talent for this. Another was to engage in more open forms of sex work with clients who didn't mind her stained reputation or were even drawn to her because of it. No doubt, she'd have considered this a degrading descent into a way of life she had tried to avoid for years.

In other words, Meg needed a miracle.

————

On June 19, Detective Pouce, one of the investigators assigned to the case, called on Meg at Vert-Logis. He told her, "An extraordinary event has taken place, a series of facts have been discovered, every one of them of such importance in the 'Impasse Ronsin Affair,' that the mystery is bound very soon to be cleared, and the three men in the black gowns and the red-haired woman you saw that night will be found and arrested… We hold the clue of clues!… Your troubles will soon cease and the murderers will be in our hands."

Then, he pulled out a photograph with two men and a woman and asked Meg, "Tell me if you see any one there who reminds you…of some one."[13]

Looking at one of them, "a bearded person with sharp shaped features and keen eyes," Meg told Pouce, "If my statement alone brought about the arrest of this man whom I don't otherwise know, I would obviously never dare to tell you anything. But I am oddly struck, and have a feeling that there is a similarity between the features of this man and the blond man who was in my room that night, near the door, and did not say a word…in general there is something in his appearance that makes me believe I have already seen him."[14] It was a very hedged yes: she wanted Pouce to be right so that her troubles would indeed cease, but she wasn't willing to have the man she claimed to recognize charged with murder solely on the basis of her words.

Pouce was thrilled. He told Meg, "We are on the right track, madame," and "I thought that was one of the men." Before he left, he promised her, "We shall run the murderers down."[15]

The story of Pouce's "right track" began the day after the murders were discovered. On June 1, an employee of the Paris metro found an invitation to Adolphe's April exhibition of his paintings in a metro station. Along with the invitation was a calling card for Jehanne Mazeline, an artist who had painted Faure's portrait. On the back of this card, someone had written a list of addresses. Thinking this might be a clue, the metro employee handed the invitation and the card over to the police.[16]

When the police investigated the addresses on Mme Mazeline's card, they found one of them belonged to a theatrical costumer named Guibert. Turns out he had lent out three felt hats and long black robes to a Yiddish-language theater a few days before the murders. Those costumes had ended up in the hands of an American journalist named Burlingham, the man Meg had recognized from the photograph. He had worn them to a dance he attended with his friend Davidson, another American, and his mistress, a chorus girl named Noretti.[17]

Davidson was an artist; this could have explained how he knew about Adolphe's exhibition. He also had a reputation as a violent crook. Burlingham had some dubious connections as well and was plenty odd by the standards of the day. He only wore sandals, loved hiking, and refused to eat meat, as if a hippie from the 1960s had traveled back in time to the Belle Époque. To top it all off, Noretti was rumored to have red hair.[18]

A miracle indeed.

As Meg learned more about this lead, she came to invest her hopes in it. It offered proof that she was neither a wildly imaginative hysteric nor an untrustworthy liar. Instead, it meant that she had been telling the truth about what she saw on the night of the crime. If it panned out, her reputation would be restored. Perhaps she fantasized about her friends explaining to her that they had always believed her, expressing their relief that the murderers had been caught, and asking her to do them the honor of telling them how she had helped the police catch the vile perpetrators.

From the police's perspective, the lead involved two disreputable foreigners and a chorus girl—the type of people who didn't count in their eyes. Hence, in the following months, they scrupulously followed this trail. The tangential connection to a Yiddish theater led them to look into foreign Jews living in Paris, despite the fact that neither Burlingham, nor Davidson, nor Noretti were Jewish. Jews, though, were seen as prone to mental illness and therefore criminality, and the police were perfectly willing to place marginalized individuals under surveillance to satisfy their xenophobia and antisemitism.[19]

Above all, the police focused on Burlingham, Davidson, and Noretti. They tracked the trio's whereabouts and arranged for Meg to see the two men on the streets of Paris to provide a more positive identification on multiple occasions. She wore disguises to avoid being recognized, dressing up as an errand girl in one instance and putting on a large cape in another.[20] Over the course of these encounters, she told the police with increasing confidence that Burlingham and Davidson were the perpetrators and lost the hesitation she had first displayed when Pouce showed her the photograph of Burlingham.[21] Likewise, in early October, Pouce brought Meg a photograph of Noretti in a crowd of singers. Meg was able to pick her out as the woman who had menaced her on the night of the murders. To add insult to injury, she also recalled that "the eyes of this woman are black and seem bad to me. Her nose is a nasty shape; the mouth, like the nose, looks ugly, horrible."[22]

There was just one minor hiccup with this lead: Noretti and Burlingham had rock-solid alibis.

As the police learned over the course of their investigation, Burlingham and a friend had set out on a long hiking trip through eastern France shortly before the murders. There were plenty of witnesses who had remembered seeing a tall, eccentric American wearing sandals in late May and early June. One who did was the proprietor of the hotel near Dijon where Burlingham stayed on the night Adolphe and Émilie were killed. Noretti, who was actually a brunette, was performing in London.[23]

The trail that led from the double murder to the invitation and card found on the metro to Burlingham, Davidson, and Noretti was no more than a series of coincidences. It was a bit of noise in the chaos of urban life that the police and Meg had wanted to see as the signal, one that reveals nothing about Adolphe's and Émilie's murders but a great deal about Meg, the authorities, and the relationship between them. None of it is good.

It shows that Meg's desperation to pin the murders on someone else was increasing over the course of the summer and fall of 1908 as her "identifications" of Burlingham and Davidson grew more and more certain. It is quite possible that Meg came to believe the lies she was telling and that she was nothing more than an innocent victim of a terrible crime. This was the dark side of Meg's propensity toward mythmaking: sometimes it led her down paths where she put others in danger in order to build the better reality she so desperately wanted to live in.

Of course, she had help from Leydet, Hamard, and his men cre-ating this fantasy world. They publicly declared her innocence and paraded men in robes and hats in front of her. Later, they took her out to the streets of Paris so she could say that she recognized Burlingham and Davidson as the two American expats went about their daily lives, totally unaware that they were being implicated in a crime that they did not commit.

If we rewind the tape to take another look at the photographic identifications of Burlingham and Noretti, we can get hints of how this collaboration between Meg and the police happened. Given that Meg could not have seen either individual on the night of the crime, the only way that she could have picked them out from group photographs is if Pouce indicated who she should single out. A nod or even his eyes lighting up when she landed on their faces would have sufficed. Worst of all, Pouce brought the photograph with Noretti to Meg after the police had learned about Burlingham's and Noretti's alibis. He knew the singer couldn't have done it but was still suggesting to Meg that Noretti was a suspect.

Pouce later maintained that he believed in his heart of hearts that Meg was innocent.[24] He may have been just another man who fell victim to her considerable charms and couldn't imagine that such an enchanting creature could lie about something so important. Hamard may also have told him to indulge Meg. If the murderer could not be arrested, it was worth giving an elite woman the sense that she was getting her way. If the taxpayers ended up paying for the police to waste their time, so be it. And if it meant intruding on the lives of innocent individuals who had few resources to defend themselves, that was just the way things worked.

Ultimately, the police propped up a very particular vision of a society. It was one where criminality lay with the dispossessed and never those close to power. The state worked to protect the rich, both from the violence of the poor and from the consequences of their own actions.

Nevertheless, by late October, the police cooperation with Meg was at an end. Once Burlingham's and Noretti's alibis had been verified, there was not much more that Leydet or Hamard could do for her.

We could imagine that Hamard could breathe a sigh of relief by this time. He had managed to convince Meg that he was on her side. If pressed, he could tell her that he and his men were simply out of leads. Journalists and members of the public had more or less given up on the case. Even if no one believed the official account, there wasn't anything to go on. From his perspective, he had done the best he could do.

He no doubt expected Meg to recognize the police inquiry was over. After giving interviews to journalists in June and July, she was now keeping her silence. As long as she remained quiet, the affair was over. Meg just needed to follow the rules.

This was something she had never been good at.

CHAPTER 14

FOR MEG, THE NEWS that the police were closing their investigation was a bitter pill to swallow. It meant an end to her hopes of clearing her name and regaining a place in high society.

Money was tight. With no generous lovers, she rented Adolphe's studio out to another artist, while cousins of her late husband moved into the villa on Impasse Ronsin to help her make ends meet.[1]

Meg was also lonely. Most of her friends had abandoned her, and she missed Borderel, who told her that clearing her name was the precondition for resuming their affair. This was probably the first time since the 1890s that she had no lover and no one on the horizon. Meg had always had a profound need for male attention; it might have been disorienting to suddenly be unable to maintain a life built around it. Now, her world on the Impasse Ronsin was dramatically reduced: there were Adolphe's cousins, there was Mariette, and, of course, there was Marthe.[2]

Of all Meg's familial relations, the mother-daughter one is the most mysterious. In her memoirs and in interviews with journalists, Meg consistently portrayed herself as a dutiful and loving mother and Marthe as adoring her in return, as nothing but innocence and devotion.

That innocence was something that Meg and Adolphe had carefully maintained. In particular, they did everything they could to keep Marthe from learning about Meg's affairs (and, presumably, Adolphe's).[3] She didn't need to know that her parents' marriage was in shambles, and she certainly shouldn't know anything about sex before she was married. Meg may have also shielded Marthe from knowing the truth because she didn't want her daughter to be disappointed in her or love her any less.

On the surface, Meg and Marthe's bond seems charming. It appears to offer proof of Meg's capacity for love and concern for others. But scratch a little deeper and it's possible to see that Meg saw herself as the sun and her daughter as a planet circling her who was incapable of casting any light of her own. What's more, Marthe sometimes had to act as Meg's caretaker, and Meg had a habit of sacrificing her daughter's interests when it suited her.

Indeed, there are signs that Marthe wasn't entirely content with the role that her mother had assigned her and that she found Meg exhausting. When she had to choose between her mother's way of doing things and her father's, she opted for the latter. A few years earlier, Marthe, who had been raised Protestant like Meg, converted to Catholicism, Adolphe's faith.[4] Her conversion might have been an expression of a desire to escape her mother's orbit, if only in a way that was entirely socially acceptable.

The double murder, though, tied Marthe's fate to Meg's. Marthe was deeply in love with Pierre Buisson and he with her, but his parents had made it very clear that their engagement was off. In her memoirs, Meg recounts that Pierre subjected her and Marthe to a terrifying scene in which he pointed a pistol at her and "told me in his usual weak, timid and despondent manner, that the murderers would have to be found, or else it would be impossible for him to marry Marthe." As a sobbing Marthe threw herself into her mother's arms, she exclaimed, "Is that real love?"[5] If this incident happened, it's clear that Marthe was struggling with her feelings for Pierre. But she may also have blamed her mother for her misfortune and wondered why Meg was telling such evident lies.

In turn, Marthe's sorrow may have wounded her mother's ego. Meg had long taken enormous pride in her ability to help friends and family members. Her daughter had suffered enormous tragedy, having lost her grandmother, her father, and her future, all in the space of a few short months. Of course, Meg would try as hard as she could to make it right for her daughter—although that meant that first she'd have to make things right for herself.

Meg made one last effort to work through official channels. In her memoirs, she describes taking Marthe with her to the district attorney and begging him not to end the investigation. He told her "in a lordly and lazy tone which clearly meant, 'This affair does not interest me in the least,'" that she was on her own and was free to follow up on any leads she thought were viable. After she indignantly replied that it was the state's job to pursue justice, he countered by saying, "Really, why don't you keep quiet... I fail to see what you expect of life!... You have your daughter, you have still a few friends... What more do you want!"[6]

It was like telling the sun not to rise. For over a decade, Meg had defined herself by refusing to settle. Against great odds, she had made a place for herself in high society and then retained it after Faure's death. She was hardly going to back down now, when so much was on the line. Once more, she would do her best to bend fate to her will.

Meg saw only one way forward: putting the case—and her future along with it—in the hands of the press.

She knew precisely where to go. For months, Marcel Hutin, a journalist for the conservative newspaper *L'Écho de Paris*, had been working on her. He had originally proposed that she write her memoirs, hoping that her need for cash would get her to open up about Faure and her other prominent lovers. As she started talking to him about her life, the story of the robes, the Americans, and the chorus singer came tumbling out, although she left out any inconvenient details about alibis or the police dropping the case.[7] Crime could sell just as well as sex, and Hutin ran with Meg's tale. He promised her "that the Press was almighty, and that he placed himself at my disposal. If the newspapers took up my case, the assassins would soon fall into the hands of the police."[8]

It was a moment when Meg's desires collided with Hutin's ambitions—and the imperatives of the press in the Belle Époque more generally. Hutin was a man whom a prominent politician described as "always on the lookout for an investigation, and in need of copy."[9] These same words could have been applied to almost any journalist of the day, one of total media saturation. In this era, there were an astonishing 79 dailies in Paris and over 250 in the provinces. There were papers for individuals of all political stripes, as well as four mass circulation dailies (*Le Journal, Le Matin, Le Petit Journal,* and *Le Petit Parisien*) that thrived on reporting crimes and sensational stories.[10]

To grab the attention of readers in this fiercely competitive environment, journalists sought to build a sense of immediacy in their stories, even to the point of producing events, not just reporting on them. They were particularly keen to unravel the secrets of criminals, celebrities, and those involved in politics—a Venn diagram that had Meg in the center.[11] As they did so, they sometimes operated in an ethical vacuum. There were newspapers that printed what was straight-up gossip and did little to verify that their reporting was accurate. In this instance, Hutin didn't check with the authorities to see if Meg was telling the truth about the state of their investigation, even though she was hardly the most credible source.

As Meg and Hutin continued talking, they decided to produce their own event. If it blended fact and fiction, it still made great copy.

In the October 31 issue of *L'Écho de Paris*, Hutin described seeing Meg and Marthe outside the Parisian police préfecture a few days before. The sight of them prompted him to write her a letter in which he asked "if, after five months, the authorities have lost any hope of finding the killers or if public opinion had some reason to think that the case had been declared dead, that is to say…covered up." Meg's response was published just below. In it, she indignantly asked him if he "was accusing her of no longer working to avenge her murdered loved ones." In fact, "*more than ever* I am helping to find our attackers." The police had a promising lead: three stolen theatrical costumes that she called "lévites" and a set of suspects "who certainly were not French."[12] While Burlingham and Davidson were foreigners, Meg did not mention their American origins. Instead, the term "lévites," which referred to the robes of Jewish priests from the House of Levi, suggested that the criminals were Jewish.

Meg's letter sent a shock wave through Paris. The public hadn't heard about the case for months. Had she been telling the truth from the very beginning?

With this exchange of letters, a period of restlessness and renewal began for Meg. In her words, it was one "of feverish, unending rushing to and fro, a nerve-racking life of hopes and fears, of constant surprise and anxieties." Journalists swarmed around her, and "each had his clue and his theory; each had made some startling discovery and wanted my views on it, each told me that his journal was the only one which was really on my side, and each craved exclusive information."[13] In return, she got attention and an endless parade of men telling her they believed her, they wanted to help her, they were at her disposal—all things she had been starved of for months.

Yet the constant coming and going, this lobbying her for access and information at all hours of the day and night, came at a cost. Bringing the case back into public view raised the stakes. If this new lead didn't pan out, the chatter about her untrustworthiness would turn into a roar.

To boost her credibility, Meg worked with journalists to paint herself as deep in grief and determined to find the murderer(s). On November 3, *Le Matin* described an interview with her in which she appeared "emaciated, wan, her features drawn but still beautiful, her face ravished with tears, her eyes surrounded by dark circles." The journalist Georges de Labruyère noted that she had difficulty answering his questions without bursting into tears. He took a photo of her in her widows' weeds with the ever-dutiful Marthe comforting her. Meg's eyes were closed, suggesting how lost in mourning she was. The tears alternated with bursts of fury. During one, she said, "Nothing will stop me from going to the end of the path that I have created: to avenge my husband, my mother, rehabilitate my name and safeguard my daughter's future." She was even willing to spend all the money she had set aside for Marthe's dowry to find the murderers.[14]

After such displays of agony and resolution, no one could think that she had been involved in the crime—unless, of course, they thought it was all a bit over the top. They might also have wondered why Meg had tapped Marthe's dowry as her source of funds, a move that would have cost Marthe a great deal but Meg nothing.

Le Matin's image of Meg from November 3

At the same time, Meg sought to cement the identity of the criminals as Jewish (or at least as foreign). She told *Le Petit Journal* that "the assassins were neither common criminals, nor *apaches*, nor even French, but instead foreigners who belonged to a special race." In her estimation, they were "Romanians or Polish Jews," no doubt "foreigners by their looks and their language" who had "physiognomies that we don't usually see in our country."[15]

Once again, Meg was keen to convey that there was something unusual about the criminals. As she did so, she drew on common tropes of antisemitism at the time, including the beliefs that Jews were a danger to society, a race apart, and physically marked by their difference.[16] It was yet another instance when Meg resorted to vicious stereotypes in the hopes that doing so would bolster her credibility.

The right-wing nationalist press eagerly took the bait and amplified the claims that Jews were responsible for the murders. *La Libre Parole* stated that the authorities had not solved the crime because Jews ran the French government and so of course covered up all instances of Jewish criminality. As it stated, "the Jew, whether he commits treason or murder, must remain sacrosanct, 'taboo' and sacred"—treason being a reference to the Dreyfus Affair.[17]

Within days, though, this whole story collapsed. The public learned that Meg's foreigners weren't Jews from Eastern Europe but Americans. Moreover, although Meg had claimed that the police hadn't investigated this lead, Hamard assured the press that his men had only stopped doing so when it became clear that Burlingham had an airtight alibi. We can imagine Hamard's frustration as he conveyed all this information.[18] He had protected Meg for months, only to have her try to make him look like he was incompetent.

Hamard was annoyed, Meg panicked, and the press was having a field day. On November 10, Burlingham even showed up to *Le Matin*'s offices. He was still being hounded by journalists and wanted to put an end to the attention. After talking to a reporter about his anarcho-pacifist political beliefs, he suggested that the paper bring Meg to their offices to see whether she still recognized him as one of the murder-ers.[19] Burlingham was a journalist, after all, and knew that everyone would want to read about this encounter, one that gave *Le Matin* the opportunity to produce an event that they could then report on.

Meg soon arrived at *Le Matin*'s offices with Marthe in tow. The young woman in no way needed to be a part of this encounter, but Meg may have brought her to remind the assembled journalists of her status as a mother and to set limits of what they would say in front of her. When the two women arrived, they found that the paper had arranged it so that Burlingham could not see Meg, but she could see him. When she did, she gasped, "No, no… If he is innocent, it would be too horri-ble… But that beard…those eyes… Oh! Oh!" and then burst into tears. Finally, she said, "Let me be… Let me be… I cannot decide." Then, the paper printed the itinerary of his hiking vacation in eastern France in late May and early June to clarify that the American could not have had anything to do with the murders.[20]

Meg's statement was ambiguous. Was she backing away from her identification of Burlingham? Or sticking to it? Whatever it meant, the public got the sense that she was either psychologically coming apart or a bald-faced liar, or both—and that she was always up for a show.

Hamard couldn't take it anymore. He told the press that Meg's the-atrics were too much and that he would no longer talk to her. If she wanted updates on the case, she'd have to speak to Leydet.[21] In other words, she was completely untrustworthy and speaking with her was not worth his time.

It was another crack in the alliance between Meg and the author-ities. Meg may well have understood that this was a warning that she needed to cool it.

For a while, she did. A few days after the encounter between Meg and Burlingham, she gave an interview with the same newspaper in which she declared, "I need to find the murderers of my husband and my mother. I will resume my investigations with more determination to solve the murders than ever."[22] But then, she stopped. No more throwing out theories to the press. Indeed, no more interviews with journalists.

———————

Meg's silence lasted for about a week. The story of the robes and the hats and the kooky American journalist had whet the public's appetite and let the press know that if they just pushed her hard enough, she'd tell them something. Maybe it would be true, probably it wasn't, but it would definitely be a wild ride.

By this point, Meg was also experiencing a complete mental collapse. She wrote in her memoirs that "the strain of my abnormal life, the constant excitement and strife around me, the ceaseless questions of journalists and visits of would-be advisers, the accumulation of clues, arguments, and suggestions, lack of sleep, and the almost complete loss of appetite, gradually brought me to a state of physical lassitude and mental agitation that bordered on madness."[23] One observer reported that even during a brief discussion, it was apparent that "she wasn't sane."[24] She had had breakdowns in the past, but this was the first in front of the public's gaze, the first that allowed her no retreat from the scrutiny that was precipitating the breakdown.

Meanwhile, she was getting a flood of anonymous letters. Many of them were hostile to her. Others were meant to be helpful and often suggested that either her valet Rémy or her cook Mariette had been involved in the murders.[25]

It was in this atmosphere that Meg and Mariette decided to look in Rémy's wallet on November 20. Meg claimed that they had done so because they were curious about where he was from, but she may have had other reasons to peek into her valet's belongings. There, she found a letter from Marthe to her ex-fiancé Pierre Buisson. Marthe had given the letter to Rémy to put in the mail, but he had kept for himself. Meg took this as proof that Rémy was suspicious, and she asked Ernest Chabrier, one of the cousins living with her, to report her valet to the police.[26]

Hamard brushed him off.[27] His feud with Meg wasn't over, and he could guess that she was up to no good. Besides, he might have thought that the unsent letter spoke more to the young man's feelings for Marthe than something nefarious.

But Meg was Meg, and a refusal was just an invitation to push harder. So once Rémy was back at the villa, she, her cousin, a female friend, and a reporter for Le Matin named Henri Barby confronted the valet and asked to see his wallet. Once again, they found the letter.

Barby's journalistic curiosity led him to press further. Undoubtedly egged on by Meg, he decided to see if Rémy was hiding anything else. As he searched the valet's wallet, he found a pearl wrapped in a piece of paper. This was a whole lot more suspicious than an unsent letter. It got worse when Meg declared that the pearl had come from one of the rings that was stolen during the murders.[28]

With that, Rémy became a suspect. Perhaps he had let the killers into the house and schemed with them in exchange for some of the spoils.

Hamard swung into action and had Rémy arrested. As the police were taking him away, the valet swore that he didn't know how the ring had found its way into his belongings and that he had played no role in the double murder. The terrified twenty-year-old kept stammering, "I am in-innocent!"[29]

Rémy had good reason to be afraid. He was from a small village in central France, where he had grown up in poverty as the son of an illiterate, unmarried mother.[30] He had no alibi, and his well-connected employer had targeted him as having a hand in the double murder. His only relatives in the Paris area were an aunt and uncle, who quickly hired a lawyer. Rémy would need a good one.

What the jailed Rémy didn't know was that the police were more favorable to his cause than the fact of his arrest suggested. Rémy wasn't charged with stealing the pearl, just taking the postage stamp affixed to Marthe's letter. Crucially, Hamard sought to sow doubt in the minds of the public regarding the valet's involvement in the murders. He told reporters that "one wonders how this paper [wrapped around the pearl] that is so clean and almost immaculate could have spent a long time in a wallet that was constantly worn and frequently opened."[31] Reading between the lines of his statement, Hamard was suggesting that Rémy hadn't been holding onto the pearl since May and that the press and the public should be skeptical of seeing him as a suspect. Rémy might have been telling the truth that he didn't know how the pearl had ended up in his belongings.

Hamard's game here isn't quite clear. He may have been so frustrated with Meg that he was willing to let his anger show and give her yet another indication that he wasn't on her side. Or he may have known that there was no other evidence tying Rémy to the murders and that the case against the valet would never stand up in court.

Meg's game, however, is entirely obvious. She now sought to cast as much suspicion on her valet as possible. Following his arrest, she fed journalists damaging information about Rémy. She told them about the anonymous letters she had received that suggested that he had been involved in the crime. She also indicated that there were "dreadful things" in his past.[32]

In truth, the dreadful things were hardly that. He had lied about how long he had lived in Paris before he got his job in the Steinheil household. At one point, he had broken a vase and not told Meg about it. He also had a mistress.[33] There was a great deal of irony in Meg's shock and horror that someone in her orbit had lied, engaged in a cover-up, and had a lover.

Meg's efforts to cast Rémy as an unsavory character found a welcome home at *Le Matin*, which eagerly reported details about the valet's background and even sent a journalist to his hometown to see what else they could dig up.[34] This newspaper, which had been founded in 1883, was known as the most innovative of the four mass-market Parisian dailies. It pioneered a journalistic style that was considered "American" because it focused on reporting the news as opposed to engaging in political debates. Interviews, like the ones they had done with Meg in the preceding weeks, helped readers feel like they were in the room with her. *Le Matin* was also an early adopter of photography, another way they strove to give readers a sense of unmediated access to events and people in the headlines.[35] Thus, after Rémy's arrest, *Le Matin* published photographs of the valet, who with his small eyes and mouth and the barest hint of a mustache looked awfully shady; his room in the attic of the Steinheils' house; the pearl ring that he may or may not have stolen; and Hamard leaving the villa after a search of the valet's quarters.

Le Matin's photograph of Rémy from November 22, 1908

On November 24, one of these searches bore fruit, which was surprising given that the police had combed through the house numerous times since May. When Hamard and his men, who were accompanied by Meg and Marthe, made their way into the cluttered attic, Meg saw something. She cried out, "There! There! Look!" Everyone saw it: a tiny diamond, not far from Rémy's room.[36] Was this another piece of jewelry that he had stolen? No one quite knew what it meant, just that it did not look great for the valet.

———

Until, even more dramatically, it did. The next day, a man named Souloy went to the police. He had seen the photograph of the pearl ring in *Le Matin* and realized that Meg was lying about a great many things. Souloy was, as it turned out, Meg's jeweler, and he told the police that she had come to him on June 12 and asked him to work on the ring with the pearl. If that was the case, then Rémy could not have been holding onto it since the murders, and Meg could not have been truthful about what the murderers had stolen.

Everyone's best guess was that Meg had planted the pearl on Rémy in an attempt to frame him. If so, Hamard had been right to point out that the paper wrapped around the pearl had been too clean to have been there since May.[37]

Meg was hauled to the Palais de Justice, the courthouse in the center of Paris. There, Rémy, Souloy, and Leydet were waiting for her. The judge started off questioning her slowly, asking her whether she still maintained that Rémy had stolen "not only letters, but was also the possessor of the pearl?"[38]

After Meg replied yes, Leydet asked her, "This pearl, are you sure you did not see it in your house after the crime?" Perhaps, he suggested, the murderers had taken the pearl and left it behind at the villa on the Impasse Ronsin as they fled. Leydet continued with this new theory: "In that case, someone could have picked it up and kept it, then placed it in Couillard's wallet?"[39]

No, she replied, that did not seem possible.

At that point, Leydet lost it. He dropped his neutral tone and took on one that was angry and cold and stated, "What! I am telling you, that this pearl which was found on Rémy on Friday, you wore it on your finger after the crime."[40]

It was an accusation: Meg was lying and Souloy was telling the truth. Leydet had tried to give her an out, one that cast both her and Rémy as innocent and the victims of some complicated scheme someone else had perpetrated. But she wouldn't take the life preserver he had thrown her to save her from drowning in her lies. Ultimately, while Leydet lasted less than two weeks longer than Hamard, he, too, had run out of patience with Meg.

From Meg's perspective, Leydet's anger was another act of desertion by a male protector. There had been those who had loved her and died (her father, Faure), one who loved her and left her because he couldn't take the hit to his reputation (Chouanard), and one who loved her but couldn't give her what she wanted (Adolphe). Each act of abandonment had been painful and destabilizing. Leydet loved her, had pledged his support, and had plenty of power. Now he was cutting her loose in the most public fashion possible while journalists looked on.

Whether because it was entirely too much for her or because some part of her knew that a display of vulnerability might get him to change his tune, she fainted.[41]

After she came to, Leydet's open fury dissolved. He pleaded with her to be honest. She was, Meg told him. It was just that there was "an inextricable mystery that I don't understand, that no one understands." She continued, "It's true that I went to M. Souloy's, but it was before the crime, not on June 12. Since then, the ring disappeared, taken by the murderers, I didn't have it in my possession anymore."[42]

Rémy wouldn't have any of this, though, and said, "I saw the ring on madame's fingers, scarcely a few weeks ago." Even worse for Meg, Souloy could prove it. He told Leydet that his records showed that Meg had given the ring to him on June 12.[43]

It went on like that for four hours. Meg vowed that she was being honest; Rémy swore that she was not. Leydet's belief that this confrontation would lead Meg to admit her lies was a lot like the idea that having a murderer see the victim's corpse would elicit a sudden confession, that the shock of the situation would lead to the collapse of the perpetrator's defenses.[44] Maybe this tactic worked in other cases, but not this one. Instead, Meg's guard was up and she wouldn't give an inch.

Finally, Leydet realized that he was getting nowhere, and he called it quits for the day. Meg was sent back home, Rémy back to jail.

It was ending the confrontation, not staging it, that softened Meg. Now she said, "it is a misfortune, a dreadful misfortune, perhaps! I am no longer so sure that Rémy Couillard is guilty."[45] She may have realized that her argument was falling apart and that she had not regained Leydet's support.

Instead, it was Rémy who won the day. He knew that his trials would soon be over.

———

When Meg arrived back home, she realized that another ordeal had begun for her. There was a swarm of journalists at the Impasse Ronsin asking her to explain how the pearl had made its way into Rémy's belongings.

In typical Meg fashion, it was a series of self-aggrandizing lies. She told the reporters, "I am devastated, discouraged, in the depths of despair. I find myself surrounded by enemies who have sworn to defeat me, who are joining forces to attack me, me, a woman, a mother. Still, I have not been undone by the horrible misfortunes that I have experienced."[46]

No, she claimed, she hadn't placed Rémy's pearl in his belongings. It must have been her enemies who were trying to discredit her and implicate her in the double murder. In her words: "Someone is pursuing a political end… I can guess where the blows are coming from, but I can't name them."[47] In other words, Rémy wasn't being framed—she was.

Once again, there were mysterious, powerful forces afoot, and Meg was at the center of some swirling, labyrinthine, political drama whose outlines were yet to be revealed. She must have been an important woman. Who else would have enemies who launched a complicated plot to undermine her credibility?

No one took these suggestions seriously.

CHAPTER 15

AN HOUR LATER, AT 9:30 p.m., Marcel Hutin of *L'Écho de Paris* and Georges de Labruyère of *Le Matin* showed up to the Steinheils' house. In the preceding weeks, no journalists had been more solicitous of Meg than these two, working with her to tell the public first about the police's lead of the missing robes and Burlingham and then about Rémy's presumed culpability.

The irony was that nothing had done more to undermine her position than their reporting. When the story of the robes unraveled, it made her look untrustworthy. Had *Le Matin* not printed a photograph of Meg's ring, one that she must have provided, Souloy would not have come to the authorities and destroyed her remaining credibility. Through an exchange of letters, interviews, and photographs, Hutin and Labruyère had sought to create an exciting narrative for readers. Yet they could not have anticipated the direction the story would go in or just how dramatic it would be.

What's more, their arrival on Meg's doorstep began a

twenty-four-hour period that was even wilder and more unpredictable than anything that had come before.

As soon as they were ushered in to see Meg, she went on the attack and blamed Hutin for urging her to publish the letter about the police's new lead. He reminded her that she was the author of her own miseries as well as the letter and said to her, "Look, you are in a bad spot, let me be honest with you: right now, the only way you can get out of this whole mess is to tell the truth. No one believes this absurd tale about the pearl being in Couillard's wallet."[1] But, he said, the public would forgive her "if she had the courage to free her conscience."[2] This was the carrot. In her account, there was a stick. They told her that the crowds gathering outside her house might lynch her if she didn't tell the truth.[3]

At first, she stuck to her story that she didn't know how the pearl had gotten into Rémy's belongings or how Souloy could say that he worked on it after the murders. But then, she burst into tears and said, "Yes, I put the pearl in the wallet." Another admission followed. No jewelry of any value had been stolen on the night of the murders: the crime had not been a robbery. By this point, Hutin and Labruyère were having a hard time following her claims as her statements became increasingly incoherent and as she was losing whatever tenuous grasp on reality she had.

So, for instance, she stated that she had planted the pearl on Rémy and placed the diamond in the attic because she needed to "divert suspicion. I knew that Rémy Couillard would be found innocent, that he could not be found guilty without any proof and that he would be released after a while."[4]

Why, though, try to implicate Rémy in the first place if she hoped that the police would find him innocent? Meg said, "Because I wanted to be able to fully justify myself to someone I do not want to name, whose love I have lost and who I can never think about again."[5] Finally, there was a grain of truth to her statements: so much of what she had done since the murders was in the vain hope that she could clear her name and resume her affairs, including her relationship with Borderel.

Hutin and Labruyère wanted to know who the real criminal was, who Meg was trying to protect. First, she couldn't say. Then, through her tears, she blamed one of Adolphe's models. Then she accused one of the model's family members. Then Mariette.

Then, finally, she settled on Mariette's son, Alexandre.[6]

Meg recounted, "He didn't think we'd be home. He came to rob the house." He killed Adolphe, then Émilie, while Meg screamed and screamed the whole time. "Then he came back to me. I yelled, I kept crying out; no one heard me, no one came to me." After he gagged her and tied her to the bed, he said, "'I spared you because of your daughter, but if you say a word, I will say that you asked me to kill your husband and mother and that you helped me do it.'"[7]

This was a tale of a brutal man who forced her to cover up his crimes as her cries for help went unanswered. For all that she was lying, there may have been an underlying truth to her account, and she may have felt she had been put in an impossible situation and abandoned.

Hutin and Labruyère were well aware that this version was as true as the other ones. They pleaded with her to be honest and asked her not to "throw this new name [i.e., Alexandre's] into the mix for public punishment."

Their skepticism of her must have come as a rude awakening. These two men had egged her on, encouraged her to come out with new versions of the crime, and promised her that they would help her prove her innocence. Now they were trying to restrain her and were telling her that they wouldn't do anything more for her. There was an angry mob outside, one that had heard about her attempts to frame Rémy. There were police officers stationed around her house, ostensibly to protect her but in fact to make sure that she didn't flee, a sign of how the alliance between her and the authorities had broken down.[8]

She had gambled and she had lost. The public, the press, and the state were all against her.

Realizing just how few options she had, she cried, "The only thing I have left to do is die, I want to die, why didn't I die like my mother! It's horrible! I am lost, what should I do?"

Hutin and Labruyère told her, "Madame, there is only one thing to do, it is to go immediately, as fast as you can, to the examining magistrate, and tell the whole truth... That is the only way to get public opinion to pity you."[9]

As they left, Meg had to ask herself: could she finally tell the truth?

————————

While Hutin and Labruyère were interviewing Meg in the dining room, Marthe and her cousins M. and Mme Chabrier were in the next room, along with Barby, another journalist for *Le Matin*. As soon as her interview was over, Meg burst in and collapsed onto a chair. Marthe knelt in front of Meg and clasped her mother's hands, an act of filial piety and perhaps protection in what was clearly her mother's hour of need. Meg was crying and through her tears said, "Protect me! Protect me!" She attempted to tell them that Alexandre was the murderer, but she was so incoherent that no one could follow her narrative. At the end of it, she exclaimed, "Oh! Kill me, kill me, please, kill me!... Find, find a way to do it, I beg of you, for Marthe!" It was not a suggestion that anyone was willing to follow.[10]

In one of her lucid moments, Meg became concerned about what Mariette might do if Meg was arrested. The two women whispered together, and eventually the cook promised her that she wouldn't say a thing if the police came for her employer, an indication that Mariette knew a great deal about the murders.[11] This was just one more of Meg's secrets that the cook would not reveal.

Eventually, Meg was persuaded to get a few hours of sleep and then go to the authorities in the morning. But even after she went to bed, there was no rest to be had in the house. At one point, M. Chabrier realized that Mariette was trying to kill herself and had turned on the gas in the kitchen where she slept. He ran to her, turned the gas off, and then heard Meg cry out, "Go find the doctor! I want to die, I want to die." So the Chabriers rushed to her side to calm her down, only to realize that they had left a suicidal Mariette all by herself. When they ran back into the kitchen, they found her seated on her bed with a revolver to her head. She grimly exclaimed to them, "I know what I need to do." Fortunately, they managed to disarm her and took her to the dining room to keep a watch on her.[12]

It was a night of terror, tears, and anguish, one that so easily could have ended in another round of horrific violence at 6 *bis* impasse Ronsin. Meg's suicidality might well have been attention seeking. For one, she kept calling for someone else to kill her, even as it was clear that no one would. In a twisted way, it was a request for someone to rescue her, for a doctor to serve as a disturbing version of the male protector she so consistently longed for.

Mariette's efforts to end her life appear to be more serious. After all, she turned on the gas and put a gun to her head. She might have been terrified about what would happen to her if the authorities started treating Meg as a suspect. Mariette was so deeply involved in Meg's affairs, sexual and otherwise, that the state might investigate her as a potential accomplice. In any case, she had been living and working in a household where the emotional temperature had been rising for months and had finally come to a boil.

Everyone knew that morning would bring no relief, only new perils and, for some, a reckoning.

———————

At 4:00 a.m., Meg, Marthe, and M. Chabrier set out in the darkness for the police headquarters. It's not clear why they decided that this was the appropriate hour for Meg to amend her account. When they arrived, they first had to wake up the sleeping police officer who complained, "What, you again? You are not going to leave us alone." In turn, he had to wake up Hamard, who greeted them in his nightdress and slippers.[13]

Hamard was evidently surprised to see Meg and undoubtedly furious at the Meg-ness of it all: her insistence that the police be at her beck and call and the complete disregard for anyone else's schedule. But whatever anger he felt, he didn't show it.

After he dressed, he ushered Meg into his office. She quickly told him, "I falsely accused Rémy Couillard of having killed my husband and my mother. I put the pearl in his wallet. It was also me who put the small diamond which your inspectors discovered the day before yesterday in the groove of the floorboard."

Meg had finally admitted guilt, and the authorities could release Rémy. That provided some measure of relief. What came next did not.

She continued, "The author of the crime is not Couillard, it's Alexandre Wolff, the son of Mariette Wolff."

To explain why she had been hiding the truth for all these months, she said that it was "Because of Mariette Wolff, the mother of the criminal. She was so good to me that I didn't want to make her sad by telling her that her son was a murderer."[14]

The story was ludicrous. Meg had made so many public declarations that she was determined to find the murderer, avenge her husband and mother, and clear her name, no one would believe that she had known who it was all along and had kept silent to spare the feelings of her cook. Yet Meg's statement was enough for Hamard to send his men to fetch Alexandre. The police already knew a bit about him, thanks to his proximity to Meg. He was a horse trader who belonged to a rough-and-tumble world and was known to be violent.[15] They also knew that he had a rock-solid alibi: on the night of the crime, he had gone to a large dance with some of his friends. Plenty of people could attest to the fact that he was nowhere near Impasse Ronsin.[16] Months before, when the police were investigating servants and models, they had concluded that there was no way Alexandre could have been involved in the double murder.[17]

On the one hand, Hamard wanted Alexandre in his office so that he could confront Meg with this latest set of lies in the hopes that she'd drop them. Unlike Rémy, Alexandre was never charged with a crime or thrown into jail, never seriously considered a suspect. On the other hand, had Meg accused a banker or a judge or someone else in her social circle, Hamard might not have rushed to bring him to police headquarters, as he did when she named Alexandre. Like Rémy—and Burlingham, Davidson, and Noretti before him—it was safe for Meg to accuse Alexandre and safe for the authorities to treat him as a suspect.

———

A few hours later, three police agents pounded on the door of Alexandre's one-room apartment in a slum on the outskirts of Paris. They woke him up, as well as the woman he had brought home for the night. "What do you want?" he asked, still groggy from what had evidently been a late night. As soon as one of the officers told him that he needed to come with them, he responded, "Oh! Yes. The story of the Impasse Ronsin again… You are from the police… Didn't I already prove my innocence? It's fine, I'll come… I'll explain myself… I am sure that I won't be kept for long." Then the police told him that his companion would have to come, too. At this, he burst into laughter, saying they had just met, but "the more the merrier."[18]

Unlike Rémy, Alexandre displayed no fear. Instead, he saw his trip to police headquarters as at worst an annoyance, at best a joke that would entertain his drinking buddies for weeks to come. Having an alibi helped, of course. Alexandre was also bold where Rémy was timid. He was decidedly a man who gave as well as—or better than—he got.

Soon, he was in Hamard's office, along with Meg and Leydet. Then, Hamard added Mariette and Rémy into the mix, just to make things more heated. It was a room bursting with animosity, frustration, exhaustion, and anxiety. And all this was heightened by class tensions and the complicated intimacy between employer and employees.

Alexandre was the first to go on the attack, telling Meg, "Madame, how can you dare say that I am the murderer of your husband and mother! A few days ago, you invited me in [to your house] and welcomed me warmly. You can't have thought [that I was the murderer] like you do now!" This was an accusation, but he was still addressing her with respect by calling her "madame."

Next up was Mariette. She turned to Meg and asked her, "Why didn't you tell me that you suspected my son? I would not have hesitated to denounce him to the police." It was a canny statement, for she was at once expressing her loyalty to Meg and her skepticism about her employer's latest version.

Rémy then repeated that he was innocent of any involvement in the murders and did not know how the pearl had ended up in his belongings.[19]

Soon it was just Meg and Alexandre duking it out. For hours, she accused him of murder and he denied it. At one point, it seemed like she was shifting her story and said, "My God! If it is not Alexandre Wolff, then the person that I saw in my home and who tied me up looks tremendously like him." But not long after, she returned to her former certainty and declared, "Yes, the murderer of my husband and my mother, it is this man, it is Wolff."[20] All this happened while journalists and officials crowded in the halls of the police headquarters, trying to see what the latest twist in the case would be and how Meg could possibly get out of the giant mess she had created for herself.

Meg was the star of the show, but Alexandre didn't disappoint. Over the course of the day, his fury rose. Here was a man with a temper who had spent hours being blamed for a crime he very clearly did not commit. Did the police know it? Absolutely. Were they still making him sit there until Meg recanted? Also yes.

Eventually he shifted from denying that he was the murderer to a full-frontal attack on Meg's character. He said, "You know that I have nothing to do with this crime, you wretch, scoundrel, crook, fallen woman."[21]

She accused him of murder again, to which he responded, "You are a liar, a monster, an infamous person. No one can believe you."

Finally, he completely lost it and launched what a journalist called "a string of insults that we could not reproduce."[22]

There is something remarkable about this exchange. Elites like Meg expected a level of deference from those beneath them on the social ladder. Those without great resources often had to navigate this expectation, if only because they lived in an inegalitarian world where the wealthy had power over them. Earlier that day, Alexandre had shown her some level of respect by calling her "madame," while Mariette had carefully worded her objections to Meg's accusation of Alexandre to make it seem that her chief loyalty was to Meg, not her son.

At the same time, many men and women of the working class took great pride in the role that they and their forebears had played in challenging entrenched social and political hierarchies through over a century of revolutionary unrest. Alexandre was here refusing to show any deference toward Meg. There were the unprintable swear words, as well as the terms like "wretch" and "fallen woman," which were all judgments on her character and her social location. The latter term was a synonym for prostitute, the others for someone who belonged to Paris's underclass, and his words cast her as the lowest of the low, a woman who was beneath him. In this one encounter, he temporarily overturned the hierarchies that structured so much of French society. And what's more, the authorities weren't weighing in on the side of power as they let him scream insults at her. Perhaps they were just as frustrated with her as he was.

Whatever went through their minds during Alexandre's tirade, Leydet and Hamard's ultimate aim was to get Meg to drop her accusation. Eventually, they realized that Alexandre would never get her to relent, and they turned to maternal love, hoping that softness and tears would work where confrontation and anger failed. When they ushered Marthe in, she immediately started sobbing, knelt in front of her mother, and pleaded, "Mother, mother, confess, say everything, say everything!"[23] Marthe, it would seem, had also lost her patience with Meg. If her mother told the truth, Marthe might be able to get some rest.

Yet Marthe's intervention was just as ineffective as everything Leydet and Hamard had tried, and Meg continued to insist that Alexandre was the murderer.

Finally, the judge took charge. He told Alexandre he could go, that the horse trader's alibi was enough to prove his innocence.[24]

It was not the solution Leydet wanted. He had hoped that he would get Meg to drop her accusation. Had she done so, she might have saved herself, might have shown the judge that she knew she had done wrong and would be more cautious in the future. He, in turn, could pass Meg's versions of the crime off as the product of a woman whose mental state had been broken by grief and stress, as a whole lot of unpleasantness the public could now forget. But Meg's refusal had narrowed his options.

Instead, all he could do was damage control. He needed to do something to put a stop to the public relations catastrophe that began with the arrest of Rémy and was making the police and the judiciary look more and more complicit with Meg's bad behavior every passing day. He also needed to prevent her from talking to reporters and coming up with new versions of the crime and new suspects.

One option was to give her a very stern lecture and then send her back home. But the past few weeks had told him that she was hardly inclined to stay silent, that she'd just keep talking to the press and finding new individuals to blame unless he took more drastic measures. He couldn't charge her with the murders, though, since there wasn't any evidence that suggested she had been responsible for them. The problem was that she had lied, but that lying wasn't exactly a crime.

Hindering the progress of an investigation was, however. So he opened his copy of the French criminal code and read a passage to Meg that stated that those who "helped or assisted" the perpetrators of a crime were complicit with that crime. Then, he told her that "I must charge you, madame, with complicity with murder" for having "misguided justice and made it impossible to find the murderers."[25]

The outcome she had feared, the outcome she and Mariette had whispered about the night before had finally come to pass. Meg was under arrest and would go to the Parisian women's prison of Saint-Lazare.

In truth, Leydet did not have the best case against Meg. Unless the government marshalled significant evidence of Meg's involvement in the murders, no jury would convict a woman for lying, something that was seen as fundamental to a woman's nature. From another perspective, the problem was not Meg's lies per se but the authorities' decision to go along with them. Following this logic, Leydet might as well have charged himself and Hamard.

But in the moment, it was the best he could do. It made it clear to the press and the public that the authorities were no longer on her side, that they knew that she was involved in a cover-up. Leydet had done everything he could to protect Meg for months and now had finally and irrevocably turned on her. He had wanted so badly to help her but had failed to understand how far she'd go and how willing she was to compromise innocent individuals, the police, and the judiciary to clear her name.

For once, she didn't burst into tears. Instead, she proclaimed her innocence but said, "I bow to your decision," and asked to speak to Marthe one last time before she went to jail.[26]

The two women embraced as Marthe told Meg that Saint-Lazare "will be good for you. It will allow you to pull yourself together…and discover the truth."[27] They were words full of care, even as they also indicated that Marthe was relieved that she and her mother would be separated, at least temporarily.

Finally, Meg was driven to Saint-Lazare. It was the first of many nights she would spend behind bars.[28]

The period between the murders and Meg's arrest offers us a wild tale of sudden reveals and the spectacle of a woman blowing up her life in an effort to save it. It's a span of time where Meg, the authorities, and the press all look terrible. Meg put innocents in danger and marshalled racism, xenophobia, and antisemitism to make herself look better; the police and the judiciary did more to uphold the social hierarchy than pursue justice; and journalists printed what they knew to be lies to sell copy.

A murderer escaped scot-free perhaps out of diplomatic considerations and very certainly because no one involved in the case valued the truth.

As a result, justice never really had a chance. Eventually—six months after the murders—Meg was charged with a crime that she had committed: complicity with murder and helping the perpetrator escape justice. This only happened because of Meg's recklessness. If she had been more cautious and risk-averse, she might have realized what seems obvious to us: avoiding the press and staying silent were in her best interest.

In the end, the fact that Meg's misdeeds and her potential involvement in the double murder only came to light due to extraordinary circumstances reveals how the authorities could so easily have buried the case and gotten their way.

PART 3

MYTHS AND LEGENDS

"No dramatist can compete with her."[1]

CHAPTER 16

AS MEG WAS BEING driven to Saint-Lazare, she was unable to recognize the city she called home. She wrote, "Paris seemed a new, a different city." She didn't know where she was going and had never even heard of the Saint-Lazare prison.[1]

There was a reason for that: it was made for poor women, not the likes of her. Many of its inmates were prostitutes who had either run afoul of the government's system of regulation and surveillance or were recovering from a venereal disease.[2] Others were awaiting trial or serving short sentences. This prison had a terrible reputation, and one inmate said, "For a woman, it is better to die than to enter Saint-Lazare."[3]

The building was enormous and unloved, located in a working-class district in the northeastern part of the city. It had a decrepit exterior, and the painful-looking spires of its metal fencing prevented anyone from getting too close. From the street, the most sinister element was a giant black door that looked like a maw threatening to consume any women passing by. The motto of the French state, "Liberty, Equality, Fraternity," was inscribed above the door, as it was on many a government-owned building. Here, it was incongruous: inmates found these qualities in short supply inside the prison's walls.

Once in prison, Meg was ushered through a series of rooms and corridors and placed in the care of the nuns who staffed Saint-Lazare. She was disoriented and asked too many questions. At one point, she went into a room with "green furniture in it; the ceiling was low. It was not a beautiful room, but it was most comfortable." She thought it was her cell, only to find out it was the prison director's office. A nun with a "kind, strong face" named Sister Léonide came in. Meg expressed her utter bewilderment by saying, "It is I, *ma sœur*; it is strange, is it not, that it should be I?"[4] Meg assumed that Sister Léonide was just as befuddled as she was about how a queen of Parisian society had ended up in Saint-Lazare.

Sister Léonide took her from the director's office and down hallways that were "filthy, evil-smelling," and cold, so very cold. She was placed in a cell with two other inmates. When they started talking to her, she couldn't understand a word of what they were saying and so burst into tears. Eventually, she fell into "a sleep almost as deep as death."[5] It was probably the first decent night's sleep she had had in weeks, if not months.

The next morning, her mental faculties returned to her and she could take in her surroundings. She saw that she had been sleeping on a mattress made of "rough straw," with a "pillow filled with dried seaweed, and the sheets made of some yellowish material that looked like sail-cloth." Her cell was dark, with pools of fetid water on the floor and vermin running everywhere. The stench of bodies, decay, and human waste was overpowering. That morning, she was served bread with insects in it and coffee that was "well-nigh undrinkable." She also learned that she would not be called Madame or Meg but inmate number 16170.[6]

At one point, she was strip searched, as all inmates were.[7] Meg wrote about many of the horrors of her life in Saint-Lazare, but not this one. It may have been too humiliating to contemplate this sign of her degradation and how she had lost the privacy typically afforded to bourgeois women.

But then again, at every moment and in every way, Meg was being told that she no longer had that status. She was in a prison for women that society didn't care about.

A few days later, 16170's situation improved slightly, and she was moved to a new cell with more light. Her cellmate was a young woman named Firmin who had been arrested for trying "to steal three blouses from a shop…to make myself beautiful for my sweetheart." Given that Meg had covered up a double murder to get back together with her lover, she could easily understand her cellmate's motive. Firmin had an air of innocence about her, and Meg found that "she reminded me a little of Marthe." One of the nuns told Meg that Firmin had been selected to be her cellmate because "she is a much nicer little woman than the others, and she is very unhappy; so, she will know how to console you."[8] According to the nuns, Meg was owed some amount of consideration, as certain hierarchies needed to be respected, even in prison.

Many of the other inmates didn't see it like that. As news of the double murder filtered into the prison, including from new inmates, many of the women in Saint-Lazare became enraged. At night, they threw their shoes "against the door of my cell; and the most abominable insults were hurled at me." They cried out, "'Murderess! You strangled your own mother, you killed your own husband… If we had you here, we would gouge your eyes out, tear you to shreds, you assassin!'"[9] Her crimes were bad enough. But Meg's fellow inmates might also have been furious at how a rich woman had been able to get away with so much for so long.[10]

This is how Meg learned that the public now suspected her of the murders, not mere complicity with murder, the crime that she had been charged with. When she entered prison, she was convinced that she wouldn't stay there for long, since lying was just what women did, what any good bourgeois woman would need to do to get through life.[11]

If she was now the chief suspect for the double murder, though, she was in a great deal more trouble than she thought.

————

The inmates' hatred of Meg was matched by an equally intense hostility toward her outside the prison's walls. Angry crowds gathered at the door of Saint-Lazare in the days following her arrest, while newspapers outright accused her of murder.[12]

The government was another target of the public's ire. The day after Meg was arrested, the press revealed that Leydet was one of her admirers and had requested to investigate the double murder to protect her. Quite obviously, he could no longer serve as examining magistrate for the case.[13]

Within the upper reaches of the French state, many feared that the crisis would metastasize if it wasn't quickly contained and that the prime minister and his cabinet might have to resign.* Meg was so well

————

*   In France, judges are not as independent as they are in the United States but instead report to the minister of justice, who is a member of the cabinet.

connected that everyone assumed she had benefitted from a cover-up: they just didn't know how far and how high it went.

The socialist left and the nationalist right worked hard to stoke the public's anger. Both saw themselves as speaking for the ordinary people of France and took Leydet's bungled investigation—and the difference between the rough treatment doled out to Rémy and Alexandre and the indulgence given to Meg—as a sign that the men who staffed the upper reaches of the government were entirely too invested in protecting their own to administer justice.[14] A socialist journalist wrote that the investigation into the double murder was proof that "the law isn't equal for everyone. Hard on the little people, the weak, it is indulgent toward the gentleman and especially the ladies of 'high society.'" How else to explain why "Rémy Couillard and Wolf [sic] were arrested on a mere suspicion, while the government spent six months not arresting Mme Steinheil"?[15] The very public failure of the authorities to treat Meg as a suspect revealed the ugly truth behind the regime's façade of egalitarianism. The government might preach its commitment to liberty and equality, but in a society riven by deep and long-standing economic and social inequalities, some were more equal than others.[16]

It fell to Leydet's replacement, Jean-Louis André, to manage the crisis. André was plenty capable and was lauded by his superiors for being "hardworking and intelligent." His social position was also key. Unlike most of his colleagues in the judiciary, he came from a modest background.[17] He might have been one of the few Parisian judges who had never been to Meg's salon.

From the beginning, he presumed that Meg had murdered Adolphe so she could marry one of her lovers. Yet he struggled to explain Émilie's death. At times, he suggested that Meg might have hated her mother so much that she had decided to kill her, too.[18] There was another, even more ghoulish theory that floated around at the time: Meg knew that if she just offed Adolphe, everyone would know that she was the murderer. But if Émilie also ended up dead, fewer people would suspect Meg. So she killed her mother to deflect attention away from her. (This theory did not come from André but instead a woman who had briefly been one of Meg's cellmates in Saint-Lazare and falsely claimed that Meg had confessed the whole thing to her.)[19]

André was industrious and distrustful, as well as a complete and utter misogynist. He looked into her childhood to dig up evidence of her innate immorality. He also investigated her brother, Julien, to see if he had helped Meg commit murder.[20] At times, his hostility toward Meg veered into the ludicrous, as when he tracked down how the Steinheils' dog had died on the suspicion that Meg might have poisoned the family pet. André may have been disappointed when he learned that the dog's death was totally unremarkable.[21]

For all this, André's investigation seemed more exhaustive than it was. Notably, he interviewed some of Meg's rich and powerful friends to get their assessment of her character but never considered them to be potential suspects.[22] André's focus on Meg was laser-like in its intensity. Because he saw Meg, and Meg alone, as responsible for the crime, he could extract the murders from her social milieu.

André may well have been convinced in his heart of hearts that Meg was the murderer. We could also imagine that he was told that his job was to demonstrate the state's hostility to Meg but not to solve the crime. She wouldn't be shielded from scrutiny, but the prominent individuals connected to her would be—including the real murderer.

———

On December 1, less than a week after Meg's arrest, her lawyer, Antony Aubin, came to Saint-Lazare to prepare her for André's first interrogation. Aubin was a star criminal attorney and had been the defense counsel for many of the most famous cases of the day.[23] Meg had hired him months ago, not long after the murders, based on Leydet's suggestion. The two men were friends, and the judge had told her that Aubin could provide her with legal advice. If the perpetrators were found, Aubin could also help her file a civil suit as part of the criminal proceedings, as was allowed by French law. From the beginning, Meg was comfortable with Aubin. There was Leydet's recommendation, for one. And he had even come to some of her soirées, back in the days when she was entertaining the cream of Parisian society, before her life of picking roaches out of her food.[24]

According to Meg's estimation, Aubin was "keen, full of life and fire and endowed with an amiable simplicity of character" and was entirely convinced of her innocence.[25] But simple doesn't seem like the way to describe him: savvy does. When Meg started speaking to the press in October 1908 and brought herself back into the public eye, he had told her to be careful. And when she accused Alexandre Wolff of the murders, Aubin had begged her not to.[26] He had known that the state's patience with her would only go so far and that Meg's best bet was to lie low. In other words, he probably suspected that his client wasn't entirely innocent of involvement in the crime. But Meg, being Meg, couldn't hear the subtext of what he was saying and didn't heed the sensible advice he had given her in the preceding months. Had she done so, she would not be sitting in Saint-Lazare.

Now, Aubin had a new set of suggestions for Meg. And this time, she was more willing to listen. He told her what he would have said to any client facing André: the judge "is no genius; but he is a relent-less, pertinacious judge who will do his utmost to make you contra-dict yourself and draw terrible conclusions against you from those contradictions… Every hesitation, every slip…every reticence will become formidable weapons in his hands." Some of it was quite partic-ular to Meg: "Don't mention your 'friendship' with M. B[ouchez]., the Attorney-General, or your intimacy with President Faure. They would only irritate him. Besides, if you did, he would only change the subject of 'conversation.' You must forget that you have received in your Salon, Ministers of State and Diplomatists, eminent politicians and eminent judges."[27] Aubin had already mastered the rules of this new game, one in which all scrutiny would fall on Meg, none on her lovers.

When Meg was ushered into André's office, she found him to be "very stout, with a red, congested face, and a greyish beard. His hair was dark and spare. His eyes seemed to jump about behind the pince-nez, and they seldom looked straight at any one." She regarded him as "vulgar and aggressive" and indelibly marked by his lower social origins.[28]

After barking at her to sit, André launched into a series of ques-tions about her marriage: How had she met Adolphe? Did she ever love him? If not, why did she agree to marry him? Why had she come to hate him?[29]

Meg tried to resist answering this last question, for she knew the judge was asking about Adolphe's relationships with men. Revealing a husband's sexual transgressions was taboo for a bourgeois woman like Meg and brought dishonor to the family.[30] She pleaded with André, "Have pity on me… I beseech you, do not force me to disclose the secrets that I hoped to take to the grave with me."

With ice in his tone, André replied, "Justice cannot show pity… Its role is to expose the truth."[31]

A few minutes later, he pressed her to talk about her own affairs and the money she earned from them, even as he let her know that she didn't have to reveal the names of her lovers.[32]

André and Leydet were like night and day. The latter was so gentle and so keen to prevent her from talking. He treated her as a lady of high society was supposed to be treated, including letting her maintain her secrets and get away with her lies. In contrast, André was intentionally rude. He blew cigarette smoke at her and varied between simmering hostility and open rage as he pressed her to reveal more.[33] He didn't care about her status and didn't see her as a woman who needed the state's protection—or even his courtesy.

André's last interrogation of Meg was in March 1909. In this four-month span defined by his obsessions and intrusions, there were times when Meg got the best of him. Once, after he yelled at her that she must have strangled her husband and mother, she showed him her tiny, delicate hands. Looming over her, he exclaimed, "'Yes, all murderers have long arms and enormous hands… Well, you are different, you are an exception, that's all… The very smallness of your hands proves that you are guilty. Even in your physique you deceive, you lie… And those little hands which look so innocent are the more criminal, since they look so innocent. There!'"

Meg knew exactly how to play it. She pointedly stared at the judge's "enormous, red, hairy hands" and told him that "'even though you were as innocent as I am, the size and look of your hands would unmistakably denounce you as a murderer—if you had to deal with a judge after your own heart!'"[34]

After these moments where Meg outwitted André, he left his own office to sulk and regroup.[35] Meg had conquered Leydet with her considerable charms; for André, she would need her just as considerable smarts.

Yet any victories were fleeting. André never let her forget that he had the upper hand. He could make her miserable with his chainsmoking and his efforts to trap her into admitting she was guilty. He'd ask her long, multipart questions and then tell her that if she was taking time to gather her thoughts, she was lying because "the truth never hesitated, but burst forth at once." He asked her the same question on different days. When her answers varied, André "jumped up with glee and exclaimed, 'I've got you!'" If she was calm, "I was cleverly concealing my hand, and therefore I was guilty." If she cried, "my weakness, my grief, were due to remorse; therefore I was guilty."[36]

Above all, André had the coercive power of the state. One day, she was taken to the courthouse and told that he was not ready to see her. Until then, she would have to wait in a part of the courthouse known as the "mouse trap." This was a series of cages, one stacked atop the other, that were "about seven feet high, five feet long, and three feet wide" and were "unspeakably filthy and foul-smelling."[37]

Meg was in the mouse trap for three hours. There, she learned that sometimes women spent up to nine hours in their cages. Suddenly, she remembered one of her former lovers who was an examining magistrate like André. She recalled that he "frequently forsook his duties to come and pay me compliments or to listen to some music in my salon." Now she saw that this courtesy to her had come at a dreadful cost: "Whenever he wasted time at my house the woman [he was interrogating], perhaps several women, had had to wait in a cage."[38] So much had been kept hidden from her when she was in high society. Having fallen down to the opposite end of the social ladder, she saw that the men around her were capable of inflicting great cruelty on some women as they showed great kindness to her.

Then there was the publicity, another sign of André's lack of consideration for Meg. While Leydet had largely kept the details of his investigation under wraps, André did not. In doing so, he damaged her reputation, as the public was treated to a stream of embarrassing information about her. They could read about her and Adolphe's affairs, as well as decades of accumulated family resentments.[39] Newspapers printed depositions from witnesses that were just as compromising, such as a transcript of André's interview with Meg's lover Borderel in which the mayor detailed how much money he spent on her and the circumstances in which they had consummated their relationship.[40] Borderel also told André that Meg hated Adolphe and had once called her husband a "bastard."[41] Rémy's deposition revealed more about Meg's mistreatment of Adolphe, how she regularly screamed at him and told him that he didn't matter in his own home.[42]

None of it looked good for Meg—and that was the point.

CHAPTER 17

ANDRÉ WASN'T THE ONLY one who wanted to spill Meg's secrets. Right after her arrest and even before he began his investigation, newspapers were filled with accounts of her many transgressions. Mariette gave interviews to journalists in which she provided them with tidbits of information about her employer's affairs and hinted that the murderer was a member of the elite.[1] Meg's lover Balincourt ungallantly described their affair to reporters at a dinner party, while friends and family members divulged what they knew about her turbulent adolescence and married life.[2] Newspapers listed the names of politicians, judges, industrialists, and high officials who had enjoyed Meg's favors over the years.[3]

Chief among them was Faure. For almost a decade, journalists had kept silent about Meg's role in the president's death. Now, what had been an open secret became simply open and not secret.[4] The press described Faure and Meg's last encounter in endless detail, discussing his use of aphrodisiacs and rumors that she left her corset behind when she fled the Élysée Palace.[5] Above all, they fixated on the detail that Faure had grasped Meg's hair so tightly that his aides had to cut it as he was dying. It was a way of suggesting that Meg had been fellating Faure without spelling it out and of describing her as marked by her affair with the president, if only temporarily.[6]

The public also read about how Faure and Meg had gone on vacation together and how everyone in her neighborhood knew about his regular visits to the Impasse Ronsin.[7] There were also stories about the influence Meg had during her affair with Faure and how she was "the great distributor of presidential favors... Officials in every part of the government and of every rank assiduously paid her court."[8]

Then there were the tales about money, including the fact that Faure had arranged for the state to pay Adolphe the extraordinary sum of thirty thousand francs a painting.[9] A newspaper reported that after the artist's death, another one of Meg's powerful lovers had the government buy one of his works to help Meg out.[10] The politicians of the Belle Époque always had a reputation for being on the take, and all these press reports gave readers the sense that the regime's sexual and financial improprieties met in Meg's body.[11]

Some of the revelations weren't exactly that. Journalists wrote that Meg had an illegitimate child who was a Parisian *apache*. André would have loved to have proven this rumor to be true but found no evidence for it.[12] Likewise, one member of the Japy family told a reporter that when Meg was an adolescent, she had a mania for putting earthworms in her mouth.[13] Given the nature of the sex act she was best known for, the tale seems more a product of the teller's vivid imagination than anything else.

And to be sure, not everything made it into the press. Although the police were convinced that Meg had been in a relationship with a woman named Mme Thors before the murders, she was never mentioned in any of the coverage of Meg's life and loves. Journalists tracked down Berthe Lefèvre, a wealthy older woman who was close to Meg beginning in the 1890s and who may have been her lover. But the press was primarily interested in Lefèvre's connection to "Aunt Lily," the relative Meg invented to hide her affairs. Lefèvre was described as so innocent that she hadn't known that Meg was taking paying lovers, a depiction that negated the possibility that Lefèvre was one of those lovers.[14] This silence about the possibility of Meg's lesbian affairs in the midst of a furious clamor about her sexual behavior might be due to the fact that Thors and Lefèvre were wealthy but not especially well known. Or it may have arisen out of the long history of lesbian invisibility in a society that often struggled to imagine that women might seek sex with one another.[15] Ultimately, too, Meg might have been seen as too conventional and too bourgeois for the public to have thought that she slept with women. In any case, the upshot was that Meg was understood as guilty of all sorts of sexual misbehavior but only and ever with men.

Still, the public couldn't get enough of all the truths, half-truths, and total falsehoods that were flying around for weeks after her arrest. This was when the case was on the front pages of the major Parisian dailies and became not just a murder investigation but a scandal known as the Steinheil Affair.[16] This is also when Meg earned the nickname of "the Red Widow," red being the color of violence, sex, and attention.[17] One journalist wrote that women were neglecting their housework: "Ordinary life is suspended while curiosity reigned… One name was obsessively on everyone's lips: Steinheil, Steinheil… The will to know, to know more and more, takes precedence over everything."[18] Politicians in the Chamber of Deputies were no different from the housewives and ignored the finance legislation they were supposed to be debating to trade the latest news and gossip about the most infamous woman in France.[19]

And ordinary life was suspended not just because everyone was fixated on the same tale of sex and murder but also because the rules of what you could and couldn't say, what you could and couldn't know suddenly shifted. Journalists could write the things they had known about for years but never dared to put in print. Headlines promised a break in the code of silence that protected the reputations of prominent individuals.[20] Those who weren't insiders and hadn't heard the gossip that had circulated for years about Meg could feel that they now had access to the truth about how the most powerful individuals in France behaved when they were behind closed doors.

This was a realm usually off-limits to outsiders, and quite intentionally so. The bourgeoisie worked hard to keep their private lives private, their secrets secret. In their minds, this ability distinguished them from the poor, who were thought to have less of a sense of shame and less of a reputation to maintain.[21]

The state also determined who benefited from silence and who was subject to scrutiny. If you belonged to Meg's world, then you knew you could probably call on officials to clean up any messes you made. Some of those same officials had a habit of surveilling the bodies and sex lives of the dispossessed. Indeed, many of Meg's fellow inmates in Saint-Lazare were poor women that the police suspected of being prostitutes and were accordingly subjected to invasive gynecological examinations.[22]

This moment when Meg's secrets came pouring out, when the

public's attention was fixed on the transgressions of the elite, was one when the direction of the surveillance was reversed. Now, ordinary citizens got an opportunity to spy into the bedrooms of the rich and powerful.[23]

It was Meg's precipitous tumble down the social ladder that was partly responsible for this shift. In one journalist's words, she was now a "fallen socialite, thrown into the dreadful jail of thieves and prostitutes."[24] As she fell from grace, she lost her privacy. The strip search, André's intrusive interrogations, and the details of her sex life appearing on the front pages of newspapers were all of a piece. Once the state started treating her like a woman with no status and no entitlement to protection, the press could, too.

———

In this moment when decades of misbehavior among the rich and powerful suddenly became visible, working-class frustration bubbled up. Workers spoke indignantly about how politicians had been running a prostitution scheme.[25] Peddlers roamed the streets of Paris singing bitterly to Meg that "there is a lot more vice in your world/ Than in that of the worker who is dying of hunger!"[26] The poor had long been told that their social superiors were also their moral betters. But if Meg slept her way to the top of society, if elites could be dishonest and licentious, if they could condone or even commit murder, it was clear that these lessons were just myths meant to prop up an inegalitarian social structure.

The left seized on the Steinheil Affair in order to decry what it saw as the atmosphere of immorality that reigned inside the elegant buildings occupied by the highest in the land.[27] A union for domestic servants sought to use the scandal to open an inquiry into what it termed the "life of corruption and crime among the bourgeoisie in general."[28] Servants were members of the working class who often knew when the seamy reality of their employers' lives didn't match their claims to propriety. Now, when the secrets of many at the top of the social hierarchy were pouring out, the union hoped that more revelations would bring down not just particular individuals but that entire hierarchy.

Meanwhile, newspapers on the nationalist right were filled with salacious details about Meg's affairs to discredit a regime they detested and a political elite they regarded as hopelessly corrupt. It also helped these newspapers position themselves as courageous truth tellers who were willing to say what no one else would.[29] They, too, railed against the elite, "this Bourgeoisie which took power by endlessly speaking about establishing probity and virtue in politics" and "stunned France by the cynicism and enormity of its scandals," in the words of the anti-Semitic journalist Édouard Drumont. As he framed it, Meg and the government were both "vicious, venal and greedy, dressed elegantly and smelling of debauchery and deprivation": there was the façade of virtue and good behavior (those fine clothes) and then there was the reality that it tried to cover up (the stench of moral rot).[30]

Sex and politics have long been inseparable in France. In the 1780s and 1840s, sex scandals led to outcries about the immorality of political figures and fueled revolutions.[31] The Steinheil Affair led to no such unrest. Indeed, the government's fear that powerful officials would have to resign because of it never became a reality.

Instead, it served as a moment of clarity that revealed unpleasant truths. The state promised to treat all citizens equally and bolster morality and the family. Likewise, the elite that held so much power within the government proclaimed that they were dedicated to duty and propriety.

It now seemed that these were all lies, that powerful men were too busy skirt-chasing to uphold their commitments to virtue or to equality. As the Steinheil Affair gave the public the ability to see what was usually hidden, they might wonder if those in power deserved their positions and if a more honest society would also be a more egalitarian one.

Meg's vertiginous fall from the heights to the depths disoriented not just her but also the world in which she lived. According to her and to so many others in the Belle Époque, society was organized around two poles that were supposed to be entirely separate from each other: that of the lofty and the good on the one hand and the base and the transgressive on the other.[32] But now that orientation made no sense. In an atmosphere where Meg was known to be a center of elite license and thought to be a murderer, high and low were jumbled in her very person. If that was the case, then the threat to society could come from elite soirées, not just the slums.[33]

———————

Although the Steinheil Affair united left and right in outrage, the scandal was a much bigger deal for the latter than the former.[34] Socialists saw it as an example of the shenanigans that the rich got up to, but their newspapers never devoted much coverage to the case. In contrast, right-wing dailies spent months using the scandal to peddle conspiracy theories and sell the public on the idea that Meg was a central node in a monstrous plot led by Jews, Freemasons, and Protestants that had ensnared France for years.

Since Faure's death, they had maintained that partisans of Captain Alfred Dreyfus had assassinated the president. Once Meg was arrested and became the chief suspect in one set of murders, these same newspapers insisted that she must have been involved in the president's death and that the crime on Impasse Ronsin was somehow linked to the Dreyfus Affair.

The details of this supposed international, decades-long conspiracy shifted on a daily basis. Sometimes Meg hadn't knowingly murdered Faure, but Émilie had. Sometimes Meg had given Faure an overdose of the aphrodisiac Spanish fly; sometimes she slipped him cyanide.[35] Then there were endless versions of the connection between the Dreyfus Affair and the double murder. Perhaps Adolphe and Émilie had been killed because the Steinheils had papers that were damning for Faure's political adversaries.[36] Maybe the reason that the judiciary and the police had tried so hard to protect Meg was that they were afraid that she would reveal that Dreyfusards had killed Faure.[37] Eventually, it would all make sense and the ghastly truth would come to light—and these newspapers assured readers that this day of reckoning would happen any day now.[38]

It never did. In fact, all these claims were baseless and said more about the fervid imaginations of those making them than anything about Meg, Faure, Adolphe, or Émilie. They posited that Jews were a danger to the nation who had captured the reins of power and that France needed a moral and political regeneration and to exclude those whom nationalists perceived as outsiders.[39]

In the short term, these conspiracy theories didn't amount to much. Other newspapers on the right, like *Le Figaro* and *L'Écho de Paris*, never indulged in them. Instead, many felt that they were idiotic and tiresome—which they were.[40] By 1908, the right-wing nationalist movement was in decline and grasping at straws in an attempt to remain relevant.[41]

Long term, however, the claim that the government was morally bankrupt and run by a Jewish conspiracy did tremendous damage. These ideas surged back to life in the interwar period and fed rising fascist currents in France in the 1920s and 1930s as well as the establishment of the Vichy government that rose out of the ashes of France's defeat in World War II. This regime was initially popular in part because it offered itself as an antidote to the corruption of the Third Republic (1870–1940). However, the Vichy government's authoritarian bent led it to collaborate with Nazi Germany—with tragic results for France's Jewish citizens.[42]

It's undoubtedly the case that had the Steinheil Affair not happened—had Adolphe and Émilie died natural, unremarkable deaths that barely made the news—fascist leagues would still have attracted plenty of adherents in the interwar period and the Vichy regime would still have willingly participated in the Holocaust. All the same, nationalists' claims about this scandal were poison in the veins of French society. And Meg was an active participant in this toxic discourse, what with her suggestions that the murderers were Jewish and part of a mysterious, international plot against her and, by extension, Faure.

For all the destruction they caused, it's possible to understand why elements of these conspiracy theories might have had some appeal in Meg's day. Powerful officials didn't commit murder, but they did countenance it, as Leydet's investigation reveals. The fact that many elites claimed to model propriety while engaging in all sorts of misbehavior behind closed doors led many to wonder what else they were lying about—and whether any of their words could be trusted. The Steinheil Affair also heightened the sense of estrangement between the ordinary citizens and the government, as it confirmed the view that real power wasn't in the ballot box but in the salons, boudoirs, and bedrooms of the rich.[43]

In essence, as the scandal allowed individuals to spill long-held truths about Meg, it also allowed members of the public to say what they felt to be true about the government and the society of the Belle Époque: that power was built on lies.

––––––––––

For all the outrage that the Steinheil Affair kicked up, it was in many cases more entertaining than infuriating. One newspaper spoke of it as "one of those good jolts of Parisian animation, without excessive disagreements…which are almost signs of health."[44]

That entertainment came in many forms. In the months that followed Meg's arrest, you could stroll down the boulevards of the capital and buy any of the newspapers whose headlines promised the latest batch of revelations. You could hear songs and jokes mocking Meg and the police as you sat in a café and listened to passersby.[45] There were postcards with photos of Meg and satirical cartoons about her life to buy, as well as plays and films about the affair to see. Some of the films featured Alexandre and Mariette Wolff playing themselves, as the boundary between art and life dissolved even further.[46]

It was a world where real life was better than any work of fiction.[47] One newspaper claimed, "Next to the 'tragic widow,' everything seems dull." The Steinheil Affair had everything: "passion, feelings, hatred, money, family and dangerous liaisons, high society and the common people, the city and the provinces, and even History," the last a reference to Meg's relationship with Faure. Faced with this, "No dramatist can compete with her."[48]

Sometimes the excitement was in the mystery of the double murder. Theatrical productions staged possible scenarios for the crime: one suggested that Meg's (nonexistent) illegitimate son was the perpetrator, another that she had paid a servant to kill her husband.[49] Films recreated Meg's initial account of the murders and key turning points in the investigation for those who wanted to relive its highlights.[50]

And sometimes, the excitement was sex. The Steinheil Affair was an opportunity to read newspaper articles filled with salacious details about the sex lives of prominent individuals, to imagine yourself in the Élysée Palace watching one of Faure and Meg's assignations—or even imagine being one of them. Many of the jokes and songs about Meg were filled with sexual innuendo and references to penises, breasts, and oral sex. And there were more than enough images of a very sexy Meg to go around. She became a sexual celebrity, a woman who was allowed to be a bit wicked as long as she was also a figure of desire.[51]

All this sex was even more thrilling because it provided answers to any number of mysteries about the government: why the Dreyfus Affair ended in the way that it did, how one artist got a whole lot of state patronage, how some civil servants got promoted, or why the authorities seemed to have been so keen to protect Meg from scrutiny in the wake of the murders.

As Meg's sex life became public property, Parisians started constructing their own version of her, weaving together details of her past with their fantasies and anxieties about sex and power. This Meg came to life through songs, images, and opinion pieces as a figure who embodied the perils and promises of female sexuality.

There was something intensely ironic to the public imagination of the mythic Meg. The real one was trapped within the grim confines of

Saint-Lazare. She was hungry, frightened, and cold. In a photograph from this time, she stands in front of a bare wall in the prison yard, the despair and exhaustion visible in her eyes. You can see how her time in prison had worn on her, how it had dulled the life and vitality that had been one of her most marked characteristics in the years before.

Meg in Saint-Lazare

But no one wanted to think about this Meg. No one wanted to reflect on what it was like to be incarcerated. And no one wanted to see Meg as a complicated woman who loved and hated, who had experienced betrayal and inflicted cruelty, who was struggling to maintain her dignity and sense of self in an institution designed to strip its inmates of those very qualities.

Instead, the public's version of Meg was as a woman who was anything but lonely or unhappy, who was the life of the party and living in the lap of luxury. After all, a woman who was dangerously alluring was a whole lot more fun to think about than one who was miserable.

And although the flesh-and-blood Meg had been stripped of her status and influence, the one who came to life in legend still held enormous sway in the halls of power. According to songs, the entire French government was in love (or lust) with this Meg. One quipped that every police officer, "up to Lépine," the head of the Parisian police, "had his baton up," a reference to both the weapon that the police used to assert their authority and these men's erect penises, as if the government's power arose from the desire of the men who ran it.[52] Another tune about Meg claimed that she frequently received "very influential members" in her salon, with "members" referring to members of the Chamber of Deputies or penises.[53] These songs were about Meg and why she got away with so much for so long, but they were also about the French government. They suggested that passion and power were one and the same, that although women could not vote or hold office, they ended up getting what they desired because they were so desirable.

As the public mulled over this mythical Meg, not many were bothered by the fact of sex, by the lust powerful men had in their hearts. Now that Meg and Faure's relationship could be openly discussed, the public was intensely curious about it but not especially condemnatory. Instead, the president was often regarded as a lucky dog who had the good fortune to have had a mistress who was a sexual virtuoso. Sure, sex killed him, but what a way to go.[54] Even Leydet could be excused. One journalist stated that the judge shouldn't have investigated a woman he was in love with, but "examining magistrates are just men like any other, subject to the same weaknesses."[55] Desire was only dangerous when it led to corruption, to officials abdicating their duties to chase women.

Illicit sex was natural and normal and maybe even good. Meg's day was one of intense concern about masculinity and fears that men were becoming weaker and less virile. These anxieties dovetailed with ones about France's plummeting birth rate and the prospect that the nation wouldn't be able to maintain its prominence on the world stage if its citizens didn't produce more babies. There was plenty of blame to go around, and homosexuality, masturbation, and opiates were all seen as dangers to the nation.[56]

At this point, everyone knew that these were the sorts of vices in which Adolphe engaged. But once Meg was arrested, he became less central to the story, and the public increasingly focused on her extramarital relations, not her marital ones. Even after death—even during the investigation into own his murder—Meg managed to eclipse her husband. As Meg's possible lesbian affairs remained hidden and as Adolphe waned in importance, heterosexual lust became the beating heart of the scandal.

And there was something very comforting about thinking about Meg's relationships with her powerful male lovers. It's true that she only had one child and wasn't exactly known for engaging in the types of sex that could raise the birth rate. But she offered proof that the men leading France were virile and entirely unlike the weak and passive Adolphe. There was reassurance in knowing that Leydet and his colleagues were "just men like any other," a phrasing that made it impossible to imagine that there were men who didn't desire women. Then there was that last encounter between Meg and Faure. Even as he was dying, he managed to assert his masculine authority over her.[57] Meg offered proof that

French politicians and officials were manly and capable of leading the nation to a brighter—and more libidinous—future.

That lust, too, wasn't just reserved for a powerful few. Her body now widely circulated, if only in image form. It's another contrast between the real Meg and the mythic one. Before her incarceration, she had reserved her charms for a paying elite. Now, the real one was living under lock and key, inaccessible to only a few visitors. But the mythic Meg was available to all, and some of the representations of her verged on the pornographic.

One of the more scantily clad Megs appears on a postcard that mocked the gap between the elite's claims to be well behaved and the sexier reality of Meg's life. It shows a haloed Meg standing on a bed of clouds as four men kneel to her and exclaim, "Saint Meg—Virgin and Martyr!!! Let us pray for her!" The words declare Meg's innocence and morality, but the image is in delicious contrast to the notion that she is in any way saintly. With her breasts exposed, she holds objects from the murder: a tray with two glasses in one hand and cords in the other. The first is a reference to the toddies she prepared for Adolphe and Émilie on the night of the crime, ones that might have contained a narcotic, the second to the cord that bound her to the bed. These props suggest that she had drugged her husband and mother and staged the crime scene. But the men around her don't care and aren't so much praying for her soul as begging for a scrap of attention from her.

These men would do anything for her. And among the four of them, they have a whole lot to offer her. There is a judge and a police officer: of course, she escaped scrutiny for so long after the double murder. There is also a highly ranked military officer and a man who looks like Faure and wears an emblem of the prestigious Legion of

Honor: of course, she held a lot of sway in the government before the crime. But with a face and a body like that, what man wouldn't fall victim to her charms?

This postcard gives another indication of just how different the mythic Meg was from the real one. In this image and in so many others from the affair, Meg was depicted as a whole lot more conventionally attractive than she was in real life, as well as a lot slimmer. The actual Meg was appealing because of how she combined the matronly and the sexualized. But here, the matron dropped out and the sex took over.

The postcard with "Saint Meg"

Another equally irresistible and impossibly thin Meg appears on a postcard titled "The Happy Widow." It imagined her life in high society prior to her arrest and then what would happen if she came to trial. Before she was thrown into Saint-Lazare, she's a center of elite sexual excess who is partying it up with well-dressed men, one of whom says, "Let's sing! Let's laugh! Let's drink!" The trial represents a brief break in the festivities, as she sits demurely in her widow's weeds, playing the role of a grieving wife. The caption, which reads, "Pretty women are never convicted," assures us that she'll be acquitted soon enough. And in the last image, she's back to her wild ways, saying, "Finally I am free! We can start again." This party is even more debauched than the one before the trial. The men are completely inebriated, and Meg lifts her skirt up to show her underwear to them—and to the viewer. Meanwhile, there is another woman on the floor, her leg poking out from underneath the table: either she's passed out drunk or she's cavorting with a lover.

There's bite in the contrast between Meg's public pretense of being a good bourgeois woman and her hard-partying ways in private. There's also bite in the idea that she'd escape any legal or social consequences for her actions, that she's too pretty for a jury to convict, too sexy to be cut off from her wealthy lovers on a permanent basis. And yet Meg is gorgeous and a whole lot of fun. Once again, it's hard to blame any of the men who surrounded her or showed her mercy.

So maybe France wasn't the most moral nation; maybe it was one where justice took a back seat to the pleasures of the flesh. On this postcard, there are the wealthy men who surround her before and after the trial. Then there is the unseen jury made up of male members of the public who can't bring themselves to convict her out of an appreciation for her charms. In the end, they'd be just as indulgent to her as Leydet had been.

This was one of the messages of the Steinheil Affair, that heterosexual desire defined France. It was an inescapable element of the political system, of the courts, of high society, and of everyday life. Sure, it could lead to corruption, but at least its women were sexy and its men lusty.[58]

And that vision of French society relied on a very particular understanding of Meg. She was all sex. It was her past, it was her future, and it was who she was, down to the marrow of her bones.

"The Happy Widow"

CHAPTER 18

MEG SPENT ALMOST A year in prison, from November 1908 to November 1909. She found Saint-Lazare to be "a place of dirt and sloth," one with an "ignoble and degrading atmosphere, a hotbed of infection for the body, as well as for the mind." She could barely sleep, thanks to the cockroaches that ran over her all night. She couldn't go into the prison yard because "when I did so, once, the other prisoners insulted and even hit me." She grew weak and was in constant physical pain and mental distress, some of which was due to her horror at being in an institution that she saw as one for "the lowest and most degraded of 'gay women [i.e., prostitutes],' the vilest viragoes of the slums."[1]

As Meg saw it, no one should have to live like this. But she, definitely, should not have to. In her words, "It was atrocious for a poor young woman 'of the people' like [her cellmate] Firmin, for instance, to live in a cell, but my fellow-prisoner would perhaps agree herself, that for a leader of society, for a woman of the world, it was almost worse. She had been used to a small shabby room or even a garret, to misery…

and I to a vast house, servants, comfort, luxury even… She was used to insults and vulgar language; they made me ill."[2] When Meg fell from grace, she fell from too great a height to be able to adjust to her new life in the depths.

Meg's drawing of her cell

She couldn't read, since that made her headaches even worse.[3] For decades, she had led a life of hustling and socializing, of entertaining and being entertained. Now that was gone.

So she sewed. It was a way "to kill time, and also to live like Firmin and the other prisoners" who needed to work in the prison to make money. They earned almost nothing: "by sewing all day and a great part of the night, [I] managed to earn seven or eight francs a *month*," a paltry sum by any standard. Meg was good at it, though, and was soon given "the more difficult sewing to do—piles of fine napkins and tablecloths for the Spring sale at the *Printemps* and the *Bon Marché*," two of the capital's chicest department stores. In her previous life, she had shopped there and marveled at the bargain basement prices of the linens.[4] Now she learned their true cost.

At least Meg's resources meant she could have meals delivered by a local restaurant and so didn't have to suffer the miseries of prison fare.[5] Her regular visits from Marthe and her lawyer also broke the monotony.[6]

There were also unexpected sources of kindness in prison. Firmin treated her with "real devotion" and "such touching attentions as I had never received from any one, except from my Mother and Marthe."[7] According to Meg, the nuns who staffed Saint-Lazare were all as saintly as their profession suggested and treated her with particular care. One time, Sister Léonide was so worried about how weak she was after one of André's interrogations that the good sister spoon-fed her a baked potato, which had been a favorite of Meg's father.[8] How strange that in Saint-Lazare, of all places, Meg found the parental, all-enveloping care that she so longed for.

Woven through Meg's account of her life in prison is a complex set of attitudes. Except for Firmin, the other inmates disgusted her on a visceral level. She felt herself to be morally and socially distant from them and fully entitled to any ounce of better treatment. At the same time, she understood that every woman in that prison deserved better.

Sometimes, she could see how she had been shielded from knowledge about how bad life was for the poor and marginalized. After all, the cruelties of incarceration weren't exactly topics for high-society pleasantries. What's more, for over a decade, she had circulated among men who could easily have made the prison a more humane place, if only they cared to do so. They hadn't, though. She had once been their darling, and now she was feeling the weight of their neglect.

And sometimes—and most interestingly—Meg came to realize that the comforts of the life that she had previously enjoyed, such as those cheap linens and the social calls that judges paid to her while prisoners waited in the mousetrap, depended on the pain of others.

———

As Meg was reflecting on the splendors and limitations of her previous life, members of the public elaborated on the mythic one in an attempt to puzzle her life out. The central mystery was what hand, if any, she had played in the Steinheil Affair. And the answer to that question always boiled down to the precise nature of Meg's sexual self. In the waning days of 1908, there were three different versions of Meg, each of which took sex to be fundamental to her character and a matter of public concern. As these discussions played out in the press, it became clear that the fate of the real Meg was tied to the public's views about the mythic one.[9]

One option—and the one that condemned both Meg and France to a horrible future—was that she was driven by greed. This view had plenty of adherents in the weeks after Meg's arrest, and many saw her as "an imperturbable and cynical schemer," in the words of one newspaper.[10] In this version of Meg, she was so coolly rational that she could plan and execute a horrific crime. What's more, her avarice meant that she was akin to a lowly streetwalker. One observer who described her as a "prostitute" wrote that she was "ambitious and perverted," with a "strong taste for showy luxury, jewels and champagne" and "villainous desires" that led her to have sex for money.[11] As a prostitute, she was beyond the pale of bourgeois society, a figure of moral degradation who reduced the most intimate of human relations to cold, hard cash.[12] Such a woman might well be so calculating and vice-ridden that she could plan and execute the murders of the woman who gave birth to her and the man she had sworn to obey. Even if she wasn't the murderer, she might have covered up the crime and lied about what she had seen because of her selfish desire to resume her affairs with rich men.

This view of Meg spelled doom for her. Juries and the public were harsh on female defendants who they saw as driven by self-interest or who weren't deemed to be as loving as a woman should be.[13] It was also doom for French society, and a greedy Meg was taken as a sign of national decline. One newspaper wrote that because of Meg's supposed "need for luxury" and willingness to trade sex for money, she was a "beautiful plant with troubling and poisonous scents [that] could only have grown on the dung of our corrupt society."[14] This statement linked Meg to one of the great bogeymen of her era: degeneration. It was a theory that sprang from Darwinism and the idea was that if a species could evolve and improve, then it must also be capable of doing the reverse. Many in the Belle Époque were convinced that as society modernized, Europeans were devolving and introducing harmful traits into the gene pool. Perhaps the French weren't having the right kind of sex (i.e., heterosexual and reproductive), or perhaps the sex that they were having was debasing them and future generations. Those anxious about the prospect of degeneration often saw prostitutes as part of the problem, for supposedly spreading vices and diseases to their well-to-do clients and for preventing men from having sex with their wives.[15] If Meg was greedy, that meant that she was one of these lower-class women corrupting the nation. Thus, while this version of Meg suggested that the nation was in danger, it did not disrupt other elements of the status quo and the idea that immorality could only come from the lower depths.

Of course, Meg had her defenders. For some who knew her well, the idea that she was a selfish schemer didn't fit with their sense that her problem was that she was too emotional, out of control, and mentally ill. A friend told reporters that the lady in question was charming, a devoted wife and mother, but had "a strange temperament," while her physician indicated that he thought she was suffering from hysteria.[16]

It was another version of Meg that put sex at her core, for hysteria was also taken as a sign of sexual dysregulation and linked to nymphomania.[17] Maybe both her affairs and efforts to pin the crime on innocent individuals were all a desperate bid for attention and a sign of overwhelming, ungovernable passions that roiled just below the surface.

There was certainly reason enough to think that Meg was suffering from a mental illness. After all, the public had witnessed her psychologically crumble in the pages of the major Parisian dailies. And yet hysteria was also a broad, nebulous diagnosis that was frequently applied to women who were seen as too much to handle and too feminine.[18]

This account of Meg's motives was laden with ambiguity. Hysteria was regarded as another sign of degeneration, but what was bad for society was good for her.[19] According to the French criminal code, "there is neither a crime nor a misdemeanor when the defendant was in a state of insanity at the moment of the act."[20] Even if a jury thought that Meg had strangled Adolphe and Émilie with her bare hands, they'd have to acquit her if they thought she was mentally ill. They would also have to excuse her lies as the natural and inevitable product of female derangement.[21]

Or maybe it was love. In the weeks after her arrest, this was the least common explanation for her actions, although some were willing to entertain this possibility. Less than a month after she had been thrown into Saint-Lazare, an article in *Le Matin* suggested that she might have been a *"grande amoureuse,"* a phrase that literally translates as "great lover" and that was used to describe a woman who loved deeply and ardently. According to *Le Matin*, if Meg was a *grande amoureuse*, then she might well have been "blinded by a passion that drives and hypnotizes her and made her lose her head."[22] This categorization didn't rule out the possibility that she was also mentally ill, but the emphasis here was less on her malady and more on her devotion to love. In this theory, she had affairs because she yearned for a man who could fulfill her in ways that Adolphe could not. That same overwhelming need for love could explain her seemingly bizarre actions after the murders: she wanted to be with Borderel so badly that her desire drove her over the edge of sanity.

This theory tied Meg to ideas that were in circulation at the time that women were fundamentally creatures of love and devotion.[23] And as a *grande amoureuse*, she joined a centuries-long line of women, many of whom were elites, who were celebrated for their love affairs with kings, aristocrats, philosophers, and writers.[24]

This version of Meg was the best possible outcome for her. It suggested that she should be freed, both because she was mentally ill and because she was pretty. The author of an article comparing her to a Parisian *grande amoureuse* of the seventeenth century who was also accused of murdering her husband implied that it would be ungallant for a jury to condemn a beautiful woman for loving too much. In his mind, whether either woman had committed a horrific crime was an open question and beside the point.[25] As the postcard titled "The Happy Widow" put it, "Pretty women are never convicted."

Meg's status as a *grande amoureuse* also offered hope for France. She tied the nation to a tradition of pleasure and passion. Maybe it wasn't doomed because its citizens were doing sex all wrong but would be saved because they had been doing sex right for centuries. In the Belle Époque, beautiful, sexy women were seen as symbols of national strength and vitality.[26] Here was a woman monopolizing all the headlines, one whose image was everywhere, whose body seemed to offer the promise that France was a lusty nation full of alluring elite women.

The prostitute, the hysteric, the loving queen of Parisian society: three different versions of the myth of Meg, three different understandings of her relationship to sex that reflected the full span of ambivalence to female sexuality in this era. This debate is another sign of how the mythic Meg flattened her. The truth was that she was ambitious, she suffered from a mental illness, and she fell in love easily. Self-interest, psychological distress, and maybe even a little bit of love combined to lead her to lie about what she had seen on the night of the murders.

But many in her day didn't want ambiguity. They craved some sort of certainty about what drove her, what the fate of their society was, and whether she belonged to the world of the high and the good or the low and the bad.

What that certainty meant for Meg wasn't clear, though. One thing was: if she came to trial, the jury would decide her guilt or innocence based on how they understood the nature of the mythic Meg.

It took months for the state to weigh in.

In March, André finally finished his investigation. He had compiled a massive dossier with around thirty-five hundred documents, including interrogations of Meg, depositions of former servants and friends, and reports on the physical evidence from the crime scene.[27] In his mind, it all led to one inescapable conclusion: Meg was the murderer.

Then it was up to a panel of judges to decide whether to indict her.[28] When they did, they combined the theory that André had pursued from the beginning with the most negative view of Meg that saw her as driven by greed. In their words, she "had never loved her husband... She was much adored in high society for her grace and beauty, but her pride suffered due to the mediocrity of her financial situation." Anxious that she was aging out of lucrative affairs, she decided "to find more secure resources in a stable and lasting relationship" with a rich man and fixed on Borderel. Since he refused to marry a divorced woman, she would make herself a widow.[29]

On this theory, the state charged her with the premeditated murder of Adolphe and the parricide of Émilie. These were two of the most grievous crimes a person could commit. If convicted of either, Meg could be sentenced to die by the guillotine. Parricide was seen as going against the laws of nature, for it destroyed the person who gave you life. But a woman's premeditated murder of her husband wasn't much better, as it was an attack on a society founded on marriage and family.[30]

The crimes were bad, but the state's case was weak. For one, there was no motive for Émilie's murder, only Adolphe's. Second, it wasn't clear how Meg was supposed to have committed the crime. Adolphe was a great deal larger than she was, so strangling him with her bare hands would have been difficult. Meg would also have needed someone to help her fake the crime scene or at the very least tie her up. The judges who wrote the indictment granted that she may have had an accomplice or two who "acted on her behalf, according to her instructions."[31] Yet they didn't have a theory of who this was.

In essence, there was a lot of damaging information about Meg's life before the murders and plenty that was worse about her lies after them. But what had happened between the evening of May 30 and the morning of May 31 went largely unexplained.

The likeliest possibility why the state decided to pursue a weak case was that the double murder—and Meg's possible role in it—had attracted so much attention that the judiciary felt they had to put her on trial. If they released her due to a lack of evidence, the public would see it as another sign of how protected she was.

Another, far less likely reason was that it was all the work of Faure's enemies. They were seeking revenge on Meg, and the state's investigative efforts were a sign of her exalted role in political life. Predictably, this was Meg's theory. At one point, she estimated how much the investigation had cost the government and exclaimed, "Certainly France would not have spent twenty-three thousand francs on any other woman."[32] She couldn't help but regard herself as special, entirely innocent, and the victim of one cruel conspiracy after another.

Still, she could see that André's case against her didn't hold water. She described it as made "of flimsy fragments of circumstantial evidence, out of vague assertions and vague assumptions, out of childish contradictions, and above all, out of his own preconceptions, a solid, impregnable charge of double murder against an unhappy, defenceless, nerve-wracked and innocent woman."[33]

So, too, did the public. André's investigation had played out so thoroughly in the press that observers knew that he had not actually solved the murders. His hostility toward Meg also backfired.[34] In the words of one author, André's "brutality...revolted the public and made them pity this woman he suspected and insulted."[35]

As the tide of opinion moved in Meg's direction, many journalists were convinced that a particular slice of the public viewed her with special regard. Men were supposedly so enchanted with her that they thought she had to be innocent, whereas women were regarded as more "severe" in their judgments.[36] The mythic Meg who was capable of charming the pants off of any man around her—sometimes quite literally—could only arouse male desire and female jealousy.

At the very least, one young woman was increasingly hostile to Meg. That was Marthe. Before her arrest, Meg had gone to great lengths to hide her affairs from her daughter. As a result, Marthe was perhaps the one person in France to have been genuinely surprised that Meg was a less-than-faithful wife.[37] Eventually, Marthe promised, "If she is found guilty, I will go to see her in prison every Sunday. If she is acquitted, she will never see me again."[38] It was a statement that expressed anger and bitterness but also a desire for distance from a woman who had treated her as an appendage and proof of her innocence as opposed to a person in her own right. Marthe would only have a relationship with her mother if she could be the one to control it, if she could determine how often she saw Meg and how long they spent with one another.

For Meg, Marthe's vow meant that whatever happened, there would be no return to normal.

———

The trial was announced for November 1909. The man presiding over it, a judge named Bernard-Théodore-Médéric de Valles, was talented and esteemed for his intelligence and speaking skills.[39] He didn't come from Meg's world but from one that was both more rarified and more restrained. Valles was a viscount whose family had a distinct scholarly bent. He himself was an amateur archaeologist who preferred the company of his Latin books to the louche crowd of Meg's salon.[40]

The prosecutor, Paul-Adolphe Trouard-Riolle, was a different matter. Called "a real creature of high society" and "superficial and a lightweight" by his superiors, he wasn't considered to be among the best magistrates.[41] He owed much of his success to his wife, a beautiful heiress. In a twist of fate—or a sign of how small the world of the judiciary was—she had also been one of Faure's mistresses, and the deceased president had sped Trouard-Riolle's career along.[42] Indeed, defendant and prosecutor had been attending the same salons for years, and Meg judged him to be a "well-groomed and boring *poseur*" who was "ambitious and scheming."[43]

Meg's drawings of Aubin (at top), Valles (on the bottom left), and Trouard-Riolle (on the bottom right)

As the trial approached, Meg was filled with a mixture of hope and anxious dread, even as her lawyer, Aubin, reassured her that "you will be triumphantly acquitted. There will remain no trace of suspicion against you."[44] Meg saw these words as proof that Aubin, who knew her case better than anyone, was convinced of her innocence. But more likely, he uttered them because he had learned how to handle Meg, learned that she yearned for a male protector who was utterly devoted to her and who would help her regain her position in high society.

Aubin was confident, Meg was apprehensive, and Parisians were all in eager anticipation.[45] They hoped they'd get some clarity as to who had murdered Adolphe and Émilie. Perhaps even more importantly, the trial promised to be wildly entertaining. In the days before the trial, it was routinely compared to a theatrical production and described as the hottest ticket in town.[46]

Valles would have none of it. He had no intention of letting his courtroom become anything other than a place for the sober work of the state. Saying "we are not in a music hall," he restricted the audience for the trial and turned away politicians, judges, and many women from high society who were bitterly disappointed at having been excluded from the best show Paris had to offer.[47]

Valles's efforts to ensure the dignity and formality of the justice system faced powerful headwinds: Parisians generally saw trials as forms of entertainment, as an exciting spectacle of events in the news.[48] French criminal procedure was also not Valles's friend. As presiding judge, Valles led the questioning of the defendant and witnesses—but the prosecutor, the defense lawyer, and the defendant could all insert themselves in the proceedings. What's more, witnesses could pretty much say whatever they wanted and were free to recount hearsay and speculate with abandon.[49]

And then, of course, there was Meg. She was wild, dramatic, and captivating. She knew that the twelve men of the jury would decide her fate based on whether or not they liked her. In this era, many maintained that at a trial, "one judges the person, not the facts."[50] She had always been able to win men over to her side. Why not now?

Maybe Valles would be able to maintain the forces of order. But maybe he, too, would fall victim to Meg's power to create chaos wherever she went.

CHAPTER 19

THE TRIAL BEGAN AT around noon on November 3, 1909. It took place in a courtroom whose high ceilings and elaborate, carved wooden moldings were meant to impress observers with the power and majesty of the state, as were Valles's and Trouard-Riolle's red robes.[1] Meg was overwhelmed, but not because of the setting or the uniforms. She was exhausted from what she called "over five hundred days of continuous mental and physical martyrdom," her term for the year-and-a-half-long period that began with the murders.[2] In a daze, she had trouble making out what she was seeing or hearing. As she listened to the reading of the indictment and the roster of over seventy witnesses who would be called, she knew she was in a bind: "I seemed to have no strength left, and yet never had I so much needed physical and moral strength."[3]

Some of the journalists in the courtroom could see it and were disappointed that she wasn't as beautiful as everyone had said she was and that almost a year in prison had dulled her charms.[4] Her status as a sex goddess made it difficult to imagine that Meg was a real person and that her body was made for more than seduction.

But most reporters were entranced and described her as alluring in precisely the ways that they expected. One wrote that "the upper half of her face is remarkably beautiful" and "it has the serenity, the eternal freshness, the grace, and the coldness of marble." In contrast, "the lower part of her face is less beautiful and above all more vulgar" and notable for "the strong jaws," which helped "denote a greedy soul" that was "carnal, greedy," and "impetuous." This contrast between high and low, the pure and the lascivious, "increases [her] strange, attractive charm."[5] It was a description that rehashed so many elements of the mythic Meg. There was the jaw that reminded everyone of her last encounter with Faure, with that one act coming to define who she was, both physically and morally. Meg herself had long played on the idea that she combined the appeal of an asexual, elite woman with the passion and availability of a lower-class one. For observers, it was now inscribed in her very features.

After a clerk read the indictment, President Valles, as he was known in the courtroom, asked Meg to rise for what would become a three-day interrogation. The judge was methodical, precise, and thorough. His task that day was to walk the jury through Meg's life up to the double murder and question Meg about her childhood, her teenage romances, and her father's death. Then he moved to a discussion of her marriage and her sex work. Throughout it all, he followed the path André and the indictment had laid out: Meg had been sexually loose since her adolescence, a bad wife, and an ambitious woman who pursued affairs for money.

Nevertheless, Valles was fair and lacked André's obsessive hostility.

At times, he was even courteous toward her. As he began to question her, he told her to talk louder because no one could hear her, and then reminded her that "you have the right to say whatever you want and that I will let you say whatever you want, when you want."[6]

Valles may have come to regret these words not long after he uttered them. Within minutes, Meg had rallied. She saw it as her task to argue with Valles whenever and however she could and pick the seams of his argument apart.

As the struggle began, she fought almost every claim he made. Sometimes it mattered; sometimes it didn't. She defended her mother's reputation against any implication that her father had married the wrong sort of woman, saying that her parents adored each other. Valles suggested that her father was an alcoholic, but Meg insisted that Édouard wasn't and was the subject of malicious gossip for having married a poor woman.[7] It was a way to ensure that the jury knew she was a dutiful daughter who would never have even dreamt of parricide and allowed her to suggest that she was raised in a family where love reigned and where greed had no place. Alcoholics were also seen as degenerates who passed deviant traits on to their descendants, so Meg was saying that she bore no such hereditary taint.[8] Meg was fighting to defend her reputation and that of her parents. But observers might have also gotten the sense that she was arguing with Valles for the sake of arguing.

Then it came to her education. Valles asked her about her tutors who said she was a habitual liar and prone to flirtation from her early childhood. According to Meg, it was another parcel of lies.[9] Her instructors were at fault for making up stories about her, but so was André for believing the worst about her.

As the narrative of Meg's life unspooled, she and Valles started arguing over terminology. There was, for instance, a long discussion of her relationship with the young army officer Édouard Sheffer when she was a teenager. Valles said it was "an affair," to which she indignantly responded, "I don't know how you can call that an affair since my father allowed me to get engaged." Then, when Valles said that after breaking up the relationship with Sheffer, Meg's father had "sent her away" to live with her sister, she replied "I was not sent away." Meg won that skirmish, and Valles conceded that she had merely been "sent" to live with her sister, that she had changed her address, not been exiled from her home.[10]

By the time Valles started asking her about her marriage, Meg was on a tear and he was on the defensive. Meg freely admitted that she didn't love Adolphe and had affairs but sharply disputed the idea that she did so for mercenary reasons, saying, "I always gave myself out of love, I never sold myself."[11] In her telling, she never asked her lovers for money. If they gave it to her, it was because they loved her and saw how domestic duties and financial anxieties were weighing on her. She also directly intervened in the debate about her status and motives by saying, "I didn't have the heart of a prostitute... I needed a friend," when asked about her affairs.[12]

Valles clearly thought that her claim had some merit. He indicated that he didn't regard her as a professional courtesan and that she could have earned a whole lot more had she been one.[13] For decades, Meg had played a long game. She had sacrificed financial gain to maintain her place in high society. Now, at a moment when the stakes could not be higher, her gamble was paying off.

Indeed, Meg often benefited from the degree to which Valles

subscribed to so many of the prejudices of the day and the fact that they shared an essential worldview. The two of them expressed a full range of horror at Adolphe's sexual liaisons with poor men and women and used words such as "repugnant," "unnatural," and "shameful" to describe his affairs with men and his penchant for masturbation. Valles's lips curled back in disgust when he described how the painter had accepted her liaisons and knowingly took money from her lovers. In the judge's words, it "showed a complete absence of dignity."[14] Adolphe should have been angry, should have demanded she be faithful, and should never have helped her have sex with other men. For the judge and for so many others, if a husband failed to show his mastery of his wife, then of course she was going to misbehave. Only a strong man could keep a woman in check—and Adolphe wasn't strong.[15] Accordingly, the murder victim was responsible for Meg's affairs and thus perhaps for his own demise.

Meg also played off Valles to cast her social ambitions in the most positive light. He might not have gone to her salon, but he was imbued with the mores of high society that saw having one as a sign of distinction and spoke admiringly of her hostessing skills. All the same, he was unnerved by her efforts to create the appearance that she and Adolphe were much wealthier than they were, for it suggested that she was unhappy with her station and wanted more. Meg, though, insisted that money and luxury were never the point. It was all done out of a devotion to family: "If I had a salon…it was because unfortunately not everyone buys art, [and] I had to take care of that myself, since my husband didn't know how to sell his paintings." Did she cultivate relationships with powerful individuals? Yes, but that, too, was a sign of her dedication to her family, for she just wanted to promote her husband's and relatives' careers. Once again, Valles admitted she was right, telling her, "There is a great deal of truth in what you just said."[16]

Again and again, Meg got Valles to concede. There were instances when she countered his allegations directly. At other times, she launched into long digressions, after which Valles urged her to spend less time arguing with him over what he saw as insignificant details.[17] Of course, she resolutely refused to do so. Ultimately, his desire to keep to an orderly account of her life crumbled under the weight of her words. He didn't get to decide what was important, she did, and she—not André or Valles or any other judge—would be the author of her own life story.

———

By the second day of her trial, Meg knew that things were going well for her. So she waltzed into the courtroom and she acted like she owned it. One reporter noted that she was "a bit like a lady of the house" who was "obliged to receive people that she doesn't know very well and are not even very likable, but to whom she has agreed to be very polite in spite of everything."[18] The Meg who had been hesitant and confused was gone, and the one who bent fate to her will was back.

It was another day of triumphs for Meg and setbacks for Valles. His goal was to point out that her story about the robed men and a redheaded woman wasn't credible and suggest that she was responsible for the murders. Her job was to make it impossible to believe or even follow the state's case. In that, she largely succeeded.

Once again, she went off on tangents. In particular, whenever she was backed into a corner, whenever she didn't want to answer a question, she deflected by crying out that she couldn't have been the murderer because she loved her mother so much and it was cruel of Valles to suggest that she might have been the perpetrator.[19]

Meg also tried out new tactics on the second day of the trial. One was antisemitism. She accused the police of not looking hard enough for the men who had taken costumes from the Hebrew Theater, on the assumption that the members of the jury were so blinded by prejudice that they'd think that the tale of the stolen robes automatically meant the criminals were Jews. As was apparent to all, the jurors were unconvinced. Ultimately, Meg was so attuned to the attitudes of others that she dropped this line of argumentation as soon as she could see that no one was buying it.[20]

Other gambits played better. The public had never seen evidence of her sense of humor, which could be scathing, and it was on full display as she took the air out of some of Valles's suppositions with her rapier-sharp wit. Again and again, he asked her how the house could have been in such good order after a robbery. Again and again, Meg asserted that Valles needed to pose that question to the real murderers and that she was in no position to explain their actions. For instance, when he pushed her to explain why there were no traces of mud in the house despite the fact that it was raining that night, she said, "Frankly, I don't even understand why you are asking me that question. How should I have known if it was raining then—I was tied up!"[21]

Meg also went on the offensive and accused Valles of mistreatment, telling him "your scale isn't fair. You put a kilo in the tray for the prosecution, but nothing in the tray for the defense." When he asked her to reconcile the fact that there were no bruises on her body with her claim that the intruders had beaten her, she told him, "It's terrible to torture a woman for such nonsense." He had to remind her that she was on trial for murder, hardly the stuff of nonsense.[22] Even still, she managed to make him look like the one breaking the rules by asking her a question she didn't want to answer. It suggested that he was violating the codes of male gallantry that structured so many social interactions between elite men and women and that his courtroom was an extension of her salon.[23] The largely working-class jury may have been skeptical of Meg's suggestion that Valles needed to show deference to her, may have found the codes of elite life an impediment to finding out the truth. But Meg knew that the aristocratic Valles would be attuned to her claims. She may also have hoped that her former friends and acquaintances would feel sympathy with her and be more inclined to let her back into their world if she was acquitted. The public claimed her as theirs, but Meg remained fixated on the milieu that had mattered the most to her for decades: Parisian high society.

As ever with Meg, there was also sex. It was like a luridly colored thread that was woven through the trial, one that held everything together but was rarely visible. After all, Valles didn't want to delve too far into Meg's affairs, lest she name names of prominent men. She didn't want to appear to be too sexualized, for that would have been a sign that she was indeed a vulgar, loose woman of the lower class. But either because she couldn't help it or because she thought it was to her benefit, she was willing to play to her mythic status as a sex goddess.

Observers noted that she made full use of her seductive talents throughout the trial, casting eyes at the jury box. At one point, the prosecutor was so worried about her ability to turn on her charm that he tried to point out that she was addressing the jurors with a "musical and loving voice" that "without even asking for your forgiveness, creeps into your heart," even as she spoke to him and Valles in a tone of "fury."[24]

He was gambling that his statement would enable these men to see the calculation behind her efforts to entice them, as opposed to reinforce their sense that she regarded them as special and uniquely worthy of her attention.

She also decided to remind everyone of her skills in the bedroom. When Valles questioned her about her story that she had been gagged during the crime and then spat out the gag after a few hours, she said, "By dint of dexterity, of skill, of cunning, I was able to push this wadding onto the pillow through the movements of my tongue."[25] It was a remarkable statement. Meg consistently denied any role in Faure's death, but here she was straight up talking about her fellatio skills. Undoubtedly, the jurors were bored at times during the trial as she and Valles argued over details for what must have seemed like an eternity. But Meg managed to turn a discussion of these particulars into a thrilling peek at her sexualized persona as she came close to confirming every legend the public had ever heard about her.

All Meg's efforts came at a cost. By the end of the second day, she was exhausted. She recalled, "Tortured by the necessity of having to reply—satisfactorily—to searching questions which to me, innocent as I was, seemed useless and incomprehensible, rendered quite ill by the long and gruesome discussion about the fatal night, I once more sank back, exhausted, on my bench, and burst into a violent fit of weeping."[26]

The next day was a low point for her, both because she couldn't muster much fight anymore and because it covered the treacherous ground of her actions between the murders and her arrest. There was almost no way to put a positive spin on her efforts to pin the crime on innocent individuals. By far the worst thing she had done was attempt to frame Rémy, an act that Valles called a "calculated trick." It was a reminder that she hadn't just lied in the heat of the moment but had planted evidence and then arranged for others to find it, that there was some truth in the indictment's claim that she could be cruel and scheming.[27]

To explain actions that seemed so heartless, Meg relied on the two acceptable excuses for a female defendant: love and weakness.[28] In her account, she was only "acting as a mother." She had lied about what was stolen on the night of the crime to hide her affairs from Marthe, since so much of her jewelry had come from her lovers. Marthe's devastation that her engagement had been called off drove Meg to implicate others in a fit of maternal frenzy. The day before, Meg had relied on her love for Émilie to cut down any suggestion that she had done wrong. Now it was Marthe's turn to be turned into a defensive weapon. At other times, Meg fell back on mental illness and stated that she had blamed Rémy and Alexandre because "I lost my head."[29]

In the end, these arguments just didn't land. It was plain to everyone that Meg was floundering and couldn't satisfactorily explain her actions after the murders. She might have known it, too. At the end of Valles's interrogation, she was in tears. One journalist wrote that there was something sad about how the "energetic, witty, superior woman" of the days before had disappeared.[30]

Yet as a whole, Meg's testimony was a bravura performance. Valles was never able to prove that she had been involved in the murders or had staged the crime scene. Just as crucially, he was rarely able to control his own courtroom.

Some observers were unsettled by what they saw as an obvious performance. One reporter said, "She is too clever, too eloquent. She uses all the methods of dramatic art," and her ability to "pray, beg, cry, moan, be outraged…be indignant, be angry…rant, scold" revealed that there was something fundamentally false in her nature and that her emotional displays were a product of calculation.[31] Meg had long been compared to an actress. After all, she had a sense of the dramatic. But it wasn't the most flattering comparison, since actresses had a reputation for being deceptive and sexually loose.[32]

Others, though, focused on the bravura and regarded Meg in a much more positive light. A journalist for *Le Figaro*, the newspaper of the Parisian bourgeoisie, wrote, "Very few defendants, however robust, have the resilience of Mme Steinheil. She has been speaking for three days and does not seem tired… If magistrates, jurors, and stenographers have limits, Mme Steinheil has none. She is inexhaustible; under a flow of words that nothing can stop she drowns, overwhelms the president [Valles]'s questions."[33]

It was this extraordinary energy that was so impressive. One commentator compared Meg and Valles to two fencers dueling with swords. His style was "tight and sharp," hers was "quick and ardent," and in the end, "She fends off and retaliates with astonishing mastery."[34] In his estimation, "the word actress doesn't suit her," for she was more like a lawyer or "a great orator; she improvises with incredible ease, she has an incomparable, varied and flexible diction."[35]

Dueling, lawyering, and orating were unexpected comparisons for Meg, since they were all seen as masculine activities. The first was proof of a man's honor, the second was a profession that had only recently opened to women, and the third was an essential element for anyone who wanted to hold an elected office, something only men could do.[36] Yet here was a woman beating the highly trained men in the courtroom at their own game.

Meg defending herself in court. Her lawyer, Aubin, is slumped below.

To a degree, Meg's triumph was a shared one. In this era, feminists were advocating for women to be granted the right to vote, for expanded professional opportunities, and to be freed from a legal system that sub-jugated them to their fathers before marriage and their husbands after it.[37] Meg offered proof that women had all the smarts and the energy needed for these new roles. Séverine, one of the most famous feminist journalists of the day, was at the trial and gleefully wrote, "The male members of the audience seem for the first time—hold on tight, my sisters, who are not on trial—to have discovered 'feminine intelligence.' I try to tell them in vain that there are many more women than they imagine…[who are] equal to this one intellectually."[38]

But Séverine was taking what she could get, because for the most part, Meg's testimony was no gift to feminists. When she defended her actions on the grounds of mental illness, it was just one more bit of proof that women were prone to psychological maladies and didn't have the mental fortitude for public life. The fact that she fell to pieces after Adolphe's death suggested that women needed husbands to guide them and that if they were freed from male domination, they might be a danger to themselves and others.[39]

If mental illness suggested that she shouldn't throw off the weight of domesticity, then the other pole of her defense, her invocations of love, reassured the public that she didn't want to. In her account, everything she did, good or bad, was for Adolphe and Marthe, and she only wanted to reinforce her household, not destabilize it.

Meg's innate conservatism served her well during her days of testimony. As much as she proved that she could beat Valles at his own game, she also indicated that she wasn't going to change the rules of that game. Had she tried to do so, he undoubtedly would have showed her far less consideration.

The question, of course, was whether it worked with the jury. Once her testimony was over, others would have their turn to speak. They might well have a different view of Meg and a different sense of what kind of woman she was.

CHAPTER 20

IF THERE WAS ANY day designed to make Meg look bad, it was the fourth day of the trial. It was when those who had been present at the crime scene on the morning of May 31 testified, a list that included Rémy and two of Adolphe's brothers-in-law. All three had plenty of reasons to dislike Meg.

Of them, Rémy's testimony was the most eagerly anticipated. Here was the first person at the crime scene and the principal victim of her efforts to reroute suspicion away from her. Rémy had a lot to say and, given his history with Meg, might well be willing to say it.

To an extent, he delivered on that promise. In a "clear, almost metallic voice," he recounted that when he found her tied to the bed on the morning of May 31, the cords that bound her were not tight. If that was true, then she could have gotten out of them without his assistance and may well have had a hand in staging the crime scene.[1]

The public already knew that. But then he dropped a bombshell and told the courtroom that in the days after the murders, Meg told

him, "Don't be afraid... Don't say much and stay away from the investigators. I will treat you as my own child, I will support you." Then
she said, "You don't have to worry about anything, I'll fix it all."[2] It was
two strikes against Meg: first, she had tried to hide something from the
police, and second, she had betrayed Rémy after making promises to
him. What's more, her attitude was all wrong. A loving woman would
have been mired in grief in the aftermath of her husband's and mother's
murders; a calculating one would have been trying to work all the angles
as Rémy said Meg was.

Meg, though, got lucky. In the end, Rémy's testimony undermined
his credibility more than hers. When Valles questioned him about the
details of the crime scene and how Meg had been tied up and what the
bedcovers looked like when he found her on the morning after the murders, the valet's responses differed from his earlier statements. The dis-
crepancies were minor and had no bearing on Meg's guilt or innocence.
But Valles was a fastidious judge who strove to tie up loose ends, even
when they didn't matter. As he asked Rémy to explain the variations in
his accounts, he made the valet look unreliable. At best Rémy couldn't
remember; at worst he was lying.[3] Either way, there were grounds for
tossing out his other, more damning statements about Meg's actions. In
her words, "These complete contradictions in my former valet's statements were naturally most favourable to me."[4]

Later that day, the jury heard from two of Adolphe's brothers-in-
law. They, too, had the potential to make her look bad, and they did
what they could to do so as they aired years of family grievances. Both
detailed their hearty dislike of Meg and how her flagrant misbehavior
led them to shun her and cause a rift in a previously united family. Even
worse was a statement from Geoffroy, the second brother-in-law to take

the stand, who recounted his dismay at seeing that Meg was wearing makeup when he arrived at the crime scene. This detail was another implicit intervention in the debate about what kind of woman she was, since it suggested that she was more concerned with her sex appeal than the loss of her husband and mother.[5]

Meg was not going to allow her disapproving in-laws to paint her as a bad wife. So she pounced on Geoffroy's statement that he had given the authorities a letter from Adolphe to Meg that discussed her affairs. With scorn and hatred in her voice, she charged Geoffroy with committing "an abomination which will remain on your conscience for the rest of your life."[6]

Meg had a point: just a few days before, Valles had condemned Adolphe for his passivity in the face of her infidelities, something this letter proved. She was no doubt furious with her brother-in-law for breaching the privacy of the family and exposing her and Adolphe's dirty laundry. But her outburst must have been intensely satisfying to her for other reasons. Adolphe's family had long disdained her and treated her as an immoral woman who brought disgrace on the Steinheil name. Now she could claim that Geoffroy was the source of the dishonor because he made Adolphe's weakness public. Although this family squabble had nothing to do with the murders, Meg was using the same strategy she had employed with Valles: seize on any opening, distract the jury with drama and fury, and get the last word in. If she did, the jury might remember her defense of Adolphe's honor and not Geoffroy's statement about her makeup.

In the end, a day that could have gone very badly for Meg wasn't the loss her defenders feared or the victory her critics anticipated. Instead, it points to two problems that bedeviled the state's case.

One was Meg herself. Thanks to her father's training, she had always known how to play to her audience, especially if it was made up of men. She had used that skill to rise in high society, with journalists after the murders, and now in the courtroom where she was fighting for her freedom and her life. Ultimately it didn't matter if what she was saying was true or even relevant, because what most people wanted was a show.

Except, of course, for Valles, who may have resented Meg's scene-stealing ability. He also begged her not to interrupt witnesses "so that we can put some order" in the proceedings.[7] But the judge was his own source of disorder, as Rémy's testimony demonstrated. Because Valles was so meticulous, he often focused on some of the finer points of an individual's testimony in an effort to pin down details. It was a style of questioning that buried observers under an avalanche of minutiae and prevented them from developing a clear narrative or an understanding of how all the facts fit together.

Between Meg's theatrics and Valles's emphasis on detail, the prosecution's case was increasingly hard to follow, even though the trial was less than halfway over. As the jury sat through long, unbroken stretches of testimony in a packed, stifling courtroom, any resolution to the question of if Meg had committed murder seemed further and further away. Instead, the trial came down to two questions: Who was Meg? And did the jurors like her?

————

Initially, observers hoped that science might provide clarity to the mystery of the double murder. Many of France's most prominent criminalists had examined the physical evidence from the crime scene and testified about their findings. This was an era when new techniques like fingerprinting offered the promise of certainty, when the public gobbled up stories of Sherlock Holmes and his claims to be a "scientific detective." If science was supposed to provide an unmediated and unbiased access to the truth, could these experts reveal who had murdered Adolphe and Émilie?[8]

The short answer was no. Instead, experts spewed facts upon facts that either raised more questions or confirmed what anyone paying the least amount of attention could have guessed. A clockmaker said that someone had stopped the clock in the Steinheils' house on the night of the crime. This was neither surprising nor illuminating, since there was no evidence as to who had intervened. Victor Balthazard, a famed professor of forensic medicine, went into scrupulous detail about his autopsies of the victims' corpses and analyses of Meg's physical condition after the murders and the physical evidence. In his testimony, he got carried away with proving his scientific prowess. For instance, he talked about measuring Meg's strength with a machine called a dynamometer and stated that she probably wasn't strong enough to have committed murder on her own but might have been. It was a conclusion that resolved nothing and didn't exactly require newfangled machinery to reach. Some of the other evidence he presented was just confusing: the ink on Meg's leg was dark purple, but the ink from the bottle in Meg's study that had spilled onto the floor was dark blue. Like the stopped clock, this meant something, but no one knew what.[9]

At other times, sloppy police procedure hamstrung the power of science. Balthazard testified that the cotton wadding that Meg said had gagged her had never been in her mouth, as there were no traces of saliva on it. This seemed to offer conclusive proof that Meg had been lying and helped stage the crime scene. But then Aubin pounced. Ever the canny operator, he knew that his best bet wasn't to attack scientific certainty but a police force that could be slapdash. He got Balthazard to admit that he wasn't sure about the chain of custody of the purported gag and didn't know if the piece of cotton he had examined was the same as the one that Meg had said had been in her mouth.[10]

It was a frustrating lesson in the limits of much-heralded, newly developed methods of scientific detection to get to the truth. As a journalist wrote, these techniques were supposed to offer "a sort of mathematical reasoning" to "minds which are eager for certainty." Yet in this case, "science could not shed light" on the many mysteries surrounding the double murder.[11]

There was another possible conclusion to take from the testimony of all these experts: perhaps the problem was silence, not science. Maybe the murderer couldn't be identified because some of the men in charge didn't want justice to be done.* One famed professor of medicine told a journalist, "It seemed to me…that the investigation was perhaps not carried out as it should have been, for undoubtedly absolutely respectable reasons… There is, on the one hand, something that is being hidden; on the other hand, something that we do not want to discover at all."[12] All the details that Balthazard and other experts offered were meant to show the public that the state was dedicated to solving the crime. Whether it was is another story.

Whatever the reason the truth never came to light, there was one clear beneficiary: Meg.

---

* Grand Duke Vladimir Alexandrovich, the man some have suggested was the murderer, died in February 1909. Even still, the revelation that he was the perpetrator would have soured the close diplomatic ties between Russia and France—ones that Faure had done much to cement.

The trial was by no means an unmitigated triumph for Meg. The lowest ebb was the day after Balthazard took the stand, when the journalists who had been present at the Impasse Ronsin the night before Meg was arrested testified. They had watched her unravel and throw accusations around. Barby, the reporter who had been there the entire night, recounted that at one point, he saw Meg and Mariette whisper to each other. When he asked Meg what they had discussed, she said that she had asked Mariette what she would do if Meg was arrested. In response, the cook said, "I will deny formally, I will deny until the end." Valles pressed Meg to clarify what Mariette planned to deny, to which Meg could only reply, "I don't remember."[13] It was plain to all that this was probably not the truth, and Meg spent much of that day "nervous" with her eyes "widened by terror."[14]

Any hopes that Mariette would reveal what she knew were dashed the next day when she stepped up to the stand. No other witness had seen so much and was so insistent on saying so little. According to Mariette, Meg and Adolphe loved each other very much. It's true that Meg wasn't faithful, but in the cook's words, "Madame didn't have that many lovers; she was described as having a lot more than she had." Valles pushed her to reveal what she had seen at Vert-Logis when Meg entertained clients to no avail. Eventually Mariette said, "When you are a servant, you must say nothing about what you see." Nor was Mariette any help when it came to the murders. Again and again, she didn't know or she couldn't recall.[15] Where Meg defeated Valles through a torrent of words, Mariette relied on stony silence.

Mariette's testimony benefited Meg in one additional way. Valles was hard on the cook, and there were none of the flashes of consideration that he occasionally showed toward Meg.[16] The contrast in his behavior undoubtedly arose from his sense that working-class women were to be treated one way, elite women another. He might not have meant to feed the argument that she belonged to the high and not the low and by implication should be acquitted, but his ingrained habits of deference to some and antagonism to others had that very effect.

After Mariette, there was a slew of witnesses who came from Meg's world of high society, all of whom said the same thing: from everything they had ever heard, everything they had ever seen, Meg was not the type of woman to have committed murder. There were relatives and friends who testified that she and Émilie adored each other, that she nursed Adolphe when he was sick and fussed over his health when he was well. If no one went as far as Mariette and said that Meg was tenderly in love with Adolphe, that only made their claims more credible.[17]

One highlight was Borderel. The state's case against Meg hinged on the idea that she had planned to marry this small-town mayor for his money, but Borderel undid it all. She wasn't greedy at all. Instead, she was "a charming woman…with very modest tastes." Yes, she had expressed a desire to find a new husband, but he had made it quite clear that he had no intention of marrying anytime soon. And despite what had been entered into evidence, she never told him that she hated Adolphe, just that she was sad about the state of her marriage. If his deposition with André said something different, this was because the judge had written down what he wanted to hear, not what Borderel said.[18]

Ultimately, Meg was protected by so many of the same forces that had shielded her in the past. There were plenty of individuals who could have made Meg look very bad. But those who stepped up to the witness stand had reasons to keep quiet about what they knew. Some, like Mariette, were mum out of loyalty to Meg. Borderel may have felt a residual affection for her as well. Even if he didn't, it would have been ungallant of him to have testified against his former mistress. His reputation would also have taken a hit if he described her as greedy and hateful, for it would have implied that he was willing to countenance her immorality for the sake of sex. Likewise, her high-society friends didn't want to suggest that they had been associating with a bad woman, for that would reflect poorly on their character.

Then there were all the men (and perhaps some women) who the state scrupulously avoided questioning, both during André's investigation and the trial. If the judiciary really wanted to paint Meg as akin to a prostitute, they could have tracked down the clients who had highly transactional, short-term liaisons with her. But that would have put a harsh spotlight on too many prominent individuals. Easier, in the end, to keep this slice of elite misbehavior under wraps.

The façade of propriety that hid the seamy reality of Meg's life had been reconstructed in the months since her arrest. Witnesses who spoke up earlier, like Mariette and some of Meg's high-society friends, might have felt that the time for spilling secrets was over. Or they may have regarded the stakes as too great. After all, it was one thing to tell a reporter what you knew, especially if you could remain anonymous, but quite another thing to do so at a trial. As had been true throughout Meg's life, in the struggle between the truth and the appearance of respectability, the latter almost always won.

As the trial went on, it became easier to see Meg as the charming society hostess that she claimed to be and harder to imagine her as a grasping murderess or base prostitute. The most you could say was that

Meg hadn't been entirely truthful in the wake of the murders and had tried to hide something. But jurors might have also gotten the sense that no one was being honest—and that that was just how society worked.

————————

When it was time for Aubin to present his witnesses, he showed that he had all Meg's flair for the theatrical but none of her excess. And unlike Valles, he knew how to build and maintain a clear narrative. He had learned how to play Meg, learned how to convince her of his unwavering support for her. Now, he started playing the jury.

First, some of Meg's relatives were called to the stand to talk about Meg's devotion to her mother. Then an accountant stated the Steinheils weren't in financial distress on the eve of the murders.[19] But no one had been dying to hear about Meg and Adolphe's different income streams. Instead, what the jury and the spectators wanted was a dash of drama and a whiff of romance.

And Aubin was more than capable of providing that in the form of his penultimate witness, who was none other than Meg's first lover, Sheffer, now a captain in the army. The two hadn't seen each other for over twenty years, not since their last encounter in a train station as Meg was being exiled to southern France for the crime of having fallen in love with him. Now, he took the stand to describe the Meg he knew as "charming, very well behaved, artistic, kind, sweet and good" and without the least interest in money. The two had gotten her father's blessing to marry until Édouard abruptly decided that the army officer was too poor for his favorite daughter. Again, it wasn't quite the truth, but it was the version of the story that was the best for both Meg and Sheffer, since it was the one in which they didn't violate any of the tenets of bourgeois propriety.[20]

Meg cried as memories of her first romance flooded back, of being "the happiest girl on earth, with a devoted mother and the best of all fathers… And the young lieutenant loved me, and I loved him… Life was beautiful, and the future smiled on me."[21] She had such high hopes back then, of making an uninterrupted transition into adulthood and marriage. It's true that she wouldn't have known what it was to be fêted by the cream of Parisian society or be an intimate of the Élysée Palace. But maybe her father wouldn't have died so precipitously; maybe she wouldn't have spent decades being buffeted by scandal and now standing trial for murder. If the tears were perhaps more for herself than for Sheffer, they would still have had a powerful effect on the courtroom as proof of her sentimental nature.

The last of Aubin's witnesses, André Paisant, cemented this impression. Paisant was a friend of the Steinheils and a well-connected lawyer known for his charisma, energy, and oratorical skills, all of which he dialed up in his defense of Meg.[22] As he described her married life, he spoke with a mixture of fondness and disapproval about Adolphe, who was totally absorbed in his work and completely passive when it came to anything else. Meg was the life force of the household and did everything she could to bolster his career and make him believe in himself as an artist. There was no mercenary motive to her affairs, only Adolphe's shortcomings and an abundance of feeling. In his words, "She had a womanly need to find someone strong, robust to support her. And what she wanted in a man is what women and children want. Children love to crawl onto their father's lap. Women want to feel like they are insignificant things who are crushed in a man's strong arms."[23] This statement combined an accurate read of Meg's desire for a man to take care of her with stereotypes that women wanted and needed men to subjugate them. Like others at the time, Paisant thought that if a husband was unable to live up to his marital duties, it was entirely expected that the wife would pursue what she needed, sexually and otherwise, elsewhere, that male weakness could unleash feminine sexual excess.[24] Paisant's testimony was so successful that Meg wasn't the only one who cried that day, as some of the spectators were so moved by his pity for Meg that they, too, were in tears.[25]

Together, Sheffer and Paisant wove a story about Meg. She was and always had been a creature of love. But in her quest for a husband who could match her energy and passion, she had been failed by the two most important men in her life. First her father had been too controlling, and then her husband hadn't been controlling enough. In search of the proper amount of masculine domination, she had affairs. She upheld so many of society's rules, from beliefs about the centrality of heterosexual couplings to the idea that women needed male authority, that she couldn't possibly have committed a crime that attacked the family and the household.

It was a vision of Meg that followed her own line of argumentation. Even better, there was some truth in it. Best of all, it offered a clear account of her life in a trial where the state's narrative had become incoherent.

———

Later that day, Trouard-Riolle began his closing argument. By that point, it was clear even to him that the case against Meg was floundering, and he urged the members of the jury to ignore the public's calls for her acquittal, ones that had only grown louder since the trial began. He also decided to downgrade the charges against Meg and now claimed that she was only complicit in Adolphe's murder and that Émilie's death was entirely accidental.[26] You could see it either as a sign of his willingness to adjust to the facts on the ground or that he knew that his case was crumbling beneath his feet.

Still, he did his best. Much of his argument followed the greatest hits of André's investigation. In his account, Meg had been immoral since her birth. He stated that she "lies as she breathes" and was an atrocious wife who alternated between neglecting and dominating her husband. If their friends thought that she was a good lady of the house, that was all a front to hide her malice behind closed doors. Her overwhelming ambition drove her to take lovers, and she was a social climber who sought what was beyond her station and who "liked to shine, to stand out."[27]

Meg was incensed. She was appalled by Trouard-Riolle's suggestion that she was "low, shrewd, [and] calculating." His tone also infuriated her, how he spoke "relentlessly, scornfully, wildly. And he seems to enjoy his 'great' task." And there was the gall of it: "While M. Trouard-Riolle goes on criticising my home-life, I wonder how *he* dare judge *me!*"[28] Meg knew perfectly well that the prosecutor owed his position in the judiciary to his wife's affair with Faure and that he wasn't exactly in a position to claim the moral high ground.

Trouard-Riolle was on his strongest footing when he talked about how the crime scene had been faked. He could remind the jury that the house hadn't been broken into, that there were few signs of disorder, and that nothing had been stolen. He suggested that Meg could easily have gotten out of the cords tying her to the bed, and the evidence pointed to the fact that she had never been gagged.[29]

The problems really started when Trouard-Riolle turned to a

narrative of the crime. He called Meg the "architect" of the murders and suggested that either Mariette or Alexandre Wolff had been her accomplice and had committed the murder according to her instructions, although he didn't go so far as to name either one. According to Trouard-Riolle, Meg had arranged for one of the Wolffs to come into the house in the middle of the night, tie up and gag both her and her mother, and then murder Adolphe. That way, Émilie could serve as a witness to the crime and testify to Meg's innocence. The plan went awry when the gag in Émilie's mouth ended up suffocating her.[30]

It was a version of the crime that made very little sense. For one, Émilie knew both Mariette and Alexandre and would have instantly recognized her assailant. Many were also aghast that at the last minute, with his case in tatters, Trouard-Riolle came very close to accusing one of the Wolffs of murder, even though neither one was on trial. As everyone knew, Alexandre had an unbreakable alibi for the night of the crime. Mariette didn't, but André had investigated her thoroughly and decided that she was innocent of any involvement in the murders.[31]

As Trouard-Riolle faltered, Aubin leapt in. He challenged the prosecutor to be more precise in his accusation and to name names. Meg recounted that as Aubin did so, "The court rings with applause; barristers and journalists climb on the benches and tables. I look at M. Trouard-Riolle… He does not reply to my counsel, but makes a wide, evasive gesture, and turns to the President, who adjourns the sitting."[32] Both the prosecutor and the presiding judge knew that the former had blown it and that the state's case was hopeless.

Finally, on November 13, it was Aubin's turn. His speech was judged to be a "true masterpiece of eloquence," and it threw Trouard-Riolle's bungling into sharp relief.[33] For one, he didn't introduce any new arguments but wove together the ones that Meg and other witnesses had made since the trial began. He started with her childhood: she had received a fine upbringing from devoted parents. He asked, "Is it possible to suppose that with the education she received, Mme Steinheil thought about killing her husband?"[34] The answer was of course no, that her status was too high for her sense of morality to be low.

Meg had innocent, entirely chaste romances until she settled on Adolphe in the hopes that he would be "a guide, a support, a [source of] energy" after her father's tragic death. No such luck, but even still, Meg upheld her end of the bargain and was "a model wife, very simple and very good" who scrimped and saved, was kind to the servants, and charitable to those in need.[35]

Then suddenly, the good housewife gave way to the mythic Meg, and Aubin provided the courtroom with a glimpse of the red thread of sex. As he recounted how she sewed her own dresses and only bought what she couldn't make herself, he stated that one such item was her corset. It was no accident that he mentioned this particular piece of clothing, for corsets were highly sexualized objects in the Belle Époque.[36] It was also a reference to her legendary past. According to the rumors that sprang up about Meg after Faure's death, she left her corset at the Élysée Palace during her last assignation with the president. When he said, "We would all like to know how Mme Steinheil was corseted," he affirmed her status as a figure of universal male desire.[37] Faure had lusted after her, and so did every man in the courtroom, including himself.

Then Aubin turned to the source of sex and the central question of whether her motivations boiled down to greed or love. She had a few lovers, but in the book of her love life, her romance with Sheffer was "not followed by numerous pages turned by dirty fingers, by the muddy fingers of a courtesan." Instead, she was a "*grande amoureuse*," one of the many elite French women celebrated for their dedication to love. Another testament to the fact that she belonged to high society was that she was received in "the best…the most honorable salons."[38] So much of his speech was designed to fix her among the high after a year of questions about where she belonged. Meg's arrest temporarily challenged the notion that vice came from below and virtue from above. Now, Aubin sought to stabilize her status and restore that hierarchical vision of society.

When Aubin turned to the actual crime, he started off by stating that Meg loved Marthe too much to deprive her daughter of a father. He also pointed out that Trouard-Riolle's version of the murders was implausible. Instead, Émilie and Adolphe had been killed by common criminals who had broken into the house to rob it. If they hadn't stolen much, that was because they were in a hurry. Had Meg told lie upon lie in the days, weeks, and months after the murders? Yes, but that was because Meg was psychologically unstable, not because she was trying to hide anything. She was a suggestible woman from a family afflicted by mental illness. It was all due to her overly sentimental nature, one that drove her love affairs and certainly would have kept her from doing anything so hateful and calculating as killing her husband.[39]

Aubin ended with another type of invocation of emotion, one that knit Meg, Marthe, and the jurors together. Speaking of mother and daughter, he said, "How many tears have they already shed and how many tears will they continue to cry! Gentlemen of the jury, I beg you… give them the means to console each other."[40]

In his estimation, acquittal would be a triumph for justice and for love.

When the jury left the courtroom to deliberate at around 11:00 p.m., Meg went to sit with the guards. She was nervous that the men deciding her fate seemed to be taking so long and wondered, "Will this martyrdom never end? What right has any one to make me suffer so?"[41]

Finally, sometime after 1:00 a.m., Meg heard the bells summoning everyone back to the courtroom. The jury had decided: Meg was innocent on all counts. The vote had been 9–3, with the dissenters being from the working class.[42] They might have been much more skeptical about her and Aubin's claims that an elite woman could never have been so heartless as to commit murder.

In the moment, though, all she heard were "the screams of enthusiasm and the frantic applause of hundreds of people," and she "saw hundreds of radiant faces shouting: 'Bravo… Bravo… Acquitted… Acquitted.'"[43] The crowd surged toward Meg, desperate to touch her, to be near her. In the background, drowned out by shouts and the general chaos, Valles said she was free to go.[44] It was the last gasp of his struggle to maintain order, defeated first by Meg and then her many admirers. He hadn't wanted his courtroom to become a place for theatrical spectacle, but that was exactly what it was in this moment.

With the acquittal, the jury had decided what kind of woman Meg was. Sure, she wasn't the best behaved woman out there. She lied, she had affairs, she covered up a horrible crime. But that didn't matter. What did matter was that she was beautiful and loved deeply and intensely. And the crowd loved her right back.

CHAPTER 21

MEG HAD BEEN ISOLATED in prison, only to be released and find that now she was a celebrity. In the immediate aftermath of the trial, she had to escape the press assembled in the courtroom who were dying to know where she'd go next. Aubin arranged for her to spend the night in a hotel and then stay at an asylum where she could recover in peace and quiet from her ordeal.[1] A journalist named Berthe Delaunay managed to pierce that privacy and slipped in to see her by claiming to be her sister; there, Delaunay learned from the staff that Meg was desperate to see Marthe, who was refusing to have anything to do with her. Even in this brief encounter, Delaunay could tell that Meg was "bewitching" and overwhelmingly charming.[2] That may well have been Delaunay's impression, but by that point it had become such a trope of newspaper coverage that almost every journalist who wrote about her had to say it.

In the aftermath of the trial, Meg had options. Men she had never met proposed to her, including a British lawyer who had seen her at the trial.[3] There were also offers to appear on the stage, to act, to sing, to star in films, to advertise products.[4] She was a celebrity, and members of the public sought access, intimacy, and everything from a whiff of sex to a life with her.[5]

Meg wanted none of it. She may have felt her health—mental and physical—was too precarious to bear the burden of fame and that she needed rest. Accepting her status as a sex goddess might have seemed demeaning. Perhaps she thought that no man who had mattered to her—her father, Bouchez, Faure, or Chouanard—would have approved of her submitting herself to the public's gaze. It is also possible that if the murderer was a highly placed individual, he or his family may have been terrified that if Meg made regular public appearances, she might let something slip about the double murders. And they might have been so terrified that they were willing to pay for her silence.

Instead, Meg sought to live a life on her own terms, as she so often did. That task had been difficult before the murders, and now it was even more so. But if anyone could manage it, it was she.

First, she left France for London to escape the constant press attention. When she arrived at Charing Cross Station, she was mobbed by reporters who chased her from hotel to hotel, a sign that even in a new country, she would have to work hard to keep out of the public's gaze.[6]

To give herself some privacy, she went by the name Mme de Serignac. It was a sign that she hadn't abandoned her social pretensions, for the "de" often indicated a person's noble status. Nor did she abandon other habits. In the coming years, she had affairs, including with a doctor and a journalist named Roger de Chateleux.[7] She had long had an international clientele and may well have been able to charge a whole lot more now that the scandal and the trial had enhanced her reputation as a femme fatale. Between the money from Adolphe's estate, her affairs, and any money she got to keep her silence, she eventually managed to buy a large house in the suburbs of London that had a garden, an orchard, and a chicken coop.[8] With her keen aesthetic sense, she decorated her new home beautifully and had plenty of old friends coming from Paris to visit her—and perhaps sleep with her.[9]

To a certain degree, life in her new home on Upper Tulse Hill was similar to life on Impasse Ronsin. It was still hard to make ends meet, and she took boarders into her new home.[10] Plenty of people knew who Mme de Serignac really was, and she regaled her friends with outrageous lies that placed her at the center of a secret, exciting political drama. She promised that as soon as certain powerful men were out of office, she'd reveal the true circumstances of Faure's death, a suggestion that those men had had a hand in it.[11] Of course, she never did. Or she claimed that King Edward VII had suggested that she move to London after the trial because she had prevented a war from erupting between France and Britain when she was with Faure.[12]

It was the same strategy as the one she had pursued before the murders: privately play on her sexualized persona while trying to remain out of the public eye. Yet it's hard to imagine that London's high society accepted her as Paris's had, both because she was now so notorious and because the codes of morality were quite a bit stricter in Britain than France.

Meg occasionally surfaced to manage her reputation. In 1912, when an author published a book titled *Woman and Crime* that claimed that Meg had committed murder, she sued him for libel and asked for the princely sum of ten thousand pounds in damages. She won the lawsuit, and the author had to remove any mentions of her from future editions of the book, although the damages were in the hundreds of pounds, not the thousands.[13]

Meg's most notable effort to control her public image came that same year when she published her memoirs in English. They were ghostwritten by her lover Chateleux, and he may have encouraged her by saying it was an opportunity to set the record straight and earn a lot of money. Members of the public couldn't wait for them to appear, and journalists predicted that they might lead to any number of duels between prominent men as Meg spilled her secrets about the rich and powerful. Meanwhile, French politicians and officials were concerned about what Meg might say, either true or false, about them.[14]

To the dismay of some and the relief of others, the memoirs turned out to be dull. There were moving passages that described her childhood and her early disappointments with her marriage to Adolphe. But when it came to the two things that everyone was really interested in—her affairs and the murders—there wasn't much that was new, revealing, or even, in some cases, true. Meg refused to air the dirty laundry of Parisian high society and named no names. She also described her relationship with Faure in professional terms. In her account, she was his political confidante, and all those hours they had spent together in a boudoir of the Élysée Palace had nothing to do with sex. Instead, she claimed, she was helping him write his memoirs.[15]

Her account of the crime was even worse. She stated that Faure had given her a pearl necklace that was connected to a diplomatic secret that would have caused a scandal if it was revealed. After he died, a German bought the pearls from Adolphe and was also after some of the papers she had from Faure. She wrote that the German had "a long Jewish nose, with scanty hair and moustache that were dyed black, small beady eyes, sly and shifty, and a sallow complexion" and "inspired me with repulsion, even with fear." He was somehow involved in the murders, which had been committed by the robed men and the redheaded woman.[16] It was a way to tie together the story she had told right after the murders with the one that put her and Faure at the center of an international, Jewish-led plot to undermine France. Even with nothing to lose, she would not stop playing to the conspiracy theories of right-wing nationalists as well as their nastiest stereotypes about the moral and physical monstrousness of Jews.[17]

The public had wanted her to tell the truth. Failing that, they wanted a story that bolstered her image as a creature of sex. When she refused to do either, the disappointment was palpable. One newspaper wrote that her memoirs were "likelier to provoke mysteries than solve them."[18]

For all that her memoirs frustrated the public, they provide a fascinating glimpse into how Meg understood herself. She was a woman of great importance who most wanted to help others around her, whether they were the civil servants who had come to her salon looking for promotions, or Marthe, whose devastation at the end of her engagement after the murders led Meg to blame Rémy and Alexandre. As she moved through the world, it was one divided between good people who were on her side and bad people who were her adversaries. In her mind, she was perpetually the victim of malicious gossip and unfair hostility and never the author of her own troubles.

Meg's most self-reflective moments come in her passages describing her time in Saint-Lazare. There, she got a glimpse at how a state that protected her for so long could also be cruel to poor women and came to realize that her privilege had blinded her to the realities of what life was like for so many. For all that, there's no evidence that she did anything with this knowledge in the years after 1909—that she changed her politics or worked to ameliorate prison conditions in either France or Britain. Instead, it seems that she returned to accepting the way things were and trying to secure a place for herself within the system.

Meg's other great concern in the years after the trial was her relationship with Marthe, who had initially refused to reconcile with her.[19] In Meg's mind, it was all the fault of another set of villains: her hateful relatives who had poisoned her daughter's mind.[20]

Marthe, though, might have seen it differently. After all, she had her own reasons to be angry with her mother. During the scandal, Marthe had learned about Meg's affairs and the cruelty her mother had displayed toward the father she so adored. Marthe may have also resented how Meg used their relationship to excuse her most inexcusable actions.

What's more, although Meg was able to reconstruct her life after the trial, Marthe was not. Very obviously, she would never marry Pierre Buisson. Instead, she rented out rooms in the villa on the Impasse Ronsin and sewed clothes for a department store to scrape by.[21] All her life, Marthe had followed the rules: she had been loving, innocent, kind, and pious. Society promised her that in return, she would be able to marry a suitable husband and live a comfortable life. But Marthe now learned that no amount of good behavior on her part could wash away the stain of her mother's and father's very public transgressions.

So Marthe started breaking the rules. She took in boarders who were Russian and Italian anarchists and adopted their far-left views. In these years, she grew especially close to a man named Raphaël del Perugia, an artist of Italian and French descent who had grown up in Odessa but had been exiled from Russia for his revolutionary fervor, and the two wed in July 1911. Despite Marthe's best efforts to keep the press away, the paparazzi came in droves, and the priest marrying them had to chase photographers out of the church.[22]

The young couple continued to be surrounded by wild, down-and-out radicals, and the neighbors objected to the constant sound of revolutionary songs and the comings and goings of strange men.[23] Marthe had always shown a favoritism for her father over her mother. By marrying an Italian artist who came from a dubious world, she was choosing a life that might have reminded her of one parent and horrified the other. The young bride might have savored the knowledge that Meg was appalled with her choices, might have felt that she finally had a chance to come out from under her mother's shadow.

It wasn't enough to keep the marriage together, however, and the young couple's relationship soon turned sour. Marthe couldn't get a divorce, for by marrying an Italian, she had forfeited her French citizenship and had to follow Italy's legal code, which did not permit divorce.[24] So she went to live with her mother in London.[25] It's hard to imagine that she eagerly anticipated reentering a life with her mother in it, but it must have been better than the one she had with her husband.

Fortunately for Marthe, her husband, who fought in the French army during World War I, died in 1915.[26] A few months later, she married another Italian named Candido Camalich; they would have three sons.[27]

The war also brought considerable changes to Meg's life. She started a factory that made food for troops and became one of the many women who took up new forms of paid labor during the war, whether because of opportunity, financial necessity, or patriotism. Meg worked tirelessly, a reminder that had she been a male member of the Japy family, she might have been quite good at managing a large enterprise.[28]

The more significant change to her life came in June 1917 when she married Robert Scarlett, the sixth Baron Abinger. He was none other than the lawyer who had fallen in love with her during her trial. While she might not have thought any more about it, Robert was enchanted with the mythic Meg. A few years after the trial, he finally met the real one and instantly renewed his proposal. This time, she took it more seriously, and the two started a romance.[29]

Robert was seven years younger and from a distinguished family, one of diplomats, politicians, and soldiers. During the war, he had volunteered to serve in the Royal Navy. The two were married in a Methodist church in London, he in his naval uniform, she in a mauve dress. After the wedding, he saluted a crowd of well-wishers while she smiled at them, while newsreel cameras caught the happy couple leaving the church.[30] It was a bit of joy in a bleak year of warfare.

Meg and Robert shortly before their marriage

Lord and Lady Abinger moved between a house in Surrey and the family's seat in the Scottish Highlands.[31] They were occasionally mentioned in society columns, such as ones that reported that he was traveling from London to Scotland or that she had attended the funeral of a woman who had decided that it was a good idea to wash her hair with petrol.[32] But they weren't received in the best circles. Morals had loosened since the prewar era, but not so much as to let a woman with her past slip through them.[33]

After ten years of marriage, tragedy struck. On June 10, 1927, the couple were in Surrey. Meg had taken the gardener's son to the seaside that day for a treat. When she returned home, she was told that Robert had died of a heart attack.[34]

In the public's mind, the sudden death of a fifty-one-year-old man married to a woman known for leaving a trail of bodies behind her might have seemed awfully suspicious, but the inquest found that he died of entirely natural causes.[35] For Meg, this loss might have recalled that of her father and Faure. Robert was the latest in a line of loving protectors who abandoned her after a sudden cardiac event.

And it was another death that required Meg to rearrange her life. The estate in the Highlands went with the baronial title and so to Robert's younger brother. She had money but also huge debts and gave up the house in Surrey for a place in Hove, a seaside city next to Brighton.[36]

If any two cities in England encapsulated Meg's life, it was Brighton and Hove. The latter was decidedly more upmarket, a place where genteel ladies went to live in their later years. It had a fashionable department store, bandstands for listening to music, and lawns by the sea to see and be seen. Meg lived in Adelaide Crescent, a giant complex of town houses by the beach built in the nineteenth century for those of means. Its white façade gleamed in the sunlight, and its residents enjoyed an extensive private garden.[37] But it, like her, had clearly been more in demand in the prewar era.[38]

In contrast, the resort town of Brighton was seedier than Hove. The playwright and wit Noël Coward quipped that it was a place for "piers, queers and racketeers."[39] As a city devoted to pleasure, it was a place to escape the constraints of normal life, including those regarding sexual behavior. In the interwar period, it gained a reputation as a locale for adulterous couples to spend a weekend cavorting with each other. Brighton had also been more fashionable before the war; by the time Meg showed up, it was a bit down at the heels and had a reputation for attracting a criminal element.[40]

Meg's life was one of constants amid unceasing disruptions. When in Hove, she was still a whole lot of fun and still told outrageous stories about her past.[41] She also continued to know a life of loss. Marthe died in 1933. One after another, Meg lost her grandsons. One died during World War II, another during a plane crash, and a third from tuberculosis.[42] Meg was a survivor, but that must have come with its own set of burdens and sorrows.

For the most part, though, she lived the life of a woman of a certain age who had some, but not great, resources. She went to church bazaars, did charity work, attended weddings and parties, and visited friends.[43] In a photograph from 1938, she's at a party, standing next to a count. Her tiara, large earrings, pearl necklace, and fur stole all speak to her status as a society lady—or her ability to project that image. The man to her right seems intent on entertaining the woman in front of him, but to his right, a balding man has his eyes fixed on Meg. She was still a figure of fascination at age sixty-nine.

In these years, the mythic Meg flourished. An Agatha Christie mystery from 1923 had a character based on Meg who lived in a house called villa Marguerite and had a daughter named Marthe, in case anyone had any doubts about the connection between Christie's version of Meg and the real one. In the French press, Meg was a cultural touchstone for crime, sex, and scandal. She was frequently invoked as a famous criminal defendant in articles from the 1920s. By the 1930s, newspapers and magazines could no longer rely on their readers to know who she was and so started retelling the story of her relationship to Faure and the tale of the double murder.[44] In an era of political strife, economic hardship, and rising international tensions, it must have been comforting to read about a woman from an era that seemed far more festive. Predictably, the nationalist right had their own view of her and now claimed that police officials had murdered Adolphe and Émilie and that the crime was more evidence that the regime was corrupt and fundamentally illegitimate.[45]

Meg, on the far right, at a party in Hove in 1938

Meg's story would circulate in the French public's mind for decades and does still today. Collectors sought out memorabilia from the affair, and plenty of authors have tried to solve the murders. Every so often, there is a television movie about her.

As ever, Meg refused to engage with the public's version of herself. She occasionally sued authors who stated that she had been involved in Faure's death or that she was a murderer.[46] In 1947, a French journalist named Jean Hamlin tracked her down in Hove, compelled by her ability to "evoke…a troubled atmosphere of drama, love and mystery" and no doubt hoping that she'd be willing to let something about Faure or the murders slip now that so much time had passed. He found her living modestly in a third-floor apartment on Adelaide Crescent, attended by just one servant, still beautiful but walking slowly with a cane and hard of hearing. Any hopes he had of her sitting for an interview were dashed when she told him, "I want nothing but to be left alone," and "I don't want to see my name in newspapers anymore."[47] That was the last word the public would hear from her.

On July 17, 1954, Meg died in a nursing home in Hove at age eighty-six.[48] The myth would remain, but she would take her secrets with her to the grave.

AFTERWORD

MEG AND THE BELLE Époque are long gone. For the most part, that's for the best. As charming as she was, she also had a capacity for destruction and even cruelty. And while Paris in the years around 1900 was a constant party for some, it was also a place of constraint, vast inequalities, and entrenched prejudices.

So much of Meg's day seems distant from us. Many women today benefit from expanded professional opportunities and a cultural climate where divorce isn't seen as a source of shame or scandal. If Meg were living in the twenty-first century, she would have faced more choices when she contemplated the failure of her marriage to Adolphe. Homophobia and antisemitism are still with us, but many in contemporary America don't see Jews and queer folks as a danger to the nation. There's a part of me that would love to be a time traveler to Meg's Paris—but only for a few hours, until I could go back to my own timeline where I can have the job that I have, love the person that I love, and move through the world with a relative amount of ease as a Jewish person.

Yet for all the changes that have occurred in the last century, we are in many ways inheritors of Meg's world. Ours is still one of double standards for men and women, a vast gulf between rich and poor, and nasty stereotypes. The sensationalist headlines of the mass press in the Belle Époque seem a whole lot like a version of today's clickbait.

Then, as now, sex sells. And Meg resembles a particular type of figure who sells really well: the sexual celebrity. These are women who capitalize on their sex appeal and high-profile liaisons, who live and love with intensity under the glare of the spotlight as drama swirls around them. Meg is different from many of today's sexual celebrities. Women like the Kardashian sisters embrace their fame, while Meg ultimately sought to run away from hers. Likewise, she stood apart from the sex goddesses of her own day. These women were often actresses or courtesans (or both) and projected an aura of availability and notoriety, whereas Meg so often sought to present herself as a society matron, even as she played up her sexualized persona behind closed doors. And yet it's easy to understand that, in eras where the rules for female behavior are rapidly changing, alluring women who break them in relatively acceptable ways hold a particular appeal.

Meg also serves as a reminder of the power of scandal. Her life was shaped by scandal from her adolescence to her death, as she sought to avoid making a scandal, capitalize on doing so, or retreat in the wake of a media frenzy. As much as we are fascinated by sex scandals, we also have a complicated relationship to that fascination. Sometimes we regard them as a distraction from what's really important, whether that's international affairs, the state of the economy, or the latest policy debate. These were arguments that could be heard in 1908 about the Steinheil Affair, with newspapers admonishing readers to pay attention to the real stuff of politics, even as their headlines promised the latest salacious revelations about Meg's life.[1]

It's true that the Steinheil Affair had plenty of tawdry elements to it. It's also true that few people's lives were affected by the precise details of what Faure and Meg were doing when he had the stroke that killed him, even as Parisians speculated endlessly about those details. But it is also the case that the Steinheil Affair allowed ordinary citizens to see the reality behind the façade of propriety, to understand the inner workings of the state, and to learn how much had been hidden from them. Scandals allow us to peer into the mess of other people's lives. Sometimes we're fascinated by them for purely voyeuristic reasons. But sometimes we're fascinated because they show us how power really operates.

What's more, the Steinheil Affair led to discussions about gender and sexuality and the line between the acceptable and the transgressive. Sex scandals often do this: I was in college in the late 1990s, an era of intense slut-shaming, including in the context of the revelations about Bill Clinton's affair with Monica Lewinsky. I'm still unlearning the toxic messages I imbibed at the time about women's sexuality. Many of us acquire a sense of what's shameful and what's not, or how men and women should behave, from sex scandals. To think of this as somehow unimportant, somehow separate from politics, would be a mistake.

The Steinheil Affair is a story about sex but also about crime, justice, and status. Here, too, elements of Meg's era are uncomfortably lodged in our own. In the Belle Époque, many of the wealthy saw themselves as inherently good, unlike the poor, who they regarded as prone to crime and sexual immorality. That's an attitude that is still alive and kicking today, one that often shapes who the criminal justice system treats with leniency and who it punishes harshly. If you are poor and Black and arrested, you're more likely to be regarded as a danger to society who needs to be punished. In contrast, if you are a rich, white person who is charged with the same crime, you are better able to argue that you deserve a second chance because you just made a mistake— the idea being that bad behavior isn't intrinsic to your person. Likewise, the media and defense lawyers sometimes frame alleged perpetrators as incapable of serious wrongdoing on the grounds that they are from a "good family."[2] It's a phrase where the association between high status and a high sense of morality remains fully intact.

Indeed, in the midst of contemporary debates about policing, Meg seems to operate as a forerunner of the figure known as the "Karen." This is the white woman who calls the cops on a Black neighbor, fellow customer, or passerby and, in doing so, polices racial boundaries. Meg's actions in the wake of the double murder are more malignant, as she tried to frame innocent individuals to reroute suspicion away from her. In doing so, she sometimes blamed Jews, Brazilians, or North Africans, all of whom were racialized others in her era. But many of her efforts were trained on those who had the protections of whiteness but not wealth: Burlingham, Davidson, Noretti, Rémy Couillard, and Alexandre Wolff. In all cases, she used her credibility, access, and privilege to put a whole host of people in danger out of a belief that the authorities were there to make her more comfortable and maintain the dividing line between who gets protected and who gets mistreated.

Meg's life also speaks to another kind of story that we've heard all too often: the one about the prominent individual who doesn't behave as they should behind closed doors. In our day, many of these stories are about the issue of consent. They gathered steam in 2002 with the reporting about Catholic priests who were sexually abusing children, erupted in 2017 when the hashtag #MeToo took over social media, and have continued pouring out since then.

The Steinheil Affair isn't a #MeToo story. Meg might have been a victim of sexual violence, but there were no allegations that she or any of the powerful men she associated with violated anyone's consent. What's more, accounts of sexual abuse at the hands of clergy and powerful figures in the media, entertainment industry, and politics came out in part because individuals decided to speak up about their experiences. They often did so despite the personal and professional risks of speaking the truth. For instance, in 2017, some of the horrors of the Hollywood system came to light when women broke nondisclosure agreements that had bound them from revealing parts of their personal history. The constraints in Meg's case were far different. Frequently, it was bourgeois codes of honor and journalistic norms—not legal documents—that prevented the truth from coming out. And in large measure, the Steinheil Affair was regarded as an entertaining spectacle of illicit sex, whereas recent revelations of sexual misconduct have been heart-wrenching, infuriating, and nauseating.

Despite all the differences between the Steinheil Affair and the stories about sexual abuse and harassment that have come out in the past few decades, there are important similarities. These contemporary cases all ask us to think about the resources the wealthy can use to manage their reputations, just as the Steinheil Affair did for the individuals of the Belle Époque. They are galling because they expose how institutions, from churches to media companies, often work to spare insiders from the consequences of their actions. That, too, was central to Meg's life. For months after the murders, she relied on a system that saw prominent individuals as worthy of protection and the poor as disposable. Meg benefited from these structures until her actions led the state to throw her under the bus—even as it's quite likely that they were doing so in part to continue shielding the murderer from scrutiny.

Indeed, many in the Belle Époque saw publicly revealing misbehavior as more disruptive than committing it. Sadly, this is an attitude many victims of sexual assault and harassment face today. When they speak up, they, rather than the perpetrators, are sometimes treated as the troublemakers. We don't live in a world where men fight duels to uphold their honor or where women are routinely discouraged from getting a divorce to protect their family's reputation. But until institutions stop protecting those who are prominent at the expense of those who are not, those who bring bad behavior to light will still be regarded as problems.

As much as the parallels between Meg's era and our own offer a depressing spectacle of how so much has remained unchanged in the past hundred years, they also provide hope. Once her transgressions came to light, members of the public became outraged and decried the hypocrisy of the elite. In our own day, we've seen how speaking up about wrongdoing can spur anger, activism, and calls for change. Because if secrets and silences help maintain inequalities, then knowing the truth allows us to imagine a more honest and fairer society.

AUTHOR'S NOTE

This is a book about a woman who lied her entire life. Meg lied to protect or enhance her reputation, she lied because she could, and she lied because she lived in a society where maintaining appearances was often more valued than telling the truth. Her story is partly about how lies and silences maintained the inequalities of this era.

Others around her told their own falsehoods about her. Some of her friends, family members, and acquaintances tried to protect their reputations by claiming that she was entirely respectable. Others spread rumors about her out of malice or because the story was simply too good not to repeat.

Even those who we tend of think of as having professional obligations to the truth—journalists and investigators—had a different sense of where their duties lay in Meg's day. Journalistic standards were lax and many newspapers had no compunctions about publishing wild speculation or unverified statements. Reporters were under such pressure to produce that they were often sloppy in their telling of events. When Leydet was directing the criminal investigation into the Steinheil Affair, the police file was compiled to make Meg look good. When André was in charge, much of the material looked much worse for her. In other words, none of the sources about Meg's life from her day provide unmediated access to the truth.

Meg's memoirs are also problematic. They were ghostwritten by the Belgian journalist Roger de Chateleux. He was her lover for years and no doubt heard many of her stories during the course of their affair.[1] A careful reading of her memoirs reveals that they include a fair amount of verifiable information that only Meg would have known, which indicates that they were not entirely his invention.[2] She was so attentive to her reputation that she would have closely monitored what information they contained. However, precisely because Meg had such a hand in writing them, they contain outright lies. For these reasons, I have used them with care. They are useful in filling in the gaps where we have very little information, such as her childhood and her life in prison. They can also provide her perspective or details in instances when other sources back up essential elements of her account. For instance, in part 2, some of the scenes from the investigation into the double murders are reconstructed by blending information that appears in her memoirs with what is in either the police investigative record or newspaper accounts.

Sometimes the untruths are fascinating. But they are also frustrating and often prevent us from knowing what happened. Throughout this book, I have tried to tell a clear narrative of Meg's life while keeping in mind the limits of the available sources. Sometimes that means reading into silences, sometimes that means making room for uncertainty, and sometimes that means privileging one account over another.

In some cases, I have presented multiple possible versions of the same event. This is true for Faure's death and the double murders. These are turning points in Meg's life, and I wanted to give the reader enough information so that they could decide what was most probable.

In other instances, however, I have privileged one conflicting account over another. For instance, Meg told one tale about why her father broke off her engagement with a young army officer at her trial, while the police report gave another. Likewise, Meg told two slightly different versions of how she met Faure, one to a newspaper in 1908 and one in her memoirs. In these instances, I have chosen the narrative that either makes the most sense or that is backed up by other independent sources.

The sources are one difficulty, language another. In this book, I sometimes use terms that are now regarded as outdated or problematic, like "prostitute," "prostitution," and "homosexuality." I use the last term to talk about Adolphe's affairs with men since our current language for queer sexuality does not match that of the Belle Époque. (In contrast, I use "lesbian," since it was around at the time, although it had a slightly different meaning than it does now, as discussed in chapter 4.) Sex workers have also rejected the words "prostitute" and "prostitution" for their negative associations. But I use them precisely because these connotations were so important to Meg's story and to how she defined herself and how others defined her. Likewise, I employ terms like "low-lifes" or "lower depths" when talking about the poorest of the poor and those who were presumed to be immoral. This is a vocabulary that has largely fallen out of use but is helpful here because Meg and so many people around her were invoking the twin concepts of low socioeconomic status and low sense of morality as they tried to make sense of her life and its many mysteries.

READING GROUP GUIDE

1. The marriage between Meg and Adolphe was contentious for a few rea-
    sons. What were they?

2. Discuss Meg's upbringing and family dynamic. How do you think it influ-
    enced her behavior as an adult?

3. How were different social classes popularly characterized in nineteenth-
    century France? Were these depictions accurate?

4. Meg wielded her sexuality to climb the social ladder. In what ways was
    she successful? In what ways did her sexual barter system backfire?

5. Characterize Meg's feelings for Adolphe Steinheil, Félix Faure, and Émile
    Chouanard. How did her feelings differ from man to man?

6. What are the prevailing theories regarding Adolphe's and Émilie's mur-
    ders? Which do you think is the truth?

7. As a woman (with a working-class mother), Meg understood what it meant to be marginalized, yet she still disdained other oppressed groups, including Jews and the lower classes. Why do you think that is?

8. Discuss the role media played in the Steinheil Affair. Did they make the situation better or worse? Can you draw any parallels to today's media?

9. In what ways do you think the trial and Meg's time in prison changed her?

10. Meg became a celebrity but never wanted to be one. Can you think of other women today who became famous without wanting to be? How might their stories be similar to Meg's?

11. Meg was simultaneously loved and hated by the public. Why do you think that is? After learning her entire story, how do you feel about her?

IMAGE CREDITS

Image on page 6: author's collection (caption: Édouard and Émilie Japy)

Image on page 16: PixPlanete (caption: Meg at 17)

Image on page 37: author's collection (caption: Adolphe Steinheil)

Image on page 39: author's collection (caption: Adolphe, Meg, and Marthe)

Image on page 62: ©National Portrait Gallery, London (caption: Félix Faure in 1895)

Image on page 68: Léon Bonnat (1833–1922)/Wikimedia Commons (caption: Bonnat's portrait of Meg)

Image on page 100: Archives de la Préfecture de Police de Paris/FRAPP_YB7_001 (caption: Bertillon's photograph of Émilie's corpse)

Image on page 101: Archives de la Préfecture de Police de Paris/FRAPP_YB7_012 (caption: Bertillon's photograph of Adolphe's corpse)

Image on page 102: Archives de la Préfecture de Police de Paris/FRAPP_YB7_016 (caption: The police floor plan…)

Image on page 106: Museum of the History of Justice, Crime and Punishment, http://criminocorpus.org (caption: The crime scene photograph of Meg's study…)

Image on page 107: Museum of the History of Justice, Crime and Punishment, http://criminocorpus.org (caption: The crime scene photograph of Adolphe's room...)

Image on page 147: Philippe Zoummeroff Collection/Museum of the History of Justice, Crime and Punishment, http://criminocorpus.org (caption: Le Matin's image of Meg from November 3)

Image on page 154: gallica.bnf.fr /Bibliothèque nationale de France (caption: Le Matin's photograph of Rémy from November 22, 1908)

Image on page 197: author's collection (caption: Meg in Saint-Lazare)

Image on page 201: Ville de Paris/Bibliothèque historique (caption: The postcard with "Saint Meg")

Image on page 203: author's collection (caption: The Happy Widow)

Image on page 205: author's collection (caption: Meg's drawing of her cell)

Image on page 215: author's collection (caption: Meg's drawings of Aubin...)

Image on page 229: Paul Renouard/Philippe Zoummeroff Collection/Museum of the History of Justice, Crime and Punishment, http://criminocorpus.org (caption: Meg defending herself in court...)

Image on page 255: Mirrorpix (caption: Meg and Robert shortly before their marriage)

Image on page 258: image courtesy of Royal Pavilion & Museums, Brighton & Hove, CC BY-SA (caption: Meg, on the far right, at a party in Hove in 1938)

NOTES

PREFACE

1   Details of this morning are taken from Service de l'identité judiciaire de la préfecture de Police de Paris, "Affaire Steinheil," Criminocorpus, 1908, https://criminocorpus.org/en/library/doc/1797/.

PART I

1   Maurice Paléologue, *An Intimate Journal of the Dreyfus Case*, trans. Eric Mosbacher (New York: Criterion Books, 1957), 204.

CHAPTER I

1   Alexis Muston, *Histoire d'un village* (Montbéliard: Barbier frères, 1882), 2:288.

2   Ivan Grassias, *Sur les traces de "l'empire" Japy* (Salins-les-Bains: Musées des techniques et cultures comtoises, 2001), 9.

3   Pierre Lamard, *Histoire d'un capital familial au XIXe siècle: le capital Japy (1777–1910)* (Belfort: Société belfortaine d'emulation, 1988), 48; Grassais, *Sur les traces,* 49–54.

4   The complicated Japy family tree can be found in Lamard, *Histoire d'un capital familial,* 305.

5   Gabriel-Louis Pringué, *30 ans de dîners en ville* (Paris: Lacurne, 2012), 26; Lela F.

Kerley, *Uncovering Paris: Scandals and Nude Spectacles in the Belle Époque* (Baton Rouge: LSU Press, 2017), 7, 119.

6   "Parricide?," *Le Journal*, December 4, 1908, 2.

7   Baronne d' Orval, *Usages mondains: Guide du savoir-vivre moderne dans toutes les circonstances de la vie*, 6th ed. (Paris: Victor-Havard, 1901), 3.

8   "Interrogatoire de l'accusée," *Le Petit Parisien*, November 4, 1909, 2.

9   Marguerite Japy Steinheil, *My Memoirs* (New York: Sturgis & Walton, 1912), 2.

10   Louis Henry and Jacques Houdaille, "Célibat et âge au mariage aux XVIIIe et XIXe siècles en France: I. Célibat définitif," *Population (French Edition)* 33, no. 1 (1978): 404, 413; Rachel Mesch, *Before Trans: Three Gender Stories from Nineteenth-Century France* (Stanford: Stanford University Press, 2020), 213.

11   Dominique Barjot, ed., *Les Patrons du Second Empire* (Paris: Editions Cénomane, 1991), 29.

12   Isabelle Bricard, *Saintes ou pouliches: L'éducation des jeunes filles au XIXe siècle* (Paris: Albin Michel, 1985), 282.

13   "La Veuve rouge," *Le Petit Parisien*, November 30, 1908, 2.

14   "Le Passé de Mme Steinheil," *Le Petit Parisien*, November 28, 1908, 2.

15   Steinheil, *Memoirs*, 2.

16   Steinheil, 5.

17   Steinheil, 2.

18   "Service Régional de l'Inventaire de Franche-Comté," Inventaire général du Patrimoine culturel de Franche-Comté, accessed August 19, 2020, http://patrimoine.franche-comte.fr/gtrudov/IA90000085/index.htm.

19   "Parricide?," *Le Journal*, December 4, 1908, 2.

20   Rapport, March 1, 1909, JA 11, Archives de la préfecture de Police, Le Pré-Saint-Gervais, France (hereafter cited as APP).

21   Steinheil, *Memoirs*, 3–4.

22   Steinheil, 4.

23   Rebecca Rogers, *From the Salon to the Schoolroom: Educating Bourgeois Girls in Nineteenth-Century France* (University Park: Pennsylvania State University Press, 2005), 174–75; Karen Offen, "The Second Sex and the Baccalauréat in Republican France, 1880–1924," *French Historical Studies* 13, no. 2 (1983): 271.

24   Steinheil, *Memoirs*, 4.

25   Steinheil, 4–5.

26 Colin Heywood, *Growing Up in France: From the Ancien Régime to the Third Republic* (Cambridge: Cambridge University Press, 2007), 132–36, 139–41, 149–50; Anne-Marie Sohn, *Chrysalides: Femmes dans la vie privée (XIXe–XXe siècles)* (Paris: Publications de la Sorbonne, 1996), 1:290–96.

27 "Le Passé de Mme Steinheil," *Le Petit Parisien*, November 28, 1908, 1.

28 Steinheil, *Memoirs*, 13.

29 Steinheil, 13.

30 Steinheil, 5, 10.

31 Steinheil, 13–14.

32 René Tavernier, *Madame Steinheil, ange ou démon: favorite de la République* (Paris: Presses de la Cité, 1976), 35; Steinheil, *Memoirs*, 17.

33 "Mme Steinheil est acquittée," *Le Petit Journal*, November 14, 1909, 1.

34 "Mme Steinheil acquittée," *Le Journal*, November 14, 1909, 2.

35 "L'Affaire Steinheil," *Le Radical*, November 29, 1908, 2; "Mme Steinheil sous les verrous," *Le Petit Journal*, November 27, 1908, 3.

36 Jann Matlock, *Scenes of Seduction: Prostitution, Hysteria, and Reading Difference in Nineteenth-Century France* (New York: Columbia University Press, 1994); Jessie Hewitt, *Institutionalizing Gender: Madness, the Family, and Psychiatric Power in Nineteenth-Century France* (Ithaca: Cornell University Press, 2020).

37 "L'Affaire Steinheil," *Le Matin*, November 28, 1908, 2.

38 Rapport, February 18, 1909, JA 11, APP.

39 Alain Corbin, "La Virilité reconsidérée au prisme du naturalisme," in *Histoire de la virilité*, ed. Alain Corbin, Jean-Jacques Courtine, and Georges Vigarello (Paris: Seuil, 2011), 2:19; Alain Corbin, "La Nécessaire Manifestation de l'énergie sexuelle," in Corbin, Courtine, and Vigarello, *Histoire de la virilité*, 2:137–54.

40 Edward Berenson, *The Trial of Madame Caillaux* (Berkeley: University of California Press, 1992), 128.

41 Rapport, March 1, 1909, JA 11, APP.

42 Rapport, February 18, 1909, JA 11, APP.

43 Berenson, *Trial of Madame Caillaux*, 130.

44 Mary Lynn Stewart, *For Health and Beauty: Physical Culture for Frenchwomen, 1880s–1930s* (Baltimore: Johns Hopkins University Press, 2001), 99.

45 Steinheil, *Memoirs*, 15.

46 Rapport, February 18, 1909, JA 11, APP.

47 Rapport, February 18, 1909, JA 11.

48 Memo to the Prefect of Police, November 30, 1908, BA 1585, Cabinet du préfet: affaires générales, APP; E. Claire Cage, "Child Sexual Abuse and Medical Expertise in Nineteenth-Century France," *French Historical Studies* 42, no. 3 (August 1, 2019): 391–421.

49 Steinheil, *Memoirs*, 7.

50 Steinheil, 15.

51 Steinheil, 15–16.

52 Rapport, March 1, 1909, JA 11, APP.

53 Sohn, *Chrysalides*, 1:76–83.

54 Rapport, March 1, 1909, JA 11, APP.

55 Berenson, *Trial of Madame Caillaux*, 131.

56 Rapport, March 1, 1909, JA 11, APP.

CHAPTER 2

1 Rapport, January 26, 1909, JA 11, APP.

2 "Mme Steinheil Sues Author and Publisher," *Dundee Evening Telegraph*, November 28, 1912, 1; "Mme Steinheil and Lord Abinger," *Yorkshire Evening Post*, June 26, 1917, 3.

3 Rapport, January 26, 1909, JA 11, APP.

4 Steinheil, *Memoirs*, 18; Rapport, January 26, 1909, JA 11, APP.

5 Rapport, January 26, 1909, JA 11, APP.

6 Steinheil, *Memoirs*, 18.

7 Steinheil, 18.

8 Steinheil, 18.

9 Rapport, January 26, 1909, JA 11, APP.

10 Rapport, January 26, 1909, JA 11, APP.

11 Rapport, January 26, 1909, JA 11, APP.

12 "Interrogatoire de Mme Steinheil," *Le Journal*, November 4, 1909, 2.

13 Stewart, *For Health and Beauty*, 99.

14 Léon Blum, *Du mariage* (Paris: Albin Michel, 1937); Anne-Marie Sohn, *Du premier baiser à l'alcôve: La sexualité des Français au quotidien, 1850–1950* (Paris: Aubier, 1996), 12–15.

15 Rapport, March 1, 1909, JA 11, APP.

16   Orval, *Usages mondains*, 5–8.

17   Rapport, January 26, 1909, JA 11, APP.

18   Tavernier, *Madame Steinheil*, 37.

19   "Les Derniers Témoins—le réquisitoire," *Le Journal*, November 12, 1909, 5.

20   Georges Claretie, "L'Affaire Steinheil," *Le Figaro*, November 12, 1909, 3.

21   "Les Derniers Témoins—le réquisitoire," *Le Journal*, November 12, 1909, 5.

22   "Le Procès Steinheil," *Le Matin*, November 4, 1909, 2.

23   "Interrogatoire de Mme Steinheil," *Le Journal*, November 4, 1909, 2.

24   Steinheil, *Memoirs*, 20; Benjamin F. Martin, *The Hypocrisy of Justice in the Belle Epoque* (Baton Rouge: Louisiana State University Press, 1984), 17.

25   "Mme Steinheil devant le jury de la Seine," *Le Petit Journal*, November 4, 1909, 2.

26   Meg Steinheil to Lucie Faure, undated, 460 AP 10, Fonds Félix Faure, Archives nationales, Pierrefitte-sur-Seine, France (hereafter cited as AN).

27   Steinheil, *Memoirs*, 20.

28   Steinheil, 20–21.

29   Steinheil, 21.

30   Steinheil, 24.

31   Anne Verjus and Denise Davidson, *Le Roman conjugal: Chroniques de la vie familiale à l'époque de la révolution et de l'empire* (Seyssel: Champ Vallon, 2011), 212.

CHAPTER 3

1   Steinheil, *Memoirs*, 22–23; Martin, *Hypocrisy of Justice*, 17; "Mme Steinheil acquittée," *Le Journal*, November 14, 1909, 2.

2   Marc Gotlieb, *The Plight of Emulation: Ernest Meissonier and French Salon Painting* (Princeton: Princeton University Press, 1996), 2.

3   "Le Peintre Steinheil & sa belle-mère étranglés," *Le Journal*, June 1, 1908, 2; *La Chronique des arts et de la curiosité* (Paris: Bureaux de la Gazette des Beaux Arts, 1882), 162.

4   Eugène Montrosier, *Les Artistes modernes* (Paris: H. Launette, 1881), 78.

5   "Assassinat du peintre Steinheil et de sa belle-mère," *Le Figaro*, June 1, 1908, 2.

6   Corbin, "Virilité reconsidérée," 19.

7   "Mme Steinheil en Cour d'Assises," *Écho de Paris*, November 12, 1909, 1.

8   Steinheil, *Memoirs*, 22.

9   Steinheil, 22–23.

10   Steinheil, 24.

11   Steinheil, 23.

12   "L'Affaire Steinheil," *Le Petit Journal*, November 7, 1909, 2; Steinheil, *Memoirs*, 25.

13   Steinheil, *Memoirs*, 25.

14   "Interrogatoire de Mme Steinheil," *Le Journal*, November 4, 1909, 2.

15   Bricard, *Saintes ou pouliches*, 279.

16   "Interrogatoire de Mme Steinheil," *Le Journal*, November 4, 1909, 2.

17   Steinheil, *Memoirs*, 26.

18   Steinheil, 26.

19   "Mme Steinheil devant le juge," *Le Matin*, December 2, 1908, 1.

20   "Vers la lumière," *L'Écho de Paris*, December 4, 1908, 1.

21   James M. Donovan, *Juries and the Transformation of Criminal Justice in France in the Nineteenth & Twentieth Centuries* (Chapel Hill: University of North Carolina Press, 2010), 125; Verjus and Davidson, *Roman conjugal*, 212.

22   Steinheil, *Memoirs*, 28.

23   Steinheil, 27–28.

24   Steinheil, 28.

25   Steinheil, 28.

26   Charles Rearick, *Pleasures of the Belle Époque: Entertainment and Festivity in Turn-of-the-Century France* (New Haven: Yale University Press, 1985).

27   Oscar Wilde, *Complete Writings of Oscar Wilde* (New York: Nottingham Society, 1909), 9:19.

28   Dominique Kalifa, *La Véritable Histoire de la "Belle Époque"* (Paris: Fayard, 2017).

29   John Merriman, *Ballad of the Anarchist Bandits: The Crime Spree That Gripped Belle Epoque Paris* (New York: Bold Type Books, 2017), 9–46.

30   Octave Uzanne, *Parisiennes de ce temps* (Paris: Mercure de France, 1910), 108–9.

31   Collections photographiques, distributed by Archives de Paris, http://archives.paris.fr/r/143/collections-photographiques/.

32   "Triple crime à Vaugirard," *Le Radical*, June 1, 1908, 1.

33   "Contrat de mariage entre M. Adolphe Steinheil, artiste peintre à Paris et Mlle Marguerite Japy de Beaucourt," July 8, 1890, AN, MC/DC/XI/1.

34   "Le Crime de l'impasse Ronsin," *Le Temps*, November 28, 1908, 2.

35   Steinheil, *Memoirs*, 29.

36   "Interrogatoire de Mme Steinheil," *Le Journal*, November 4, 1909, 2.

37 Steinheil, *Memoirs*, 30.

38 Steinheil, 31–32.

39 "Le Crime de l'impasse Ronsin," *Le Temps*, November 28, 1908, 2.

40 "Interrogatoire de Mme Steinheil," *Le Journal*, November 4, 1909, 6.

41 Anne Martin-Fugier, *La Bourgeoise: Femme au temps de Paul Bourget* (Paris: B. Grasset, 1983), 185. The terminology of their status comes from a statement made by the presiding judge of Meg's trial; "Interrogatoire de Mme Steinheil," *Le Journal*, November 4, 1909, 6.

42 Georges Claretie, "L'Affaire Steinheil," *Le Figaro*, November 6, 1909, 2.

43 "Parricide?," *Le Journal*, December 4, 1908, 2.

44 "Mme Steinheil sur la sellette," *Le Petit Parisien*, December 4, 1908, 1.

45 "Interrogatoire de Mme Steinheil," *Le Journal*, November 4, 1909, 2.

46 "Contrat de mariage entre M. Adolphe Steinheil, artiste peintre à Paris et Mlle Marguerite Japy de Beaucourt."

47 "On exhume les corps de M. Steinheil et de Mme Japy," *Le Journal*, November 30, 1908, 2.

48 Sarah C. Maza, *Violette Nozière: A Story of Murder in 1930s Paris* (Berkeley: University of California Press, 2011), 59–63.

49 "Mme Steinheil est acquittée," *Le Petit Journal*, November 14, 1909, 1.

50 Steinheil, *Memoirs*, 32.

51 "Mme Steinheil devant le jury de la Seine," *Le Petit Journal*, November 4, 1909, 2.

52 Rachel Mesch, "Housewife or Harlot?: Sex and the Married Woman in Nineteenth-Century France," *Journal of the History of Sexuality* 18, no. 1 (2009): 65–83; Andrea Mansker, *Sex, Honor and Citizenship in Early Third Republic France*, Genders and Sexualities in History (Houndmills: Palgrave Macmillan, 2011), 110.

53 Commission rogatoire, January 20, 1909, JA 11, APP; "L'Assassinat du peintre Steinheil et de sa belle-mère Mme veuve Japy," *Le Figaro*, June 1, 1908, 2. On working-class wages, see Mary Lynn Stewart, *Women, Work, and the French State: Labour Protection and Social Patriarchy, 1879–1919* (Kingston: McGill-Queen's Press, 1989), 26.

54 Andrew Israel Ross, *Public City/Public Sex: Homosexuality, Prostitution, and Urban Culture in Nineteenth-Century Paris* (Philadelphia: Temple University Press, 2019); Dominique Kalifa, *Paris: Une histoire érotique, d'Offenbach aux sixties* (Paris: Payot, 2018).

55   Vernon A. Rosario, *The Erotic Imagination: French Histories of Perversity* (Oxford: Oxford University Press, 1997), 76; Robert A. Nye, *Masculinity and Male Codes of Honor in Modern France* (Berkeley: University of California Press, 1998), 107.

56   "Histoire de Mme Steinheil par Mariette Wolff," *Le Matin*, December 1, 1908, 2 (ellipsis in original).

57   Commission rogatoire, January 20, 1909, JA 11, APP.

58   Ed Cohen, *Talk on the Wilde Side: Towards a Genealogy of a Discourse on Male Sexualities* (New York: Routledge, 1993), 61; Nye, *Masculinity*, 101; Rosario, *Erotic Imagination*, 39.

59   "Mme Steinheil en Cour d'Assises," *L'Écho de Paris*, November 9, 1909, 2; "Interrogatoire de Mme Steinheil," *Le Journal*, November 4, 1909, 2.

60   Steinheil, *Memoirs*, 34.

61   "L'Interrogatoire de Mme Steinheil," *Le Radical*, December 2, 1908, 1.

62   Steinheil, *Memoirs*, 35.

63   Sohn, *Chrysalides*, 2:995–98.

64   Steinheil, *Memoirs*, 35.

65   Michele Plott, "The Rules of the Game: Respectability, Sexuality, and the Femme Mondaine in Late-Nineteenth-Century Paris," *French Historical Studies* 25, no. 3 (July 1, 2002): 531–56; Gail L. Savage, "Divorce and the Law in England and France Prior to the First World War," *Journal of Social History* 21, no. 3 (April 1988): 510; Mansker, *Sex, Honor and Citizenship*, 95.

66   Steinheil, *Memoirs*, 35.

67   "L'Affaire Steinheil," *Le Petit Journal*, December 5, 1908, 3.

68   Steinheil, *Memoirs*, 36.

69   Sohn, *Chrysalides*, 2:6, 47; Berenson, *Trial of Madame Caillaux*, 112; Mary Louise Roberts, *Disruptive Acts: The New Woman in Fin-de-Siècle France* (Chicago: University of Chicago Press, 2002), 12.

70   Roberts, *Disruptive Acts*.

71   Martin-Fugier, *Bourgeoise*, 10.

CHAPTER 4

1   Steinheil, *Memoirs*, 34.

2   "Mme Steinheil en Cour d'Assises," *L'Écho de Paris*, November 12, 1909, 2; "Le Procès Steinheil," *Le Matin*, November 4, 1909, 2.

3   "Le Crime de l'impasse Ronsin," *Le Temps*, November 28, 1908, 2.

4   Paléologue, *Intimate Journal*, 204.

5   "L'Affaire Steinheil," *La Libre Parole*, December 1, 1908, 2; "Mystérieuse Tragédie à Vaugirard," *Le Journal*, June 1, 1908, 2; "Mauvaise Journée pour Mme Steinheil," *Le Journal*, December 15, 1908, 2.

6   Marcel Rousselet, *Histoire de la magistrature française des origines à nos jours* (Paris: Plon, 1957), 201.

7   *Tout-Paris: Annuaire de la Société parisienne* (Paris: A. La Fare, 1905), 84.

8   Steinheil, *Memoirs*, 36–37.

9   Steinheil, *Memoirs*, 35.

10   Thomas Piketty, "Income, Wage, and Wealth Inequality in France, 1901–98," in *Top Incomes over the Twentieth Century: A Contrast between Continental European and English-Speaking Countries*, ed. A. B. Atkinson and Thomas Piketty (Oxford: Oxford University Press, 2007), 43–81.

11   Thierry Billard, *Félix Faure: biographie* (Paris: Julliard, 1995), 515; Christophe Charle, *Les Élites de la République* (Paris: Fayard, 2006); Maza, *Violette Nozière*, 59–61.

12   "L'Interrogatoire a pris fin sur une scène dramatique," *Le Journal*, November 6, 1909, 6.

13   "Les Derniers Témoins—le réquisatoire," *Le Journal*, November 12, 1909, 5.

14   "Les Derniers Témoins—le réquisatoire," *Le Journal*, November 12, 1909, 5; "Mme Steinheil acquittée," *Le Journal*, November 14, 1909, 2.

15   Steinheil, *Memoirs*, 38.

16   Steinheil, 41.

17   Ernest Dudley, *The Scarlett Widow* (London: F. Muller, 1960), 172; Rapport, February 18, 1909, JA 11, APP.

18   Fernand Vandérem, "Le Programme de Bayonne," *Le Figaro*, November 9, 1909, 1.

19   "Mme Steinheil devant le juge," *Le Matin*, December 2, 1908, 1.

20   Présentation pour le grade de Chevalier de l'Ordre de la Légion d'honneur, Parquet de la cour d'appel de Paris, September 1, 1882, BB/6(II)/456, dossier on Camille-Joseph Bouchez, Ministère de la Justice, Cours et tribunaux, Dossiers personnels de magistrats, AN.

21   Steinheil, *Memoirs*, 36–37.

22   "Interrogatoire de Mme Steinheil," *Le Journal*, November 4, 1909, 5.

23 "Interrogatoire de Mme Steinheil," *Le Journal*, November 4, 1909, 5.

24 "Interrogatoire de Mme Steinheil," *Le Journal*, November 4, 1909, 5; "L'Affaire Steinheil," *La Libre Parole*, December 13, 1908, 2.

25 "Mme Steinheil se dit innocente," *Le Journal*, December 2, 1908, 1.

26 "Le Procès Steinheil," *Le Matin*, November 4, 1909, 1.

27 *Tout-Paris*, 84.

28 Plott, "Rules of the Game"; Anne-Marie Sohn, "The Golden Age of Male Adultery: The Third Republic," *Journal of Social History* 28, no. 3 (April 1, 1995): 469–90.

29 Pringué, *30 Ans*, 69.

30 "Chez M. Martin-Feuillée," *Le Matin*, November 4, 1909, 4.

31 "Interrogatoire de Mme Steinheil," *Le Journal*, November 4, 1909, 5.

32 "Mme Steinheil est bien une criminelle," *Le Petit Journal*, November 29, 1908, 1.

33 Paléologue, *Intimate Journal*, 204.

34 See Chapter 10 for her relationships with Balincourt and Borderel, which followed this timeline.

35 Alain Corbin, *Les Filles de noce: Misère sexuelle et prostitution: 19e et 20e siècles* (Paris: Aubier Montaigne, 1978); Lola Gonzalez-Quijano, *Capitale de l'amour: Filles et lieux de plaisir à Paris au XIXe siècle* (Paris: Vendémiaire, 2015); Andrew Israel Ross, "Serving Sex: Playing with Prostitution in the Brasseries à Femmes of Late Nineteenth-Century Paris," *Journal of the History of Sexuality* 24, no. 2 (2015): 292.

36 "La Tragédie de l'impasse Ronsin," *Le Petit Journal*, November 3, 1909, 1.

37 Evidence of her concurrent partners can be found in "L'Affaire Steinheil," *Le Petit Parisien*, December 15, 1908, 3.

38 "L'Affaire Steinheil," *Le Journal*, November 29, 1908, 2; "Renseignments confidentiels," April 1896, BB/6(II)/1009, dossier on Joseph-Charles-Louis-Athanase-Abel Lemercier, Ministère de la Justice, Cours et tribunaux, Dossiers personnels de magistrats, AN; letter from the premier president, Cour d'appel d'Aix, to the Garde des Sceaux, Ministre de la Justice, March 9, 1886, BB/6(II)/668, dossier on Paul-Joseph-Jules Bertulus, Ministère de la Justice, Cours et tribunaux, Dossiers personnels de magistrats, AN.

39 "Le Crime de l'impasse Ronsin," *Le Temps*, December 15, 1908, 2.

40 Hannah Frydman, "Reading Incognito: Periodicals, Sapphic Fictions, and Lesbian Communication," *Dix-Neuf* (forthcoming).

41 Benjamin F. Martin, *Crime and Criminal Justice under the Third Republic: The*

Shame of Marianne (Baton Rouge: Louisiana State University Press, 1990), 44; Memo to the Prefect of Police, November 30, 1908, BA 1585, APP.

42 Nicole Albert, *Lesbian Decadence: Representations in Art and Literature of Fin-de-Siècle France* (New York: Harrington Park Press, 2015), 62–63.

43 José Esteban Muñoz, "Ephemera as Evidence: Introductory Notes to Queer Acts," *Women & Performance: A Journal of Feminist Theory* 8, no. 2 (January 1, 1996): 5–16.

44 "Mauvaise Journée pour Mme Steinheil," *Le Journal*, December 15, 1908, 2.

45 Albert, *Lesbian Decadence*; Gretchen Schultz, *Sapphic Fathers: Discourses of Same-Sex Desire from Nineteenth-Century France* (Toronto: University of Toronto Press, 2014).

46 "L'Interrogatoire de Mme Steinheil," *Le Radical*, December 8, 1908, 2.

47 "Interrogatoire de Mme Steinheil," *Le Journal*, November 4, 1909, 2.

48 "La Journée de Rémy Couillard," *Le Journal*, November 7, 1909, 4; Steinheil, *Memoirs*, 37–38.

49 Aaron Freundschuh, *The Courtesan and the Gigolo: The Murders in the Rue Montaigne and the Dark Side of Empire in Nineteenth-Century Paris* (Stanford: Stanford University Press, 2017), 73; Gabrielle Houbre, *Le Livre des courtisanes: Archives secrètes de la police des moeurs, 1861–1876* (Paris: Tallandier, 2006), 37.

50 "Interrogatoire de Mme Steinheil," *Le Radical*, December 2, 1908, 2.

51 "Interrogatoire de Mme Steinheil," *Le Journal*, November 4, 1909, 5.

52 "Histoire de Mme Steinheil par Mariette Wolff," *Le Matin*, December 1, 1908, 1.

CHAPTER 5

1 "La Veuve rouge," *Le Petit Parisien*, November 29, 1908, 1.

2 Steinheil, *Memoirs*, 38.

3 Fernand Vandérem, "Le Programme de Bayonne," *Le Figaro*, November 9, 1909, 1.

4 Undated calling card of Meg Steinheil, 460 AP 10, Fonds Félix Faure, AN.

5 Orval, *Usages mondaines*, 96, 112–13, 134; Elizabeth C. Macknight, "Cake and Conversation: The Women's Jour in Parisian High Society, 1880–1914," *French History* 19, no. 3 (September 1, 2005): 355.

6 Rapport général, September 16, 1908, JA 11, APP.

7 "Propos d'un parisien," *Le Matin*, December 13, 1908, 1.

8 Pierre Montal, *L'Affaire Steinheil* (Paris: Imprimeries, Édition et Publicités Belleville, 1909), 35; "L'Affaire Steinheil," *Le Matin*, December 18, 1908, 1.

9   Steinheil, *Memoirs*, 43–52.

10 Armand Lanoux, *Madame Steinheil, ou, la connaissance du Président* (Paris: Bernard Grasset, 1983), 204–6; Steinheil, *Memoirs*, 43, 50, 59.

11 Steinheil, *Memoirs*, 188; "Les Derniers Témoins—le réquisitoire," *Le Journal*, November 12, 1909, 5; Pierre Lepage, *André Paisant, député d'Oise* ([Chantilly?]: Association de Sauvegarde de Chantilly et de son Environnement, 2011), 16.

12 Steinheil, *Memoirs*, 59–63.

13 Carolyn C. Lougee, *Le Paradis des Femmes: Women, Salons, and Social Stratification in Seventeenth-Century France* (Princeton: Princeton University Press, 1976); Dena Goodman, *The Republic of Letters: A Cultural History of the French Enlightenment* (Ithaca: Cornell University Press, 1994); Antoine Lilti, *Le Monde des salons: Sociabilité et mondanité à Paris au XVIIIe siècle* (Paris: Fayard, 2005); Steven D. Kale, *French Salons: High Society and Political Sociability from the Old Regime to the Revolution of 1848* (Baltimore: Johns Hopkins University Press, 2006); Anne Martin-Fugier, *Les Salons de la IIIe République: Art, littérature, politique* (Paris: Librairie Académique Perrin, 2003).

14 Hollis Clayson, *Painted Love: Prostitution in French Art of the Impressionist Era* (New Haven: Yale University Press, 1991); Corbin, *Filles de noce*; Charles Bernheimer, *Figures of Ill Repute: Representing Prostitution in Nineteenth-Century France* (Cambridge: Harvard University Press, 1989); Sander L. Gilman, *Difference and Pathology: Stereotypes of Sexuality, Race, and Madness* (Ithaca: Cornell University Press, 1985), 94–99; T. J. Clark, *The Painting of Modern Life: Paris in the Art of Manet and His Followers*, (Princeton: Princeton University Press, 1999), 79–146; Ross, *Public City*, 12–13, 27–60.

15 Jill Harsin, *Policing Prostitution in Nineteenth-Century Paris* (Princeton: Princeton University Press, 1985); Jean-Marc Berlière, *La Police des mœurs sous la IIIe République* (Paris: Editions du Seuil, 1992).

16 Freundschuh, *Courtesan and the Gigolo*, 90; Clayson, *Painted Love*, 63–67.

17 Liane de Pougy, *My Blue Notebooks*, trans. Diana Athill (New York: Harper & Row, 1979), 49.

18 Lenard R. Berlanstein, *Daughters of Eve: A Cultural History of French Theater Women from the Old Regime to the Fin de Siècle* (Cambridge: Harvard University Press, 2001), 123; Virginia Rounding, *Grandes Horizontales: The Lives and Legends of Marie Duplessis, Cora Pearl, La Païva and La Présidente* (London: Bloomsbury,

2003), 130; Nina Kushner, *Erotic Exchanges: The World of Elite Prostitution in Eighteenth-Century Paris* (Ithaca: Cornell University Press, 2013); Courtney Ann Sullivan, "Classification, Containment, Contamination, and the Courtesan: The Grisette, Lorette, and Demi-Mondaine in Nineteenth-Century French Fiction" (PhD diss., University of Texas, Austin, 2008), http://hdl.handle.net/2152/982.

19 Catherine Guigon, *Les Cocottes: Reines du Paris 1900* (Paris: Parigramme, 2012), 78; Clayson, *Painted Love*, 63; Freundschuh, *Courtesan and the Gigolo*, 90; Sullivan, "Classification, Containment, Contamination"; Bernheimer, *Figures of Ill Repute*.

20 Quoted in Vandérem, "Le Programme de Bayonne," *Le Figaro*, November 9, 1909, 1.

21 Gonzalez-Quijano, *Capitale de l'amour*, 49–51.

22 Sohn, "Golden Age of Male Adultery"; Plott, "Rules of the Game"; Lela F. Kerley, *Uncovering Paris: Scandals and Nude Spectacles in the Belle Époque* (Baton Rouge: LSU Press, 2017), 7.

23 Pringué, *30 Ans*, 26.

24 Pringué, *30 Ans*, 27; Martin, *Crime and Criminal Justice*, 192, 195.

25 Sylvia Schafer, *Children in Moral Danger and the Problem of Government in Third Republic France* (Princeton: Princeton University Press, 1997), 9–11.

26 Letter from the premier president, Cour d'appel d'Aix, to the Garde des Sceaux, Ministre de la Justice, March 9, 1886, BB/6(II)/668, AN.

27 Plott, "Rules of the Game," 552–53.

28 Harsin, *Policing Prostitution*, 323–57.

29 Martin, *Crime and Criminal Justice*, 51.

30 Judith Surkis, *Sex, Law, and Sovereignty in French Algeria, 1830–1930* (Ithaca: Cornell University Press, 2019), 153; Orval, *Usages mondains*, 183; Plott, "Rules of the Game."

31 Steinheil, *Memoirs*, 40.

CHAPTER 6

1 Tavernier, *Madame Steinheil*, 84; Memo to the Prefect of Police, June 1, 1908, BA 1584, APP.

2 Steinheil, *Memoirs*, 70–71; Emile-Auguste-François-Thomas Zurlinden, *Mes Souvenirs depuis la guerre: 1871–1901* (Paris: Perrin, 1913), 141.

3 "L'Affaire Steinheil," *La Libre Parole*, November 9, 1908, 1; Billard, *Faure*, 294.

4 Steinheil, *Memoirs*, 71.

5   Steinheil, 71.

6   Steinheil, 71.

7   Zurlinden, *Mes Souvenirs*, 142.

8   Steinheil, *Memoirs*, 71.

9   Steinheil, 71.

10   Martin, *Hypocrisy of Justice*, 19; Pierre Darmon, *Marguerite Steinheil, ingénue criminelle?* (Paris: Perrin, 1996), 9.

11   Guy Saigne, *Léon Bonnat: Le portraitiste de la IIIe République* (Paris: Mare & Martin Editions, 2017), 165–66.

12   Billard, *Faure*, 515.

13   Charles Braibant, ed., *Félix Faure à l'Élyseé: Souvenirs de Louis Le Gall* (Paris: Hachette, 1963), 11, 226; Dudley, *Scarlett Widow*, 22; Martin-Fugier, *Salons de la IIIe République*, 95; Billard, *Faure*, 294.

14   Billard, *Faure*, 294, 500, 527, 903, 909.

15   Jean-Denis Bredin, *The Affair: The Case of Alfred Dreyfus*, trans. Jeffrey Mehlman (New York: G. Braziller, 1986), 395.

16   Steinheil, *Memoirs*, 80.

17   Avner Ben-Amos, *Funerals, Politics, and Memory in Modern France, 1789–1996* (Oxford: Oxford University Press, 2005), 197.

18   Tracy Adams and Christine Adams, *The Creation of the French Royal Mistress: From Agnès Sorel to Madame Du Barry* (University Park: Penn State University Press, 2020), 1; Marie Colombier, *Mémoires: Fin de siècle* (Paris: Ernest Flammarion, 1899), 122–23.

19   Billard, *Faure*, 902–3.

20   Braibant, *Félix Faure*, 24.

21   Quoted in Bredin, *Affair*, 200.

22   Quoted in Billard, *Faure*, 909–10.

23   Billard, *Faure*, 910; Paléologue, *Intimate Journal*, 204.

24   Steinheil, *Memoirs*, 116–17.

25   Paléologue, *Intimate Journal*, 204.

26   Dudley, *Scarlett Widow*, 24.

27   Steinheil, *Memoirs*, 89–90.

28   Steinheil, 77.

29   Steinheil, 75–76.

30 "Mme Steinheil est incarcérée à la prison de Saint-Lazare," *Le Petit Journal*, November 28, 1908, 1.

31 Certificat d'inscription, Édouard Charles Adolphe Steinheil, July 25, 1898, LH/2549/12, Grande Chancellerie de la Légion d'honneur, AN.

32 "L'Affaire Steinheil," *La Libre Parole*, December 6, 1908, 2.

33 Cover sheet, BB/6(II)/1008, dossier on Georges Leloir, Ministère de la Justice, Cours et tribunaux, Dossiers personnels de magistrats, AN.

34 "Nos Échos," *L'Intransigeant*, December 4, 1908, 2.

35 Steinheil, *Memoirs*, 76.

36 Robert de Jouvenel, *La République des camarades* (Paris: Bernard Grasset, Éditeur, 1914).

37 Steinheil, *Memoirs*, 77.

38 "Propos d'un parisien," *Le Matin*, December 13, 1908, 1; see also Christine Adams, "'Venus of the Capitol': Madame Tallien and the Politics of Beauty Under the Directory," *French Historical* Studies 37, no. 4 (October 2014): 603.

39 Madeleine Pelletier, *La Femme vierge* (Paris: Indigo & Coté-femmes éditions, 1996), 65.

40 Adams and Adams, *Creation of the French Royal Mistress*; Karen Offen, *The Woman Question in France, 1400–1870* (Cambridge: Cambridge University Press, 2019), 31–32.

41 Adams and Adams, *Creation of the French Royal Mistress*, 14.

42 Steinheil, *Memoirs*, 76; Lanoux, *Madame Steinheil*, 151; Kalifa, *Paris: Une histoire érotique*, 54.

43 "L'Affaire Steinheil," *L'Action française*, November 28, 1908, 2.

44 Luc Boltanski, *Mysteries and Conspiracies: Detective Stories, Spy Novels and the Making of Modern Societies*, trans. Catherine Porter (Cambridge: Polity Press, 2014), 111.

45 "Les Étrangleurs de Vaugirard," *Le Petit Journal*, June 3, 1908, 2.

46 "Félix Faure et Mme Steinheil," *La Libre Parole*, December 1, 1908, 1.

47 Images of sex workers and sexually available women with open-mouthed slides can be found in Nienke Bakker, *Splendeurs & misères: Images de la prostitution, 1850–1910* (Paris: Flammarion, 2015), 76, 95, 112, 141, 190, 197, 271, 273.

48 Myriam Tsikounas, "Marguerite Steinheil," Histoire par l'image, October 2011, http://www.histoire-image.org/de/etudes/marguerite-steinheil; Saigne, *Bonnat*, 155.

CHAPTER 7

1   "La Temperature," *Le Temps*, February 17, 1899, 3.

2   Saigne, *Bonnat*, 583.

3   Quoted in Dudley, *Scarlett Widow*, 29.

4   Paléologue, *Intimate Journal*, 204.

5   Quoted in Dudley, *Scarlett Widow*, 29.

6   Dudley, *Scarlett Widow*, 29–30.

7   Louis Le Gall, *Félix Faure à l'Élyseé. Souvenirs de Louis Le Gall*, ed. Charles Braibant (Paris: Hachette, 1963), 249.

8   Paléologue, *Intimate Journal*, 204–5.

9   Martin, *Hypocrisy of Justice*, 19.

10 "Les Minutes tragiques," *L'Intransigeant*, December 6, 1908, 1.

11 Billard, *Faure*, 7–16; Christophe Deloire and Christophe Dubois, *Sexus politicus* (Paris: Albin Michel, 2006), 212.

12 Dudley, *Scarlett Widow*, 28.

13 "Mort de Félix Faure," *Le Petit Journal*, February 26, 1899, 7.

14 Memo to the Prefect of Police, November 27, 1908, BA 1584, APP.

15 "Mort de Félix Faure," *Gil Blas*, February 17, 1899, 1.

16 E. Janvoin, "La Vérité sur la mort de Félix Faure," *Le Journal du Peuple*, February 23, 1898, 2.

17 Quoted in Dudley, *Scarlett Widow*, 28.

18 Steinheil, *Memoirs*, 117.

19 Steinheil, 116.

20 "Le Crime de l'impasse Ronsin," *Le Temps*, November 28, 1908, 2.

21 Saigne, *Bonnat*, 583; "L'Affaire Steinheil," *Le Matin*, November 28, 1908, 3.

22 Berlanstein, *Daughters of Eve*, 195.

23 Darmon, *Marguerite Steinheil*, 49.

24 Berlanstein, *Daughters of Eve*.

25 Darmon, *Marguerite Steinheil*, 49.

CHAPTER 8

1   Steinheil, *Memoirs*, 130.

2   Steinheil, 130.

3   Steinheil, 131.

4   "L'Affaire Steinheil," *Le Petit Journal*, November 7, 1909, 3.

5   Rapport, March 1, 1909, JA 11, APP.

6   Ari Adut, *On Scandal: Moral Disturbances in Society, Politics, and Art* (Cambridge: Cambridge University Press, 2008), 24–31.

7   "L'Affaire Steinheil," *Le Journal*, January 2, 1909, 2.

8   "Les Dessous de l'affaire Steinheil," *L'Intransigeant*, November 29, 1908, 3rd ed., 1.

9   "Les Dessous de l'affaire Steinheil," *L'Intransigeant*, November 29, 1908, 3rd ed., 1.

10 "L'Affaire Steinheil," *Le Matin*, December 21, 1908, 2.

11 "Comment Mme Steinheil a vécu," *Le Petit Journal*, November 3, 1909, 1.

12 Sohn, *Du premier baiser à l'alcôve*, 96–97; *The Pretty Women of Paris: Their Names and Addresses, Qualities and Faults, Being a Complete Directory or Guide to Pleasure for Visitors to the Gay City* (Ware: Wordsworth Editions, 1996), 14, 50, 64, 82.

13 Leonore Davidoff, "Class and Gender in Victorian England: The Diaries of Arthur J. Munby and Hannah Cullwick," *Feminist Studies* 5, no. 1 (1979): 87–141.

14 Robin Mitchell, *Vénus Noire: Black Women and Colonial Fantasies in Nineteenth-Century France* (Athens: University of Georgia Press, 2020); Sabrina Strings, *Fearing the Black Body: The Racial Origins of Fat Phobia* (New York: NYU Press, 2019).

15 Bram Dijkstra, *Idols of Perversity: Fantasies of Feminine Evil in Fin-de-Siècle Culture* (New York: Oxford University Press, 1986).

16 Lanoux, *Madame Steinheil*, 168–70.

17 "Le Crime de l'impasse Ronsin," *Le Temps*, December 21, 1908, 3.

18 "L'Affaire Steinheil," *La Libre Parole*, December 1, 1908, 1.

19 "L'Affaire Steinheil au Palais-Bourbon," *La Croix*, November 28, 1908, 2.

20 "Chez M. Martin-Feuillée," *Le Matin*, November 4, 1909, 4.

21 Rapport, February 23, 1909, JA 13, APP.

22 "L'Affaire Steinheil," *Le Matin*, December 18, 1908, 2; Cabinet de M Andre Copie, Commission rogatoire, JA 14, APP.

23 Rapport, March 1, 1909, JA 11, APP.

CHAPTER 9

1   "Quelques clartés dans les ténèbres," *Le Journal*, November 29, 1908, 1; "Le Mystère Steinheil," *L'Humanité*, November 30, 1908, 2.

2   Steinheil, *Memoirs*, 132.

3   "Interrogatoire de Mme Steinheil," *Le Journal*, November 4, 1909, 5.

4   Procès-verbal du February 5, 1909, JA 14, APP; "Interrogatoire de Mme Steinheil," *Le Journal*, November 4, 1909, 5.

5   "Interrogatoire de Mme Steinheil," *Le Journal*, November 4, 1909, 6.

6   "Mme Steinheil devant le jury de la Seine," *Le Petit Journal*, November 4, 1909, 3.

7   "Autour de 'l'ami de Mme Steinheil,'" *Le Petit Journal*, November 28, 1908, 1.

8   "Interrogatoire de Mme Steinheil," *Le Journal*, November 4, 1909, 6

9   Freundschuh, *Courtesan and the Gigolo*, 72–73.

10   "Interrogatoire de Mme Steinheil," *Le Journal*, November 4, 1909, 6.

11   "Interrogatoire de Mme Steinheil," *Le Journal*, November 4, 1909, 6.

12   "Quelques clartés dans les ténèbres," *Le Journal*, November 29, 1908, 1.

13   Steinheil, *Memoirs*, 136, 209.

14   Dossier Caisse d'Epargne postale and Rapport, Paris, December 19, 1908, JA 11, APP; "L'Affaire Steinheil," *Le Petit Journal*, February 7, 1909, 4.

15   "L'Enquête continue…," *Le Petit Journal*, December 5, 1908, 1; Louis Latzarus, "Préparatifs de débats," *Le Figaro*, November 3, 1909, 4; Martin-Fugier, *Bourgeoise*, 62–63.

16   Jean de Paris, "Le Drame de l'impasse Ronsin," *Le Figaro*, December 4, 1908, 4; Jean de Paris, "Le Drame de l'impasse Ronsin," *Le Figaro*, December 5, 1908, 3.

17   Dossier Caisse d'Epargne postale, JA 11, APP.

18   "L'Affaire Steinheil," *Le Journal*, November 7, 1908, 4.

19   Rapport, December 18, 1908, JA 14, APP.

20   "L'Affaire Steinheil," *Le Petit Journal*, December 19, 1908, 3; see also Mariette's testimony on "Histoire de Mme Steinheil par Mariette Wolff," *Le Matin*, December 1, 1908, 1.

21   "L'Affaire Steinheil," *L'Action française*, November 28, 1908, 2; "Le Mystère Steinheil," *L'Humanité*, November 30, 1908, 2.

22   "L'Affaire Steinheil," *Le Petit Journal*, December 5, 1908, 3.

23   "L'Affaire Steinheil," *Le Petit Journal*, February 7, 1909, 4.

24   Darmon, *Marguerite Steinheil*, 57–58.

25   "L'Affaire Steinheil," *Le Journal*, January 2, 1909, 2.

26   "Mme Steinheil se dit innocente," *Le Journal*, December 2, 1908, 1.

27 Sohn, *Du premier baiser à l'alcôve*, 89.

28 "Mme Steinheil se dit innocente," *Le Journal*, December 2, 1908, 1.

29 Uzanne, *Parisiennes de ce temps*, 413–14; Kalifa, *Paris: Une histoire érotique*; Gonzalez-Quijano, *Capitale de l'amour*; Ross, *Public City*.

30 Uzanne, *Parisiennes de ce temps*, 23.

31 Edmond Locard, *Le Crime et les criminels* (Paris: La Renaissance du livre, 1925), 240.

32 "Mme Steinheil devant le jury de la Seine," *Le Petit Journal*, November 4, 1909, 3; Rapport, July 18, 1908, in dossier on Dominique-Marie-Joseph de Balincourt, JA 13, APP.

33 "Mme Steinheil devant le jury de la Seine," *Le Petit Journal*, November 4, 1909, 3; Rapport, July 18, 1908, in dossier on Dominique-Marie-Joseph de Balincourt, JA 13, APP.

34 Rapport, December 9, in dossier Dominique-Marie-Joseph de Balincourt, JA 13, APP.

35 Memo from December 4, 1908, in dossier on Dominique-Marie-Joseph de Balincourt, JA 13, APP.

36 "La Confession d'un amant," *L'Intransigeant*, January 25, 1909.

37 "Histoire de Mme Steinheil par Mariette Wolff," *Le Matin*, December 1, 1908, 1.

38 Berlanstein, *Daughters of Eve*, 99–100.

39 "Mme Steinheil est bien une criminelle," *Le Petit Journal*, November 29, 1908, 1.

40 "Mme Steinheil est bien une criminelle," *Le Petit Journal*, November 29, 1908, 1.

41 "Mme Steinheil est bien une criminelle," *Le Petit Journal*, November 29, 1908, 1.

42 "Mme Steinheil est bien une criminelle," *Le Petit Journal*, November 29, 1908, 1.

43 "L'Affaire Steinheil," *Le Matin*, November 28, 1908, 3.

44 "Mme Steinheil est bien une criminelle," *Le Petit Journal*, November 29, 1908, 1; "L'Interrogatoire de Mme Steinheil" *Le Radical*, December 2, 1908, 2.

45 "Mme Steinheil est bien une criminelle," *Le Petit Journal*, November 29, 1908, 1.

46 "Les Importantes Dépositions d'hier," *Le Petit Journal*, December 1, 1908, 1.

47 "L'Affaire Steinheil," *Le Matin*, November 28, 1908, 3.

48 "Interrogatoire de Mme Steinheil," *Le Journal*, November 4, 1909, 4.

49 "La Veuve aurait eu un complice," *Le Petit Journal*, March 10, 1909, 3; "Quelques clartés dans les ténèbres," *Le Journal*, November 29, 1908, 1.

50 Montal, *Affaire Steinheil*, 35.

51 Rapport, December 14, 1908, JA 14, APP.

52 "Interrogatoire de Mme Steinheil," *Le Journal*, November 4, 1909, 4; Darmon, *Marguerite Steinheil*, 56–57.

53 "Vers le dénouement," *Le Petit Parisien*, November 13, 1909, 1.

PART 2

1 "Le Plus horrible des crimes mais surtout le plus étrange," *Le Matin*, June 2, 1908, 1.

CHAPTER 10

1 Rapport, February 18, 1909, JA 11, APP; "Conversation avec Mme Herr," *Le Journal*, March 9, 1909, 1.

2 "La Nuit tragique," *Le Journal*, November 5, 1909, 6.

3 "Interrogatoire de Mme Steinheil," *Le Journal*, 4 November 1909, 1–2, 4–6.

4 "La Journée de Rémy Couillard," *Le Journal*, November 11, 1909, 1. Except when otherwise noted, the account of the crime is from Lanoux, *Madame Steinheil*; Darmon, *Marguerite Steinheil*; Martin, *Hypocrisy of Justice*; Rapport, February 18, 1909, JA 11, APP.

5 Frédéric Delacourt, *L'Affaire Steinheil* (Paris: De Vecchi, 2006), 12; Steinheil, *Memoirs*, 174–75.

6 "L'Interrogatoire a pris fin sur une scène dramatique," *Le Journal*, November 6, 1909, 8.

7 Delacourt, *Affaire Steinheil*, 11.

8 Delacourt, *Affaire Steinheil*, 11.

9 Simon Cole, *Suspect Identities: A History of Fingerprinting and Criminal Identification* (Cambridge: Harvard University Press, 2001), 32–59.

10 "L'Affaire Steinheil," *Le Figaro*, November 7, 1909, 2.

11 Lela Graybill, "The Forensic Eye and the Public Mind: The Bertillon System of Crime Scene Photography," *Cultural History* 8, no. 1 (March 20, 2019): 96.

12 Steinheil, *Memoirs*, 173.

13 "Nuit d'épouvante de crime et de mystère," *Le Matin*, June 1, 1908, 1.

14 "Mme Steinheil parle," *L'Intransigeant*, June 2, 1908, 1.

15 Impasse Roncin [*sic*] 6 bis, May 31, 1908, JA 14, APP; "Nuit d'épouvante de crime et de mystère," *Le Matin*, June 1, 1908, 1.

16 Impasse Roncin [*sic*] 6 bis, May 31, 1908, JA 14, APP; "Nuit d'épouvante de crime et de mystère," *Le Matin*, June 1, 1908, 1.

17 Martin, *Hypocrisy of Justice*, 37, 41; Service de l'identité judiciaire de la préfecture de Police de Paris, "Affaire Steinheil."

18 Flyer from Agence Azur, June 15, 1908, F7 14665, Affaire Steinheil, Police Générale, AN; Martin, *Hypocrisy of Justice*, 27; Darmon, *Marguerite Steinheil*, 11–16.

19 Martin, *Hypocrisy of Justice*, 37; Service de l'identité judiciaire de la préfecture de Police de Paris, "Affaire Steinheil."

20 Delacourt, *Affaire Steinheil*, 14.

21 Martin, *Hypocrisy of Justice*, 27; Darmon, *Madame Steinheil*, 11–16.

22 Service de l'identité judiciaire de la préfecture de Police de Paris, "Affaire Steinheil."

23 Martin, *Hypocrisy of Justice*, 37.

24 Martin, *Hypocrisy of Justice*, 28.

25 Darmon, *Marguerite Steinheil*, 11.

26 Delacourt, *Affaire Steinheil*, 23.

27 Delacourt, *Affaire Steinheil*, 23.

28 Martin, *Hypocrisy of Justice*, 75.

29 "La Nuit tragique," *Le Matin*, November 4, 1908, 1.

30 "La Mystérieuse Tragédie de l'impasse Ronsin," *Le Petit Journal*, June 2, 1908, 1.

31 "Vers le dénouement," *Le Petit Parisien*, November 13, 1909, 1.

CHAPTER II

1 Memo to the Prefect of Police, December 12, 1908, BA 1585, APP; "Pour retrouver les assassins," *Le Petit Parisien*, April 11, 1909, 118; "Mme Steinheil est bien une criminelle," *Le Petit Journal*, November 29, 1908, 1.

2 Martin, *Hypocrisy of Justice*, 59–60.

3 "Les Derniers Témoins—le réquisitoire," *Le Journal*, November 12, 1909, 1.

4 Lindsay Steenberg, *Forensic Science in Contemporary American Popular Culture: Gender, Crime, and Science* (London: Routledge, 2013), 35; Lanoux, *Madame Steinheil*, 312.

5 Locard, *Crime et les criminels*, 241.

6 Armand Lanoux, "Meg Steinheil était bien innocente," *Paris-Presse, L'Intransigeant*, December 28, 1955, 12 (emphasis in original).

7 Locard, *Crime et les criminels*, 241; Lanoux, *Madame Steinheil*, 312, 315.

8 Delacourt, *Affaire Steinheil*, 135.

9 Locard, *Crime et les criminels*, 241.

10   Lanoux, "Meg Steinheil était bien innocente," 12.

11   Martin, Hypocrisy of Justice, 75; "La Question d'argent," *Le Petit Parisien*, December 5, 1908, 1; Procès Verbal, December 20, 1908, JA 11, APP.

12   "Le Mystère Steinheil," *L'Humanité*, November 30, 1908, 2.

13   "Mauvaise Journée pour Mme Steinheil," *Le Matin*, November 10, 1909, 4.

14   Georges Bourdon, "Comme à l'impasse Ronsin," *Le Figaro*, January 13, 1909, 1–2; Georges Bourdon, "Comme à l'impasse Ronsin," *Le Figaro*, January 14, 1909, 2–3.

15   Louis Ulbach, *Les Cinq Doigts de Birouk* (Paris: Michel Lévy frères, 1875), 308–20; Martin, *Hypocrisy of Justice*, 49.

16   Dominique Kalifa, *L'Encre et le sang: Récit de crimes et société à la Belle Époque* (France: Fayard, 1995), 140.

17   Elizabeth Wilson, *Bohemians: The Glamorous Outcasts* (New Brunswick: Rutgers University Press, 2000), 24; Jerrold E. Seigel, *Bohemian Paris: Culture, Politics, and the Boundaries of Bourgeois Life, 1830–1930* (New York: Viking, 1986), 4–5.

18   William A. Peniston, *Pederasts and Others: Urban Culture and Sexual Identity in Nineteenth-Century Paris* (New York: Harrington Park Press, 2004), 2.

19   "Les Cambrioleurs de Vaugirard demeurent insaisisables," *L'Intransigeant*, June 6, 1908, 2.

20   Rosario, *Erotic Imagination*; Nye, *Masculinity*, 107.

CHAPTER 12

1   Kalifa, *Encre et le sang*; Robert Nye, "Two Capital Punishment Debates in France: 1908 and 1981," *Historical Reflections/Réflexions Historiques* 29, no. 2 (July 1, 2003): 211–28.

2   "Le Triomphe de Sherlock Holmes," *L'Humanité*, June 8, 1908, 2; Arthur Dupin, "On les a vu," *Le Journal*, June 7, 1908, 1–2; Léon Daudet, "Crime politique ou crime crapuleux?," *L'Action française*, June 10, 1908, 1; "L'Assassinat du peintre Steinheil et de sa belle-mère Mme veuve Japy," *Le Figaro*, June 1, 1908, 2.

3   Martin, *Crime and Criminal Justice*, 76; Thierry Saint-Joanis, "Sherlock Holmes et la France: Un amour réciproque," in *Sherlock Holmes et la France: Une étude en bleu, blanc, rouge*, ed. Société Sherlock Holmes de France (Paris: Bibliothèque des littératures policières, 1996), 4–9.

4   Martin, *Crime and Criminal Justice*, 61, 76.

5   Quoted in Martin, *Crime and Criminal Justice*, 51.

6 Martin, *Crime and Criminal Justice*, 142–45; Adut, *On Scandal*, 143.

7 Benjamin F. Martin, "The Courts, the Magistrature, and Promotions in Third Republic France, 1871–1914," *American Historical Review* 87, no. 4 (1982): 989.

8 "Notice du Président et du Procureur," July 31, 1907, BB/6(II)/1025, dossier on Félix-Pierre-Joseph Leydet, Ministère de la Justice, Cours et tribunaux, Dossiers personnels de magistrats, AN.

9 Martin, *Crime and Criminal Justice*, 208.

10 "Remise du dossier de l'affaire Ullmo. Remerciements addressés à M. le juge de l'instruction Leydet," December 18, 1908, BB/6(II)/1025, AN; Martin, *Crime and Criminal Justice*, 76, 42–43, 50–51.

11 Léon Daudet, "Crime politique ou crime crapuleux?," *L'Action française*, June 10, 1908, 1.

12 Steinheil, *Memoirs*, 180.

13 Memos to the Prefect of Police, November 24 and December 2, 1908, BA 1585, APP; Édouard Bernaert, "L'Affaire Steinheil," *L'Action française*, January 13, 1909, 2; "Après l'arrestation de Mme Steinheil," *L'Humanité*, November 28, 1908, 1.

14 Georges Berry, "Justice égale pour tous!," *L'Intransigeant*, November 9, 1909, 1.

15 Steinheil, *Memoirs*, 180.

16 Vanessa R. Schwartz, *Spectacular Realities: Early Mass Culture in Fin-de-Siècle Paris* (Berkeley: University of California Press, 1998).

17 "Un Nouveau Récit de Mme Steinheil," *Le Journal*, June 2, 1908, 1.

18 Lisa Downing, *The Subject of Murder: Gender, Exceptionality, and the Modern Killer* (Chicago: University of Chicago Press, 2013); Berenson, *Trial of Madame Caillaux*, 100–132.

19 "La Tragédie de l'impasse Ronsin," *L'Écho de Paris*, June 2, 1908, 1.

20 Dominique Kalifa, *Les Bas-fonds: Histoire d'un imaginaire* (Paris: Seuil, 2013).

21 Isidore Alauzet, *Essai sur les peines et le système pénitentiaire*, 2nd ed. (Paris: Cosse et Marchal, 1863), 261; Stephen Toth, *Mettray: A History of France's Most Venerated Carceral Institution* (Ithaca: Cornell University Press, 2019), 18–19.

22 "Mme Steinheil parle," *L'Intransigeant*, June 2, 1908, 1.

23 Quoted in Michelle Perrot, "Dans la France de la Belle Époque, les 'apaches,' premières bandes de jeunes," in *Les Marginaux et les exclus dans l'histoire* (Paris: Union générale d'éditions, 1979), 395. See also Louis Chevalier, *Classes laborieuses et classes dangereuses à Paris pendant la première moitié du XIXe siècle*

(Paris: Plon, 1958); Kalifa, *Bas-fonds*; James Cannon, *The Paris Zone: A Cultural History, 1840–1944* (Farnham: Ashgate, 2015), 31–76, 81, 88; Locard, *Crime et les criminels*, 19–21; Robert A. Nye, *Crime, Madness and Politics in Modern France: The Medical Concept of National Decline* (Princeton: Princeton University Press, 1984).

24 Ann Laura Stoler, *Race and the Education of Desire: Foucault's History of Sexuality and the Colonial Order of Things* (Durham: Duke University Press, 1995).

25 "Les Affirmations de M. Hamard," *L'Humanité*, June 7, 1908, 2; "Un peu plus de lumière," *Le Matin*, June 6, 1908, 1.

26 A sampling of rumors from the time can be found in memos to the Prefect of Police, BA 1584, APP.

27 "Échos," *L'Action française*, June 4, 1908, 1.

28 For comparison, see "Les Soupçons se précisent," *Le Matin*, June 11, 1908, 1–2.

29 Steinheil, *Memoirs*, 209–10.

30 Rapport, June 13, 1908, JA 12, APP.

31 Jennifer Sessions, *By Sword and Plow: France and the Conquest of Algeria* (Ithaca: Cornell University Press, 2011), 235.

32 Rapport, June 13, 1908, JA 12, APP.

33 Rapport, June 13, 1908, JA 12, APP; "L'Affaire Steinheil," *Le Matin*, July 7, 1908, 2; "La Tragédie de Vaugirard," July 8, 1908, *Le Matin*, 1–2; "Interrogatoire de Mme Steinheil," *Le Journal*, November 4, 1909, 2.

34 Some of this amateur detection can be gleaned from anonymous letters to the police in JA 13, APP.

35 Interview of Georges Émile Félix Perriot, January 25, 1909, and interview with Louis Marie Camille Perriot; Rapport, December 14, 1908, JA 13, APP.

36 "Assassinat du peintre Steinheil," *Le Figaro*, June 2, 1908, 1.

37 "Le Triomphe de Sherlock Holmes," *L'Humanité*, June 8, 1908, 2.

38 "La Tragedie de Vaugirard," *Le Matin*, July 10, 1908, 1.

CHAPTER 13

1 Rapport general to Monsieur Leydet, juge d'instruction, September 16, 1908, JA 11, APP.

2 Rapport general to Monsieur Leydet, juge d'instruction, September 16, 1908, JA 11, APP

3   Dorothy Hoobler, *The Crimes of Paris: A True Story of Murder, Theft, and Detection* (New York: Little, Brown, 2009), vii; Seigel, Bohemian Paris, 339–41.

4   Rapport general to Monsieur Leydet, juge d'instruction, September 16, 1908, JA 11, APP.

5   Rapport general to Monsieur Leydet, juge d'instruction, September 16, 1908, JA 11, APP; Rapport, July 18, 1908, in dossier on Dominique-Marie-Joseph de Balincourt, JA 13, APP.

6   Steinheil, *Memoirs*, 208.

7   Steinheil, 187–88 (ellipses in original).

8   Letter from the procureur général to Garde de Sceaux, November 30, 1908, Ministère de la Justice, BB/18/2369, Correspondance générale de la division criminelle, AN.

9   Steinheil, *Memoirs*, 209–10, 227.

10   Steinheil, *Memoirs*, 207 (ellipsis in original).

11   Procureur général to Garde des Sceaux, November 30, 1908, BB/18/2369, AN.

12   Steinheil, *Memoirs*, 193.

13   Steinheil, *Memoirs*, 193.

14   Steinheil, *Memoirs*, 193; Pouce to I Iamard, Rapport, June 19, 1908, JA 12, APP.

15   Steinheil, Memoirs, 193.

16   Pouce to Hamard, Rapport, June 19, 1908, JA 12, APP.

17   Pouce to Hamard, Rapport, June 19, 1908, JA 12, APP; D'un correspondant, November 14, 1908, F7 14665, Affaire Steinheil, Police Générale, AN.

18   Pouce to Hamard, Rapport, June 19, 1908, JA 12, APP; D'un correspondant, November 14, 1908, F7 14665, Affaire Steinheil, Police Générale, AN.

19   Gilman, *Difference and Pathology*, 131–62.

20   "Le Mystère Steinheil," *Le Matin*, November 12, 1908, 2; Steinheil, *Memoirs*, 217.

21   Reconnaissance de Burlingham, September 16, 1908, JA 12, APP; Reconnaissance de Davidson par Mme Steinheil, September 21 and 22, 1908, JA 12, APP.

22   Rapport, October 2, 1908, JA 12, APP.

23   Rapport, October 30, 1908, JA 12, APP; Rapport, October 29, 1908, JA 12, APP.

24   "Le Défilé des témoins continue," *Le Matin*, November 9, 1909, 6.

CHAPTER 14

1   "L'Affaire Steinheil," *Le Matin*, November 1, 1908, 2.

2   Steinheil, *Memoirs*, 214.

3   "Interrogatoire de Mme Steinheil," *Le Journal*, November 4, 1909, 5.

4   "Le Crime de l'impasse Ronsin," *Le Temps*, November 28, 1908, 2.

5   Steinheil, *Memoirs*, 214.

6   Steinheil, 220–21 (ellipses in original).

7   Procureur général près la cour d'appel de Paris to Garde des Sceaux, Ministre de la Justice, Paris, November 30, 1908, BB/18/2369, AN.

8   Steinheil, *Memoirs*, 226.

9   Procureur general to Garde de Sceaux, November 30, 1908, BB/18/2369, AN.

10   Judith Lyon-Caen, "Lecteurs et lectures: les usages de la presse au XIXe siècle," in *La Civilisation du journal: Histoire culturelle et littéraire de la presse française au XIXe siècle*, ed. Dominique Kalifa et al. (Paris: Nouveau monde, 2011), 24–26; Vincent Robert, "Périodiser: Paysages politiques, cohérences médiatiques," in Kalifa et al., Civilisation du journal, 264.

11   Jean-Marie Seillan, "L'Interview," n Kalifa et al., *Civilisation du journal*, 1034–36; Dominique Kalifa, "L'Envers fantasmé du quotidien," in Kalifa et al., *Civilisation du journal*, 1330–31.

12   Marcel Hutin, "Mme Steinheil croit avoir découvert la piste des assassins de sa mère et de son mari," *L'Écho de Paris*, October 31, 1908, 1 (ellipsis and emphasis in original).

13   Steinheil, *Memoirs*, 229.

14   "Sur la piste," *Le Matin*, November 3, 1908, 1.

15   "Mme Steinheil précise ses accusations," *Le Petit Journal*, November 4, 1908, 1.

16   Gérard Noiriel, *Immigration, antisémitisme et racisme en France, XIXe–XXe siècle: Discours publics, humiliations privées* (Paris: Fayard, 2007), 216–31; Stephen Wilson, *Ideology and Experience: Antisemitism in France at the Time of the Dreyfus Affair* (Rutherford: Fairleigh Dickinson University Press, 1982), 456–508.

17   "Le Secte," *La Libre Parole*, November 6, 1908, 1.

18   "Le Mystère Steinheil," *Le Matin*, November 5, 1908, 1–2.

19   "Le Mystère Steinheil," *Le Matin*, November 11, 1908, 1–2.

20   "Le Mystère Steinheil," *Le Matin*, November 11, 1908, 1–2 (ellipses in original).

21   "La Nuit tragique," *Le Matin*, November 4, 1908, 1; "Le Mystère Steinheil," *Le Matin*, November 12, 1908, 1.

22   "Le Mystère Steinheil," *Le Matin*, November 13, 1908, 2.

23   Steinheil, *Memoirs*, 231.

24   Rapport, January 18, 1909, JA 13, APP.

25   "Interrogatoire de Mme Steinheil," *Le Journal*, November 4, 1909, 5.

26   Déclarations de M. Chabrier, November 20, 1908, JA 11, APP.

27   Déclarations de M. Chabrier, November 20, 1908, JA 11, APP.

28   "Coup de théâtre," *Le Matin*, November 21, 1908, 1.

29   Martin, *Hypocrisy of Justice*, 31.

30   "Extrait des registres des actes de naissance de la commune de Cluis," 603 AP 5, Affaire Rémy Couillard, Fonds Géraud, AN; "L'Affaire Steinheil," *Le Matin*, November 23, 1908, 2.

31   "Après l'arrestation de Rémy Couillard," *Le Petit Journal*, November 23, 1908, 1.

32   "L'Affaire Steinheil," *Le Matin*, November 22, 1908, 2.

33   "Les Bijoutiers et les journalistes," *Le Journal*, November 10, 1909, 2.

34   "L'Affaire Steinheil," *Le Matin*, November 22, 1908, 1–2; "L'Affaire Steinheil," *Le Matin*, November 23, 1908, 1–2; "L'Affaire Steinheil," *Le Matin*, November 24, 1908, 1–2; "L'Affaire Steinheil," *Le Matin*, November 25, 1908, 1–2.

35   Gilles Feyel, *La Presse en France des origines à 1944: Histoire politique et matérielle* (Paris: Ellipses, 1999), 123-7.

36   "L'Affaire Steinheil," *Le Matin*, November 25, 1908, 1–2.

37   "Journée fâcheuse pour Mme Steinheil," *Le Petit Journal*, November 26, 1908, 3.

38   "Journée fâcheuse pour Mme Steinheil," *Le Petit Journal*, November 26, 1908, 1.

39   "Journée fâcheuse pour Mme Steinheil," *Le Petit Journal*, November 26, 1908, 1.

40   "Journée fâcheuse pour Mme Steinheil," *Le Petit Journal*, November 26, 1908, 1.

41   "Journée fâcheuse pour Mme Steinheil," *Le Petit Journal*, November 26, 1908, 1.

42   "On accuse Mme Steinheil," *Le Journal*, November 26, 1908, 1.

43   "On accuse Mme Steinheil," *Le Journal*, November 26, 1908, 1.

44   Timothy Verhoeven, *Sexual Crime, Religion and Masculinity in Fin-de-Siècle France: The Flamidien Affair* (Basingstoke: Palgrave Macmillan, 2019), 38.

45   "On accuse Mme Steinheil," *Le Journal*, November 26, 1908, 1.

46   "Les Dénigations de Mme Steinheil," *Le Petit Journal*, November 26, 1908, 3.

47   "Les Dénigations de Mme Steinheil," *Le Petit Journal*, November 26, 1908, 3.

CHAPTER 15

1   "Les Bijoutiers et les journalistes," *Le Journal*, November 10, 1909, 2.

2   Marcel Hutin, "Mme Steinheil avoue," *L'Écho de Paris*, November 26, 1908.

3   Steinheil, *Memoirs*, 277.

4   "Aveux de Madame Steinheil," *Le Matin*, November 26, 1908, 1.

5   "Aveux de Madame Steinheil," *Le Matin*, November 26, 1908, 1.

6   "Mme Steinheil en cour d'assises," *L'Echo de Paris*, November 10, 1909, 2.

7   "Aveux de Madame Steinheil," *Le Matin*, November 26, 1908, 1.

8   Martin, *Hypocrisy of Justice*, 33.

9   "Les Bijoutiers et les journalistes," *Le Journal*, November 10, 1909, 2.

10   "L'Affaire Steinheil commence," *Le Matin*, November 27, 1908, 1.

11   "Mauvaise Journée pour Mme Steinheil," *Le Matin*, November 10, 1909, 4.

12   "L'Affaire Steinheil commence," *Le Matin*, November 17, 1908, 1.

13   "L'Affaire Steinheil commence," *Le Matin*, November 17, 1908, 1.

14   "Effroyable Confrontations," *Le Journal*, November 27, 1908, 4.

15   "L'Affaire Steinheil," *La Libre Parole*, December 19, 1908, 2.

16   "Autour de l'instruction," *Le Figaro*, November 27, 1908, 2.

17   "L'Affaire Steinheil commence," *Le Matin*, November 27, 1908, 1.

18   "L'Affaire Steinheil commence," *Le Matin*, November 27, 1908, 1 (ellipses in original).

19   "L'Affaire Steinheil commence," *Le Matin*, November 27, 1908, 1.

20   "Effroyables Confrontations," *Le Journal*, November 27, 1908, 4.

21   "Effroyables Confrontations," *Le Journal*, November 27, 1908, 4.

22   "Effroyables Confrontations," *Le Journal*, November 27, 1908, 4.

23   "Effroyables Confrontations," *Le Journal*, November 27, 1908, 4.

24   "Mme Steinheil est arrêtée," *Le Petit Parisien*, November 27, 1908, 2.

25   "Mme Steinheil est arrêtée," *Le Petit Parisien*, November 27, 1908, 2.

26   "Mme Steinheil est arrêtée," *Le Petit Parisien*, November 27, 1908, 2.

27   "Mme Steinheil est arrêtée," *Le Petit Parisien*, November 27, 1908, 2.

28   "Mme Steinheil est arrêtée," *Le Petit Parisien*, November 27, 1908, 2.

PART 3

1   "Le Trottoir roulant," *L'Echo de Paris*, December 7, 1908, 1.

CHAPTER 16

1   Steinheil, *Memoirs*, 289.

2   Harsin, *Policing Prostitution*, 266–67.

3   Quoted in Ch. Morizot-Thibault, "De La Détention préventive," *Revue du droit public et de la science politique en France et à l'étranger* (Librairie générale de droit et de jurisprudence, 1904), 69. See also Elissa Gelfand, *Imagination in Confinement: Women's Writings from French Prisons* (Ithaca: Cornell University Press, 1983), 76; Patricia O'Brien, *The Promise of Punishment: Prisons in Nineteenth-Century France* (Princeton: Princeton University Press, 1982).

4   Steinheil, *Memoirs*, 292.

5   Steinheil, 289–91.

6   Steinheil, 292–95.

7   "Mme Steinheil à Saint-Lazare," *Le Matin*, January 2, 1908, 5.

8   Steinheil, *Memoirs*, 303–4.

9   Steinheil, 305 (ellipsis in original).

10   Evidence of working-class investment in the class dynamics of the affair can be found in postcards workers sent to Rémy Couillard after his release from jail in 603 AP 5, Affaire Rémy Couillard, Fonds Géraud, AN.

11   "M. le juge Leydet se récuse," *Le Petit Parisien*, November 28, 1908, 1.

12   "Le Cercle se resserre autour de Mme Steinheil," *Le Matin*, December 6, 1908, 1; "Nous assistons à l'exhumation du cadavre, Mme Steinheil et les assassins: pas d'erreur possible; elle a des complices," *L'Intransigeant*, November 30, 1908, 1; "Mme Steinheil est bien une criminelle," *Le Petit Journal*, November 30, 1908, 1.

13   "L'Affaire Steinheil," *Le Matin*, November 28, 1908, 1.

14   Memo to the Prefect of Police, December 2, 1908, BA 1585, APP.

15   Raymond Figeac, "Mme Steinheil à Saint-Lazare," *L'Humanité*, November 27, 1908, 1.

16   Thomas Piketty, *Capital in the Twenty-First Century*, trans. Arthur Goldhammer (Cambridge: Harvard University Press, 2014), 141–248.

17   Notice individuelle, 1896, BB/6(II)/620, dossier on Jean-Louis André, Ministère de la Justice, Cours et tribunaux, Dossiers personnels de magistrats, AN; Martin, "Courts."

18   "Mme Steinheil sur la sellette," *Le Petit Parisien*, December 4, 1908, 1.

19   "L'Affaire Steinheil," *Le Matin*, January 17, 1909, 1.

20   Rapport, February 18, 1908, JA 11, APP.

21   Commission rogatoire and Rapport, January 13, 1909, in Chiens: Dick et Turc, JA 14, APP.

22   Rapport, January 23, 1909, JA 13, APP; Procès-verbal, February 5, 1909, JA 14, APP; Dossier on Chouanard, JA 14, APP; Steinheil, *Memoirs*, 395–97.

23   Martin, *Hypocrisy of Justice*, 45.

24   Steinheil, *Memoirs*, 188.

25   Steinheil, 189.

26   Steinheil, 240, 285.

27   Steinheil, 340–41.

28   Steinheil, 340–41.

29   Steinheil, *Memoirs*, 343; "Mme Steinheil devant le juge," *Le Matin*, December 2, 1908, 1.

30   Mansker, *Sex, Honor and Citizenship*, 99; William M. Reddy, *The Invisible Code: Honor and Sentiment in Postrevolutionary France, 1814–1848* (Berkeley: University of California Press, 1997), 7, 72, 111.

31   "Mme Steinheil devant le juge," *Le Matin*, December 2, 1908, 1 (ellipses in original).

32   "Mme Steinheil devant le juge," *Le Matin*, December 2, 1908, 1–2.

33   Steinheil, *Memoirs*, 344–45.

34   Steinheil, 340, 346–47.

35   Steinheil, 346–47.

36   Steinheil, 349.

37   Steinheil, 358.

38   Steinheil, 359.

39   "Mme Steinheil sur la sellette," *Le Petit Parisien*, December 4, 1908, 1.

40   "Mme Steinheil est bien une criminelle," *Le Petit Journal*, November 29, 1908, 1.

41   "Interrogatoire de Mme Steinheil," *Le Journal*, November 4, 1909, 4, 6.

42   "L'Affaire Steinheil," *Le Petit Journal*, December 19, 1908, 3.

CHAPTER 17

1   "Le Mystère Steinheil," *L'Humanité*, November 30, 1909, 2.

2   "'La Confession d'un amant,'" *L'Intransigeant*, January 25, 1909, 1; "L'Affaire Steinheil," *Le Matin*, December 18, 1908, 1–2; "L'Affaire Steinheil," *Le Radical*, December 8, 1908, 2.

3   "Quelques clartés dans les ténèbres," *Le Journal*, November 29, 1908, 1; "Plus d'initiales: Des noms!," *L'Action française*, November 29, 1908, 1.

4   "L'Affaire Steinheil," *Le Petit Journal*, December 5, 1908, 1.

5   "L'Affaire Steinheil," *Le Petit Journal*, December 5, 1908, 3; "L'Affaire Félix Faure," *Le Matin*, November 30, 1908, 1; "On exhume les corps de M. Steinheil & Mme Japy," *Le Journal*, November 30, 1908, 2.

6   "Les Minutes tragiques," *L'Intransigeant*, December 6, 1908, 1; *L'Oeil de la Police*, no. 47, 1908.

7   "Félix Faure et Mme Steinheil," *La Libre Parole*, December 1, 1908, 1; "L'Affaire Steinheil," *L'Action française*, November 28, 1908, 2.

8   "Nos Échos," *L'Intransigeant*, December 4, 1908, 2.

9   Jean Péheu, "Elle acquittée… Saint-Lazare?," JA 13, APP.

10   "Autour de l'affaire," *L'Humanité*, November 30, 1908, 2; "Toute la lyre!," *L'Intransigeant*, November 29, 1908, 2nd ed., 1.

11   Billard, *Faure*, 579–83; Theodore Zeldin, *France, 1848–1945* (Oxford: Clarendon Press, 1988), 1:570; Paul Jankowski, *Shades of Indignation: Political Scandals in France, Past and Present* (New York: Berghahn Books, 2008), 56; Paul Jankowski, *Stavisky: A Confidence Man in the Republic of Virtue* (Ithaca: Cornell University Press, 2002), 264.

12   "Mme Steinheil acquittée," *Le Journal*, November 14, 1909, 2; Rapport, January 26, 1909, JA 11, APP.

13   "Le Passé de Mme Steinheil," *Le Petit Parisien*, November 28, 1908, 1.

14   "Mauvaise Journée pour Mme Steinheil," *Le Journal*, December 15, 1908, 2.

15   Frydman, "Reading Incognito."

16   Uses of the term "scandal" to describe this case after Mme Steinheil's arrest include "Le Drame de l'impasse Ronsin," *Le Figaro*, November 29, 1908, 1, and "Rémy Couillard depose chez le nouveau juge," *L'Intransigeant*, November 28, 1908, 2.

17   "La Veuve rouge," *Le Petit Parisien*, November 29, 1908, 1.

18   "Paris en fièvre," *Le Matin*, November 27, 1908, 2.

19   Memo to the Prefect of Police, November 28, 1908, BA 1585, APP.

20   "Plus d'initiales: Des noms!," *L'Action française*, November 29, 1908, 1.

21   Deborah Cohen, *Family Secrets: Shame and Privacy in Modern Britain* (Oxford: Oxford University Press, 2013); Reddy, *Invisible Code*, 111. See also Marcela

Iacub, *Through the Keyhole: A History of Sex, Space and Public Modesty in Modern France*, trans. Vinay Swamy (Oxford: Oxford University Press, 2016).

22 Michel Foucault, *The History of Sexuality*, trans. Robert Hurley, vol. 1 (New York: Vintage Books, 1988); Frank Mort, *Dangerous Sexualities: Medico-Moral Politics in England Since 1830*, 2nd ed. (London: Routledge, 2000); Harsin, *Policing Prostitution*; Berlière, *La Police des mœurs sous la IIIe République*.

23 Annette K. Joseph-Gabriel, *Reimagining Liberation: How Black Women Transformed Citizenship in the French Empire* (Urbana: University of Illinois Press, 2020), 97.

24 "Mme Steinheil à Saint-Lazare," *Le Matin*, January 2, 1908, 5.

25 Péheu, "Elle acquittée... Saint Lazare?"; "Autour de l'affaire," *L'Humanité*, November 30, 1908, 2.

26 Quoted in Jules Claretie, "La Vie à Paris," *Le Temps*, December 4, 1908, 2.

27 "Tante Lily," *Le Radical*, December 3, 1908, 1.

28 "Interrogatoire de Mme Steinheil," *Le Radical*, December 2, 1908, 2.

29 Michel Winock, *Nationalism, Anti-Semitism, and Fascism in France*, trans. Jane Marie Todd (Stanford: Stanford University Press, 2000), 27; Sandrine Sanos, *The Aesthetics of Hate: Far-Right Intellectuals, Antisemitism, and Gender in 1930s France* (Stanford: Stanford University Press, 2012), 51; Grégoire Kauffmann, *Édouard Drumont* (Paris: Perrin, 2008), 251.

30 Édouard Drumont, "La Menteuse," *La Libre Parole*, December 1, 1908, 1.

31 Sarah Maza, "The Diamond Necklace Affair Revisited: The Case of the Missing Queen," in *Eroticism and the Body Politic*, ed. Lynn Hunt (Baltimore: Johns Hopkins University Press, 1991); Sarah Horowitz, "The End of Love: Politics, Emotions and Domestic Violence in the Choiseul-Praslin Affair," *Journal of Family History* 42, no. 4 (October 2017): 381–400.

32 Kalifa, *Bas-fonds*; Jerrold E. Seigel, *Modernity and Bourgeois Life: Society, Politics, and Culture in England, France and Germany since 1750* (Cambridge: Cambridge University Press, 2012), 338.

33 See also Anne-Emmanuelle Demartini, *L'Affaire Lacenaire* (Paris: Aubier, 2001), 68–74, 177–212.

34 "Crimes et scandales," *Le Radical*, December 24, 1908, 1.

35 "Le Mystère s'épaissit," *L'Intransigeant*, November 28, 1908, 2nd ed., 2; "L'Autre Nuit tragique," *L'Intransigeant*, December 7, 1908, 1.

36 Léon Daudet, "Crime politique ou crime crapuleux?," *L'Action française*, June 10, 1908, 1.

37 Léon Daudet, "Les Mystères d'une instruction," *L'Action française*, January 22, 1909, 1.

38 Henri Vaugeois, "Trop de zèle!," *L'Action française*, November 30, 1908, 1.

39 Winock, *Nationalism, Anti-Semitism, and Fascism in France*, 13, 29–30.

40 "Le Revenant l'assassin. Interview de M. Félix Faure de M. Steinheil & Madame Japy." ([Paris?]: Imprimerie Edgard Klotz, n.d.).

41 Willa Z. Silverman, *The Notorious Life of Gyp: Right-Wing Anarchist in Fin-de-Siècle France* (Oxford: Oxford University Press, 1995), 169–75.

42 Michael Robert Marrus and Robert O. Paxton, *Vichy France and the Jews* (Stanford: Stanford University Press, 1995).

43 Pierre Birnbaum, *Le Peuple et les gros: Histoire d'un mythe* (Paris: B. Grasset, 1979).

44 "Notes d'un parisien," *Le Figaro*, November 4, 1909, 4.

45 Some of these jokes are reprinted in "Nouvelles a la main," *L'Écho de Paris*, December 3, 1908, 1, and Urbain Gohier, "La Haute Pègre," *L'Intransigeant*, December 5, 1908, 1.

46 "Au théâtre," *Le Matin*, May 2, 1909, 4; "Au théâtre," *Le Matin*, May 16, 1909, 4; *L'Affaire Steinheil* (Joinville-le-Pont: 1908), film; Jean Lecoq, "L'Affaire Steinheil et le cinématographe," *Le Petit Journal*, December 5, 1908, 1.

47 Schwartz, *Spectacular Realities*.

48 "Le Trottoir roulant," *L'Echo de Paris*, December 7, 1908, 1.

49 "Au théâtre," *Le Matin*, May 2, 1909, 4; "Au théâtre," *Le Matin*, May 16, 1909, 4.

50 Jean de Paris, "Le Drame de l'impasse Ronsin," *Le Figaro*, December 13, 1908, 5; *L'Affaire Steinheil* (Joinville-le-Pont: 1908), film, and *L'Affaire Steinheil* (3ème partie) (Joinville-le-Pont: 1908), film.

51 Sharon Marcus, *The Drama of Celebrity* (Princeton: Princeton University Press, 2019), 94–119; Antoine Lilti, *The Invention of Celebrity*, trans. Lynn Jeffress (New York: Polity, 2018), 7, 49; Lenard Berlanstein, "Historicizing and Gendering Celebrity Culture: Famous Women in Nineteenth-Century France," *Journal of Women's History* 16, no. 4 (2004): 72–73.

52 Péheu, "Elle acquittée… Saint-Lazare?."

53 Serpieri, Plébus and Danerty, "Les Mémoires de Madame Steinheil," Paris: Pèle-Mêle Édition, 1914.

54 "Le Revenant l'assassin. Interview de M. Félix Faure de M. Steinheil & Madame Japy."

55 Leon Bailby, "Les Larmes du Juge," *L'Intransigeant*, November 28, 1908, 2nd ed., 1.

56 Christopher E. Forth, *The Dreyfus Affair and the Crisis of French Manhood* (Baltimore: Johns Hopkins University Press, 2004); Howard Padwa, *Social Poison: The Culture and Politics of Opiate Control in Britain and France, 1821–1926* (Baltimore: Johns Hopkins University Press, 2012), 72; Venita Datta, *Heroes and Legends of Fin-de-Siècle France: Gender, Politics, and National Identity* (Cambridge: Cambridge University Press, 2011), 207; Nye, *Masculinity*; Rosario, *Erotic Imagination*, 39, 75.

57 Julie Peakman, *The Pleasure's All Mine: A History of Perverse Sex* (London: Reaktion Books, 2013), 371.

58 Judith Surkis, *Sexing the Citizen: Morality and Masculinity in France, 1870–1920* (Ithaca: Cornell University Press, 2006); Robert A. Nye, "Sexuality, Sex Difference and the Cult of Modern Love in the French Third Republic," *Historical Reflections/Réflexions Historiques* 20, no. 1 (January 1, 1994): 57–76.

CHAPTER 18

1 Steinheil, *Memoirs*, 333–35.

2 Steinheil, 331–32.

3 Steinheil, 335.

4 Steinheil, 331, 334, 335.

5 "Mme Steinheil trahie par ses bijoux," *Le Petit Journal*, November 28, 1908, 1.

6 Steinheil, 335–36.

7 Steinheil, 334–35.

8 Steinheil, 348.

9 Gelfand, *Imagination in Confinement*, 9; Lisa Downing, "Murder in the Feminine: Marie Lafarge and the Sexualization of the Nineteenth-Century Criminal Woman," *Journal of the History of Sexuality* 18, no. 1 (2009): 121–37.

10 "L'Affaire Steinheil," *Le Matin*, December 21, 1908, 2.

11 "L'Affaire Steinheil," *Le Matin*, December 21, 1908, 2.

12 Bernheimer, *Figures of Ill Repute*; Clayson, *Painted Love*; Clark, *Painting of Modern Life*, 79–146.

13 Donovan, *Juries*, 139; Ruth Harris, *Murders and Madness: Medicine, Law, and*

Society in the Fin de Siècle (Oxford: Oxford University Press, 1989); Downing, *Subject of Murder*; Anne-Emmanuelle Demartini, *Violette Nozière, la fleur du mal: Une histoire des années trente* (Paris: Editions Champ Vallon, 2017), 51.

14 "Mme Steinheil lutte avec l'accusation," *L'Humanité*, November 4, 1909, 1. See also J. Clair-Guyot, "La Journée de Mme Steinheil," *L'Echo de Paris*, November 15, 1909, 1.

15 Margaret Cook Andersen, *Regeneration through Empire: French Pronatalists and Colonial Settlement in the Third Republic* (Lincoln: University of Nebraska Press, 2015); Gilman, *Difference and Pathology*; Sullivan, "Classification, Containment, Contamination"; Bernheimer, *Figures of Ill Repute*; Clark, *Painting of Modern Life*, 79–146.

16 "Le Crime de l'impasse Ronsin," *Le Temps*, November 28, 1908, 2; Jean de Paris, "Autour de l'instruction," *Le Figaro*, November 28, 1908, 2.

17 Carol Groneman, "Nymphomania: The Historical Construction of Female Sexuality," *Signs: Journal of Women in Culture and Society* 19, no. 2 (January 1994): 337–67.

18 Matlock, *Scenes of Seduction*; Janet L. Beizer, *Ventriloquized Bodies: Narratives of Hysteria in Nineteenth-Century France* (Ithaca: Cornell University Press, 1994); Jessie Hewitt, *Institutionalizing Gender*.

19 Andersen, *Regeneration through Empire*, 31.

20 Quoted in Harris, *Murders and Madness*, 6.

21 Harris, *Murders and Madness*, 155–207; Berenson, *Trial of Madame Caillaux*, 13–42.

22 "L'Affaire Steinheil," *Le Matin*, December 21, 1908, 2.

23 Berenson, *Trial of Madame Caillaux*, 100–132.

24 See for instance Louise Colet, *Lui* (Geneva: Slatkine Reprints, 1973), 97; Simone de Beauvoir, *The Second Sex*, trans. H. M. Parshley (New York: Knopf, 1953), 644.

25 Ernest Laut, "Procès de femmes: Une affaire Steinheil au XVIIe siècle," *Le Petit Journal*, November 7, 1909, 351.

26 Holly Grout, *The Force of Beauty: Transforming French Ideas of Femininity in the Third Republic* (Baton Rouge: Louisiana State University Press, 2015).

27 "Réquisitoire," *Le Matin*, November 12, 1909, 2.

28 Martin, *Hypocrisy of Justice*, 26–27.

29 Arrêt qui prononce la mise en accusation et renvoie la veuve Steinheil aux assises

de la Seine, June 18, 1909, D5 U9 194, no. 4898, Cour d'appel de Paris, Chambre des mises en accusation, Archives de la Seine, Paris, France.

30   Downing, "Murder in the Feminine," 125; Maza, *Violette Nozière*, 108; Demartini, *Violette Nozière*, 44–45.

31   Arrêt qui prononce la mise en accusation et renvoie la veuve Steinheil aux assises de la Seine.

32   "Interrogatoire de Mme Steinheil," *Le Journal*, November 4, 1909, 2.

33   Steinheil, *Memoirs*, 372–73.

34   "On veut clôturer l'affaire Steinheil par un non-lieu," *L'Intransigeant*, April 11, 1909, 1.

35   Montal, *Affaire Steinheil*, 18.

36   Foemina, "L'Ame double," *Le Figaro*, November 11, 1909, 1.

37   Martin, *Hypocrisy of Justice*, 39.

38   Louis Latzarus, "Où est Mme Steinheil?," *Le Figaro*, November 16, 1909, 2.

39   Présentation pour un poste de subtitut au Tribunal de la Seine en prévision de la nomination de M. Lefuel à d'autres fonctions, February 23, 1894, BB/6(II)/1267, dossier on Bernard-Théodore-Médéric de Valles, Ministère de la Justice, Cours et tribunaux, Dossiers personnels de magistrats, AN.

40   Steinheil, *Memoirs*, 395; Louis Latzarus, "Le Dimanche de M. de Valles," *Le Figaro*, November 8, 1909, 1.

41   "Renseignments confidentiels," undated, BB/6(II)/1257, dossier on Paul-Adolphe Trouard-Riolle, Ministère de la Justice, Cours et tribunaux, Dossiers personnels de magistrats, AN.

42   Memo to the Prefect of Police, November 12, 1909, BA 1585, APP.

43   Steinheil, *Memoirs*, 36 (emphasis in original).

44   Steinheil, 394.

45   "Mme Steinheil songe déjà au lendemain de la Cour d'assises," *Le Matin*, August 28, 1909, 1.

46   "Avant le lever du rideau," *L'Humanité*, November 3, 1909, 1.

47   Louis Latzarus, "Préparatifs de débats," *Le Figaro*, November 3, 1909, 1; "Demain s'ouvre un des plus grands procès du siècle," *Le Matin*, November 2, 1909, 1.

48   Katherine Fischer Taylor, *In the Theater of Criminal Justice: The Palais de Justice in Second Empire Paris* (Princeton: Princeton University Press, 1993), 10, 21–23.

49 Donovan, *Juries*, 13; Berenson, *Trial of Madame Caillaux*, 5.

50 Quoted in Donovan, *Juries*, 14.

CHAPTER 19

1 Steinheil, *Memoirs*, 421–22, 412–13.

2 Steinheil, 414.

3 Steinheil, 413. For the unfolding of the trial, I have relied on Martin, *Hypocrisy of Justice*, chapter 1.

4 Edgard Troimaux, "Mme Steinheil en Cour d'assises," *L'Écho de Paris*, November 4, 1909, 1.

5 "Mme Steinheil devant le jury de la Seine," *Le Petit Journal*, November 4, 1909, 2.

6 "Interrogatoire de Mme Steinheil," *Le Journal*, November 4, 1909, 1.

7 "Interrogatoire de Mme Steinheil," *Le Journal*, November 4, 1909, 1.

8 Nye, *Crime, Madness & Politics*, 172.

9 "Interrogatoire de Mme Steinheil," *Le Journal*, November 4, 1909, 2.

10 "Interrogatoire de Mme Steinheil," *Le Journal*, November 4, 1909, 2.

11 "Interrogatoire de Mme Steinheil," *Le Journal*, November 4, 1909, 6.

12 "Interrogatoire de Mme Steinheil," *Le Journal*, November 4, 1909, 6.

13 Fernand Vandérem, "Le Programme de Bayonne," *Le Figaro*, November 9, 1909, 1.

14 "Interrogatoire de Mme Steinheil," *Le Journal*, November 4, 1909, 2.

15 Mesch, "Housewife or Harlot," 67–69.

16 "Interrogatoire de Mme Steinheil," *Le Journal*, November 4, 1909, 2.

17 "Interrogatoire de Mme Steinheil," *Le Journal*, November 4, 1909, 2.

18 "La Nuit tragique," *Le Matin*, November 5, 1909, 1.

19 "La Nuit tragique," *Le Matin*, November 5, 1909, 2.

20 "La Nuit tragique," *Le Matin*, November 5, 1909, 2.

21 "La Nuit tragique," *Le Matin*, November 5, 1909, 2.

22 "Les Débats de l'affaire Steinheil," *Le Petit Journal*, November 5, 1909, 2.

23 Claude Habib, *Galanterie française* (Paris: Gallimard, 2006); Mona Ozouf, *Les Mots des femmes: essai sur la singularité française* (Paris: Fayard, 1995).

24 Edgard Troimaux, "Mme Steinheil en Cour d'assises," *L'Écho de Paris*, November 12, 1909, 2.

25 "L'Affaire Steinheil," *Le Figaro*, November 5, 1909, 2.

26 Steinheil, *Memoirs*, 417–18.

27   "Mme Steinheil se débat dans le cercle qui l'étreint," *Le Matin*, November 6, 1909, 6.

28   Berenson, *Trial of Madame Caillaux*, 100–132.

29   "Mme Steinheil se débat dans le cercle qui l'étreint," *Le Matin*, November 6, 1909, 6.

30   "Mme Steinheil se débat dans le cercle qui l'étreint," *Le Matin*, November 6, 1909, 6.

31   "Mme Steinheil devant le jury de la Seine," *Le Petit Journal*, November 4, 1909, 1.

32   Berlanstein, *Daughters of Eve*; Roberts, *Disruptive Acts*, 54–55.

33   Georges Claretie, *Drames et comédies judiciaires* (Paris: Berger-Levrault, 1909), 382.

34   "Les Débats de l'affaire Steinheil," *Le Petit Journal*, November 5, 1909, 1.

35   "L'Affaire Steinheil," *Le Petit Journal*, November 6, 1909, 1.

36   Nye, *Masculinity*; Julie Fette, "Pride and Prejudice in the Professions: Women Doctors and Lawyers in Third Republic France," *Journal of Women's History* 19, no. 3 (2007): 60–86.

37   Karen Offen, *Debating the Woman Question in the French Third Republic, 1870–1920* (Cambridge: Cambridge University Press, 2018).

38   Séverine, "Impressions féminines," *L'Intransigeant*, November 7, 1909, 1.

39   Berenson, *Trial of Madame Caillaux*, 100–132.

CHAPTER 20

1   "La Journée de Rémy Couillard," *Le Journal*, November 7, 1909, 1–2.

2   "La Journée de Rémy Couillard," *Le Journal*, November 7, 1909, 5.

3   "La Journée de Rémy Couillard," *Le Journal*, November 7, 1909, 2.

4   Steinheil, *Memoirs*, 421.

5   "La Journée de Rémy Couillard," *Le Journal*, November 7, 1909, 4; Grout, *Force of Beauty*, 19.

6   "La Journée de Rémy Couillard," *Le Journal*, November 7, 1909, 4.

7   "La Journée de Rémy Couillard," *Le Journal*, November 7, 1909, 1.

8   Harris, *Murders and Madness*, 93; Saint-Joanis, "Sherlock Holmes et la France," 4–9; Cole, *Suspect Identities*, 6–59; Ronald R. Thomas, *Detective Fiction and the Rise of Forensic Science* (Cambridge: Cambridge University Press, 2000); Frédéric Chauvaud, *Les Experts du crime: La médecine légale en France au XIXe siècle* (Paris: Aubier, 2000).

9   "Médécins & policiers," *Le Journal*, November 9, 1909, 4.

10   "Médécins & policiers," *Le Journal*, November 9, 1909, 4.

11   Georges Claretie, "L'Affaire Steinheil," *Le Figaro*, November 7, 1909, 1–2.

12 "Après le verdict," *Le Radical*, November 14, 1909, 2.

13 "Mauvaise Journée pour Mme Steinheil," *Le Matin*, November 10, 1909, 4.

14 "Mauvaise Journée pour Mme Steinheil," *Le Matin*, November 10, 1909, 1.

15 "Mariette—Alexandre Wolff—M. Borderel," *Le Journal*, November 11, 1909, 2.

16 Martin, *Hypocrisy of Justice*, 61.

17 "Mariette—Alexandre Wolff—M. Borderel," *Le Journal*, November 11, 1909, 4, 6. "Les Derniers Témoins—le réquisitoire," *Le Journal*, November 12, 1909, 1–2.

18 "Les Derniers Témoins—le réquisitoire," *Le Journal*, November 12, 1909, 1–2.

19 Martin, *Hypocrisy of Justice*, 63.

20 "Les Derniers Témoins—le réquisitoire," *Le Journal*, November 12, 1909, 5.

21 Steinheil, *Memoirs*, 431 (ellipses in original).

22 Lepage, *André Paisant*, 7, 16.

23 "Les Derniers Témoins—le réquisitoire," *Le Journal*, November 12, 1909, 5.

24 Mesch, "Housewife or Harlot," 67–69.

25 Martin, *Hypocrisy of Justice*, 64.

26 "Les Derniers Témoins—le réquisitoire," *Le Journal*, November 12, 1909, 1.

27 "Les Derniers Témoins—le réquisitoire," *Le Journal*, November 12, 1909, 5–6.

28 Steinheil, *Memoirs*, 433 (emphasis in original).

29 "Le Réquisitoire est terminé," *Le Journal*, November 13, 1909, 2, 5.

30 "Le Réquisitoire est terminé," *Le Journal*, November 13, 1909, 4.

31 Steinheil, *Memoirs*, 436.

32 Steinheil, 436 (ellipsis in original).

33 "Mme Steinheil acquittée," *Le Journal*, November 14, 1909, 1.

34 "Acquittement," *Le Figaro*, November 14, 1909, 2.

35 "Mme Steinheil acquittée," *Le Journal*, November 14, 1909, 2.

36 Clayson, *Painted Love*, 89–90; Sohn, *Chrysalides*, 1:783.

37 "Mme Steinheil acquittée," *Le Journal*, November 14, 1909, 2.

38 "Mme Steinheil acquittée," *Le Journal*, November 14, 1909, 1–2.

39 "Mme Steinheil acquittée," *Le Journal*, November 14, 1909, 5–6.

40 "Mme Steinheil acquittée," *Le Journal*, November 14, 1909, 6.

41 Steinheil, *Memoirs*, 447.

42 "Acquittée," *Le Matin*, November 14, 1909, 2.

43 Steinheil, *Memoirs*, 447–48.

44 "Acquittement," *Le Figaro*, November 14, 1909, 1.

CHAPTER 21

1   "Après l'acquittement," *L'Illustration*, November 20, 1909, 368–69.

2   "Mme Steinheil rêve encore..." *Le Matin*, November 17, 1909, 1–2.

3   Dudley, *Scarlett Widow*, 186; Lilti, *Invention of Celebrity*, 7.

4   Steinheil, *Memoirs*, 453–54.

5   Lilti, *Invention of Celebrity*, 7, 49; Marcus, *Drama of Celebrity*, 94–119.

6   "Madame Steinheil in London," *Times* (London), December 1, 1909, 15.

7   Dudley, *Scarlett Widow*, 186.

8   "A Famous Cause Celebre Now Recalled by a Romance," *Liverpool Echo*, June 25, 1917, 2.

9   "Mme Steinheil and Lord Abinger," *Yorkshire Evening Post*, June 26, 1917, 3.

10   "Lord Abinger's Bride," *Hull Daily Mail*, June 26, 1917, 6.

11   Memo to the Prefect of Police, January 24, 1910, BA 1585, APP.

12   "Mme Steinheil est devenue lady Abinger," *Excelsior*, June 27, 1917, 5.

13   "Mme Steinheil Sues Author and Publisher," *Dundee Evening Telegraph*, November 28, 1912, 1; Dudley, *Scarlett Widow*, 188.

14   "Lovers and Duels," *Pall Mall Gazette*, February 9, 1912, 7; Memo to the Prefect of Police, February 15, 1912, BA 1585, APP.

15   Steinheil, *Memoirs*, 76–79; Anna Norris, *L'Écriture du defi: Textes carceraux feminins du XIX et XXe siecles* (Birmingham: Summa, 2002), 34.

16   Steinheil, *Memoirs*, 106–10, 121–26, 160–72.

17   Silverman, *Notorious Life of Gyp*, 131–32.

18   "Les Mémoires de ma vie," *Le Journal*, May 18, 1912, 2.

19   "Le Retour de Mme Steinheil," *Le Matin*, March 9, 1910, 1.

20   Steinheil, *Memoirs*, 465.

21   "Madame Rafaël del Pérugia," *Gil Blas*, July 26, 1911, 1; "Les Revenants de l'affaire Steinheil," *Le Matin*, January 9, 1914, 5.

22   Memos to the Prefect of Police, October 11, 1911, and May 5, 1911, BA 1585, APP; del Perugia et Steinheil, July 25, 1911, 15M 235 acte 1215, Archives de Paris, Paris, France; "Mariage de Mlle Steinheil," *La Liberté*, July 27, 1911, 3.

23   "Les Revenants de l'affaire Steinheil," *Le Matin*, January 9, 1914, 5.

24   "L'Ex-Mlle Steinheil plaide en séparation de corps," *Le Matin*, November 4, 1912, 1.

25   "Madame Steinheil," *Western Mail*, February 9, 1914, 5.

26 Base des Morts pour la France de la Première Guerre mondiale, Ministère des Armées, https://www.memoiredeshommes.sga.defense.gouv.fr/.

27 England & Wales, Civil Registration Marriage Index, 1837–1915, s.v. "Cammalich, Candido," ancestry.co.uk; Dudley, *Scarlett Widow*, 187.

28 "Mme Steinheil est devenue lady Abinger," *Excelsior*, June 27, 1917, 5; "Mme Steinheil and Lord Abinger," *Yorkshire Evening Post*, June 26, 1917, 3; Deidre Beddoe, *Back to Home and Duty: Women Between the Wars* 1918-1939 (London: Pandora Press, 1989).

29 "Mme Steinheil to wed Lord Abinger," *Daily Mirror*, June 26, 1917, 2.

30 Dudley, *Scarlett Widow*, 185; "The New Lady Abinger," *Pall Mall Gazette*, June 26, 1917, 8; "Mme Steinheil—Wedding (1917)," British Pathé, April 13, 2014, YouTube video, 0:30, https://www.youtube.com/watch?v=bsAmtvGVeXs.

31 Dudley, *Scarlett Widow*, 189–90.

32 *Dundee Courier*, November 16, 1926, 6; "The Late Mrs. Huntley-Walker," *Bury Free Press*, July 3, 1926, 9.

33 Dudley, *Scarlett Widow*, 189; Lisa Z. Sigel, *Making Modern Love: Sexual Narratives and Identities in Interwar Britain* (Philadelphia: Temple University Press, 2012).

34 "Death of Lord Abinger," *Western Gazette*, June 17, 1927, 16; "Lord Abinger Dead," *Leeds Mercury*, June 13, 1927, 6; "Lord Abinger's Sudden Death," *Newcastle Journal*, June 14, 1927, 9.

35 "Death of Lord Abinger," *Western Gazette*, June 17, 1927, 16.

36 Dudley, *Scarlett Widow*, 190.

37 Margaret Powell, *Below Stairs: The Classic Kitchen Maid's Memoir That Inspired "Upstairs, Downstairs" and "Downton Abbey"* (New York: St. Martin's Griffin, 2012), 34.

38 Judith Middleton, *A History of Women's Lives in Hove and Portslade* (Havertown: Pen & Sword Books, 2018), 3, 22, 64–66, 95–107; Judith Middleton, "Hove in the Past: Adelaide Crescent, Hove," *Hove in the Past* (blog), January 12, 2016, http://hovehistory.blogspot.com/2015/11/adelaide-crescent-hove.html.

39 Tim Ridgway, "Opinion: Majestic, Symbolic—and Still Standing. The Beautiful and Iconic West Pier," *The Argus*, October 6, 2016, https://www.theargus.co.uk/news/14784480.majestic-symbolic-and-still-standing-the-beautiful-and-iconic-west-pier/.

40 Rob Shields, "The 'System of Pleasure': Liminality and the Carnivalesque at

Brighton," *Theory, Culture & Society* 7, no. 1 (February 1, 1990): 39–72; Janet Cameron, *LGBT Brighton and Hove* (Stroud: Amberley Publishing, 2009).

41   Dudley, *Scarlett Widow*, 190–91.

42   England & Wales, Civil Registration Death Index, 1916–2007, s.v. "Marthe Camalich," ancestry.co.uk; Dudley, *Scarlett Widow*, 187.

43   "Helping the County Hospital," *Mid Sussex Times*, September 6, 1932, 7; "Staying at Hove," *Eastbourne Gazette*, November 27, 1935, 3; "Charming Bride," *West Sussex County Times*, February 19, 1934, 5.

44   "Une dernière visite à Saint-Lazare," *Paris-Soir*, December 14, 1923, 2; "Mestorino devant le jury," *Paris-Soir*, June 5, 1928, 3; Victor Faure, "De quelques beautés fatales: Marguerite Steinheil," *Être Belle*, January 1, 1938, 24–25; "Hier et aujourd'hui," *Ric et Rac: Grand Hebdomadaire pour Tous*, June 3, 1933, 2.

45   Léon Daudet, "Sur trois crimes policiers," *L'Action française*, November 29, 1931, 1; "Débâcle de la sûreté générale et de la Maçonnerie," *L'Action française*, April 8, 1934, 1.

46   Dudley, *Scarlett Widow*, 190.

47   Jean Hamlin, "Oubliez-moi, c'est tout ce que je vous demande," *Ici Paris Hebdo*, April 15–21, 1947, 5.

48   "Dies at Age of 86," *Belfast News-Letter*, July 19, 1954, 6; "'The Tragic Widow' is Dead," *Northern Whig*, July 19, 1954, 3.

AFTERWORD

1   "Le Cabinet rouge," *L'Intransigeant*, December 8, 1908, 1; Bracke, "Sensation!," *L'Humanité*, November 27, 1908, 1.

2   Luis Ferré-Sadurní, "Teenager Accused of Rape Deserves Leniency Because He's From a 'Good Family,' Judge Says," *New York Times*, July 2, 2019, sec. New York, https://www.nytimes.com/2019/07/02/nyregion/judge-james-troiano-rape.html.

AUTHOR'S NOTE

1   Martin, *Hypocrisy of Justice*, 15, note 1; Dudley, *Scarlett Widow*, 186.

2   One example of this is the jewelry that Faure gave her, information about which is also in Faure's personal papers; Billard, *Faure*, 910. Another instance is the existence of her lover Balincourt's accomplice, Delpit, mentioned in Steinheil, *Memoirs*, 147; Rapport, December 9, 1908, JA 13, APP.

ACKNOWLEDGMENTS

I first heard about Meg in 2013, when I was on a tour of Père Lachaise cemetery in Paris with friends. When we stopped at the tomb of Félix Faure, our tour guide told us about how he died, the double murder, and Meg's connection to both events. At first, I thought he must have been making these stories up, but as soon as I did some digging, I found that he was telling the truth and that her life was even more interesting than the brief version I had heard.

I've spent much of the years since researching and writing about Meg and have incurred numerous debts in the process, and it's a great pleasure to acknowledge them here. Extra special thanks go to Jon Michael Darga, my agent, and Anna Michels and Jenna Jankowski, my editors at Sourcebooks, for seeing the potential in this project, making it so much better, and being wonderful people to work with. I'm also grateful for Jessica Thelander and Alison Marcotte for their work copyediting the manuscript.

W&L University provided financial support to research and write this project, while the History Department and the Women's, Gender, and Sexuality Studies Program gave me an intellectual home. I am also thankful to the archivists at the Archives de la préfecture de police, the Archives nationales, and the Archives de la Seine. There is absolutely no way I could have done this project without the help of the W&L Library, and I am particularly grateful to Mackenzie Brooks, Emily Cook, and Elizabeth Teaff for being rock-star librarians and to Brandon Walsh for undertaking a digital humanities project with me that fed into this book. I presented portions of the manuscript at Harvard University's Center for European Studies Visiting Scholars Seminar, the Symposium on the Art of Friendship in France from the Revolution to the First World War at Oxford, Sciences-Po in Le Havre, and the 2019 French Historical Studies conference and benefited greatly from the comments I received in all forums. Members of the Gender in Modern France group and the Crime in Modern France group also kindly read parts of this book and provided amazingly helpful suggestions; I'd like to thank Margaret Andersen and Briony Neilson for facilitating these discussion forums.

This project is immeasurably better from the feedback that Christine Adams, Naomi Andrews, Nimisha Barton, Judith DeGroat, Hannah Frydman, Julie Kane, Robin Mitchell, Jake Reeves, Greg Shaya, and Robin Walz provided on previous drafts. Extra special thanks to Christine, Naomi, and Julie for reading the entire thing.

Annabelle Allouch, Andrew Counter, Denise Davidson, Elizabeth Everton, Lela Graybill, Daniel Harkett, Gabrielle Houbre, Nina Kushner, Elisabeth Ladenson, Andrea Mansker, Jann Matlock, Jean Pedersen, Michèle Plott, Tip Ragan, Andrew Israel Ross, and Nick White were all generous with their expertise at various points during the research and writing process. Much of this book was written during the COVID-19 pandemic, a period when the hot mess of Meg's life was often a welcome distraction. I was fortunate to find a Zoom cowriting group whose regulars included Amy Freund, Kate Hamerton, Judith Miller, Cassidy Puckett, Rebecca Scales, and Jen Sessions. I'm also grateful to Jacques Maillard for sending me material and James Abinger and Maitena Horiot-Ortega for answering my questions. Vanda Wilcox and Jean-Philippe Miller-Tremblay saved the day by undertaking research for me when I could not get to France, and Suzie Tibor researched images for me. I had the good fortune to work with three extraordinary undergraduate research assistants who were beyond talented and truly delightful: Megan Doherty, Sam Gibson, and Chase Isbell. I'm also grateful to Paul Youngman and Jessica Wager for facilitating my research in so many ways.

Friends near and far provided support and advice and answered any number of seemingly random questions, and it's a pleasure to thank Christa and Nathan Bowden, Mark Bradley, Mikki Brock, Ron Fuchs, Meredith McCoy, Molly Michelmore, Jayne Reino, Melissa Vise, Taylor Walle, and Ricardo Wilson. Ever farther afield, Thibaut Clément, Hélène Cottet, Nam Le Toan, Solène Nicolas, and Antoine Quint are all dear friends and on that tour on Père Lachaise. Daniel Horowitz, Helen Horowitz, Ben Horowitz, Judy Liebman, Aaron Horowitz, Adam Liebman, Leslie Field, and Morris Weiner all make me realize how lucky I am to have a family much different from Meg's. Last but never, ever least, I couldn't have done this without Lucie Fielding, whose love, support, enthusiasm, and balance of Chaos-Muppet energy and Order-Muppet energy make my life so much better.

INDEX

Note: Illustrations are indicated by *italics*.

ABOUT THE AUTHOR

© Jen Fox

Sarah Horowitz is a professor of history at W&L University in Virginia, where she is also head of the Women's, Gender, and Sexuality Studies program. She has a PhD in history from the University of California, Berkeley, and has published in scholarly journals as well as the *Washington Post*. This is her second book.